WOMEN IN LATE M
REFORMATION EU

European Culture and Society
General Editor: Jeremy Black

Published

Lesley Hall *Sex, Gender & Social Change in Britain since 1880*
Helen M. Jewell *Women in Dark Age and Early Medieval Europe c.500–1200*
Helen M. Jewell *Women in Late Medieval and Reformation Europe 1200–1550*
Keith D. Lilley *Urban Life in the Middle Ages: 1000–1450*
Jerzy Lukowski *The European Nobility in the Eighteenth Century*
Neil MacMaster *Racism in Europe, 1870–2000*
Noël O'Sullivan *European Political Thought since 1945*
W. M. Spellman *European Political Thought 1600–1700*
Gary K. Waite *Heresy, Magic and Witchcraft in Early Modern Europe*
Diana Webb *Medieval European Pilgrimage, c. 700–c.1500*

European Culture and Society Series
Series Standing Order
ISBN 0–333–74440–3
(outside North America only)

You can receive future titles in this series as they are published by placing a standing order. Please contact your bookseller or, in case of difficulty, write to us at the address below with your name and address, the title of the series and the ISBN quoted above.

Customer Services Department, Macmillan Distribution Ltd
Houndmills, Basingstoke, Hampshire RG21 6XS, England

Women in Late Medieval and Reformation Europe 1200–1550

Helen M. Jewell

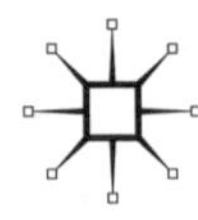

First published 2007 by
PALGRAVE MACMILLAN
Houndmills, Basingstoke, Hampshire RG21 6XS and
175 Fifth Avenue, New York, N.Y. 10010
Companies and representatives throughout the world

PALGRAVE MACMILLAN is the global academic imprint of the Palgrave Macmillan division of St. Martin's Press, LLC and of Palgrave Macmillan Ltd. Macmillan® is a registered trademark in the United States, United Kingdom and other countries. Palgrave is a registered trademark in the European Union and other countries.

ISBN–13: 978–0–333–91256–0 hardback
ISBN–10: 0–333–91256–X hardback
ISBN–13: 978–0–333–91257–7 paperback
ISBN–10: 0–333–91257–8 paperback

This book is printed on paper suitable for recycling and made from fully managed and sustained forest sources.

A catalogue record for this book is available from the British Library.

Library of Congress Cataloging-in-Publication Data

Jewell, Helen M.
Women in late Medieval and Reformation Europe, 1200–1550 / Helen M. Jewell.
p. cm. — (European culture and society series)
Includes bibliographical references and index
ISBN–13: 978–0–333–91256–0 (cloth)
ISBN–10: 0–333–91256–X (cloth)
ISBN–13: 978–0–333–91257–7 (pbk.)
ISBN–10: 0–333–91257–8 (pbk.)
1. Women—Europe—History—Middle Ages, 500–1500. 2. Women—Europe—History—Renaissance, 1450–1600. I. Title.

HQ1147.E85J47 2007
305.409′0902—dc22 2006048583

10 9 8 7 6 5 4 3 2 1
16 15 14 13 12 11 10 09 08 07

Printed in China

Contents

Preface

When I was writing *Women in Medieval England* (1996) I read through Chaucer's *Troilus and Criseyde* and came across Criseyde's startlingly modern statement of independence – 'I am myn owene woman, wel at ese – I thank it God – as after myn estat' (Book II, lines 750–1). Extending my interest into Europe, I found the words leaping out of the text at me again in David Nicholas's *The Domestic Life of a Medieval City: Women, Children and the Family in Fourteenth-Century Ghent* (1985), where he quotes (his p. 89) Alice van den Plassche's heirs' description of her as 'her own woman, free business-woman'. Two swallows do not make a summer, nor two women (one fictional) a trend, but this 100 per cent increase in my observations of the phrase 'own woman' in a late fourteenth-century context was thought provoking. There was obviously rather more to medieval women than we pick up from the reiterated catalogues of female faults peddled by jaded misogynists. In writing both *Women in Dark Age and Early Medieval Europe c.500–1200* and this book I have enjoyed piecing together my version of that fuller picture. This later volume takes up the story from where the earlier volume left off, but it must be stressed that both volumes have been devised to stand alone and may be read completely independently of each other. It is not necessary to have read the earlier volume in order to understand and appreciate this one.

Women's history first attracted my attention over 40 years ago, when Lynette Ramsay encouraged me to pursue my choice of 'Women in medieval France' as a Sixth Form project. I am pleased to acknowledge her influence here, along with my more recent indebtedness to participants in many women's history sessions at the International Medieval Congresses held annually since 1994 at the University of Leeds.

My policy with regard to names of both people and places has been to standardize them in their simplest commonly used spelling. Where names have not been widely simplified, they are left as per source. Monetary terms are similarly left in the currencies cited, with no attempt to value them consistently against each other or from one period to another. Only the English (pre-decimal) currency with 240 pence (d) to the pound (£) and 12d to the shilling (s) is given in abbreviated form.

Feeling the English Authorized King James Bible inappropriate for a work on Catholic Europe I was directed by Catholic friends to The New Jerusalem Bible, which I have found a most informative edition.

Helen M. Jewell

1

INTRODUCTION

The Geographical Range and Timescale

The geographical focus for this book is the territory definable as the Latin West or Catholic Europe. By the start of the period Western Christianity already extended east of the Empire, across Poland and Hungary, and as the period progressed it embraced areas further east, reaching the Black Sea in the south-east, pushing north-east up the Baltic and bordering with the eastern church on the land boundary with the Russians, and with Muslims on the frontier with the Turks. It is not proposed to push this study of women further east than the Holy Roman Empire, which keeps the focus on western Europe: the women of the German, Swiss, French, Italian, Iberian and Scandinavian territories plus Britain with Ireland.

Neither of the terminal dates for this volume is a year of particular significance. Both are rounded cut-off points in periods of significant change. Round about 1200 the unsettling factor of Viking activity in the west may be seen to have stopped, the regularity of record keeping in church, state and civic communities really took off, leaving more evidence, and the papal dominance of western Europe reached its apogee under Innocent III. Thus 1200 seems an apt date for dividing earlier from later medieval European history. By 1550, on the other hand, the Protestant Reformation had completely broken the unity of Catholic Europe, and other developments, in politics, diplomacy and economics, all pull the later sixteenth century into what is called the early modern period.

In a seminal article 'Did women have a renaissance?' Joan Kelly-Gadol made the key point that the significant periodizations traditionally imposed on history have to be questioned in relation to women's history.[1] Trends that may seem to indicate universal progress, or liberation, characteristic of an era have been identified in the long male-dominated perspective of history but may not actually have brought the same consequences for the women of the day. Many of the features which differentiate the early modern from the late medieval period – such as the rise of bureaucracy and state armies – meant little for women who had no career path in either. However, no apology is offered for taking traditional break points for the parameters of this book, nor for considering traditionally defined characteristic periods within it. After all, watersheds affect all people living at the time. Periods of war, disease or famine, familiar to some 14 generations whose lives spanned this volume, have such wide repercussions that they affect both sexes even if men do most of the fighting and women most of the nursing and scrimping.

The Variety of Social Groupings and Communities within Europe

The modern geographical identities of Italy, Spain, France, Germany, Belgium and the Netherlands do not match up precisely with the political geography of western Europe in the period reviewed, but the territorial boundaries by 1550 certainly come closer to the modern situation than they had in earlier times. Boundaries went on being redefined, for example Provence and Dauphiné changed from the imperial side of the frontier with France to the French side during the period but other territories of modern France such as Franche Comté still remained beyond its border at the end. The Holy Roman Empire was an unwieldy collection of kingdoms, principalities, duchies and lower titled power bases, with the imperial free cities and the Swiss Confederation contained within, the latter virtually independent after 1499. Italy's identity was particularly fragmented throughout the period. The territory was split into three distinct political zones – the north, within the boundary of the Holy Roman Empire, the middle, temporally controlled by the papacy, and the south, for most of the period dominated by the Angevins (in Naples until 1435) and the Aragonese (in Sicily from 1282 and Naples from 1435). City states, especially in the north (most obviously Venice, outside the imperial boundary), struggled for independence, in league or at war with each other. Towards the end of the period French invasion added to the political disturbance. Spanish territory was politically fragmented and regionally diverse. Thus it is hazardous to think of women as Italian or French or German or Spanish just because they may be found in an identifiable geographical location, or under a certain rule, at a particular moment. Their speaking a particular language or dialect may identify them more satisfactorily but even this is a quicksand of fashion and influence, with Catalan, Basque, Spanish, Portuguese and Mozarabic spoken by the Iberian Christians, *langue d'oc* and *langue d' oïl*, not to omit Breton and Flemish, by the people of France. The British Isles and the Scandinavian countries, including of course Iceland, had more continuity of identity through the period, along with Portugal. Women in any one particular country also resist generalization because of regional variation, differences in altitude and climate, pastoral and agricultural specializations, rural and urban contrast, and pious or heretical leanings.

However, there are signs that people were beginning to feel more sense of national identity than previously, and the admittedly extraordinary career of Joan of Arc shows that a peasant girl could feel this as keenly as any man. One of the many remarkable aspects of her story is that an uneducated girl from Domrémy on the very edge of France on the marches of Lorraine should have developed so driving an urge to secure the dauphin's coronation as Charles VII, and to eject the English invaders. A young country girl seems unlikely to have had access to information to get a grasp on the situation. Unless we fall back on direct divine revelation, we have to assume Joan's rather more indirect divine instruction – priests being used to preach patriotically, and to publicize news of war, as they were in England – plus personal experience and travellers' tales and rumour.

If the political geography presents ever changing challenges, the settlement geography of Europe in this period is easier to identify. By 1200 the characteristics of the most developed urban zones in medieval Europe (northern Italy and the Low Countries) were clearly distinguishable from the less active towns scattered in more rural areas, while the landscapes of villages and hamlets differed yet again. Sufficient structures survive to give us imaginative leads into the varied life styles of their inhabitants, as will be indicated in surveying the evidence for the period: there is enough *in situ* material, pictorial representation and verbal description to make the reader much more confident about placing the women of later medieval Europe into the various social groupings and communities of the time than is possible for the pre-1200 period despite the best efforts of archaeology. It is easier to recreate how physical conditions interplayed with the necessary activities carried out in them. Women lived in a great variety of conditions, but their overall treatment permits many generalizations despite particularities of detail.

The Effects on Women of Political, Economic, Demographic and Religious Developments

The period 1200–1550 was much less migratory than earlier times. For the most part, women were born into stable communities which stayed put. Individuals were mobile. The merchant of Prato's wife Margherita was a Florentine whom he met in Avignon, who mainly kept his Prato house in his absences, but joined him occasionally in Florence and Pisa, moved with him to Bologna fleeing plague, and after his death in 1410 spent most of her widowhood in Florence. Women in the mass were not involved in any tribal movement nor did they have to face mass invasion by others. However, there was a great deal of warring, with inevitable disruption and particular atrocities. War brought less threat of invasion with view to settlement than in earlier times, and was in some areas almost a tidying up operation to smooth out anomalies from past history, such as ejecting English interests (remnants of the Angevin Empire) from France and recovering Granada from the Moors. More limited in objective than the earlier migrations, war was no less turbulent for those living where it was fought. Right through the period the two leading powers of France and England were intermittently at war, mostly fought on French soil, with accompanying devastation. Invading armies lived off the countryside and plundered it. The invention of the *chevauchée* in the Hundred Years' war intensified deliberate destruction of the invaded enemy's agricultural activity. *Écorcheurs* is another term indicating the damage wreaked. After the English Thiérarche campaign of 1339, Benedict XII's agent Bertrand Cant operated relief funds, giving out aid to nearly 8000 victims. In the dioceses of Laon, Reims, Noyon and Cambrai 174 parishes had been devastated. There had been burning, looting and laying waste. At Easter 1360 Jean de Venette watching the English approach to Paris commented on seeing men, women and children desolate.[2] Occasionally there was a pitched battle, as at Agincourt (1415) and Verneuil (1424), but much early fifteenth-century military activity in northern France was siege warfare. Technical changes to arms, armour, military recruitment and fortification affected the men who fought, and crippling injuries must have left some campaign veterans in beggary, but women were affected at one remove, by the belt-tightening effects of war taxation and food shortage, and directly if in the path of an army, when their homes and persons were at risk; both situations are attested in the *Parisian Journal*. The military participation of their close menfolk – husbands, brothers or sons – might leave women either temporarily or in widowhood running estates and raising ransoms, or labouring in communities with a workforce drained of men. Several examples of 'ethnic cleansing' for religious motives occurred in the period, affecting men and women. The most striking example was the early sixteenth-century expulsion of Moors from Catholic Spain. Earlier localized precedents for such activity were focused on Jews in towns in the Empire, France and England. At the start of the period the Albigensian Crusade against Cathars in the south of France amounted to savage repression.

Much warring arose out of the political and dynastic ambitions of leading royal and princely families, and the traditional idea of the diplomatic marriage to bring peace held up right through the period. The most politically demanding of all marriages was surely that of Katherine of Valois to Henry V in 1420, which required her parents, Charles VI and his wife Isabeau of Bavaria, to disinherit her brother the dauphin and pass his rights to the French throne to their new son-in-law, the son of the very man who had toppled their daughter Isabelle's husband Richard II. Whether Katherine and Henry had any personal attraction for each other was obviously immaterial with stakes like these. Another obvious match, with a less overambitious purpose, was that of Ferdinand of Aragon and Isabella of Castile in 1469, which achieved the desired political result. Daughters of great feudatories were welcomed into royal families (Jeanne of Champagne into the French in 1284 for one) and royal daughters likewise into ducal dynasties (another of Charles VI's daughters married John V Duke of Brittany). The less pedigreed nobility of the city states began marrying upwards into foreign royalty in the fourteenth century: Bernabo Visconti's niece Violante brought two million gold florins and towns and castles in Piedmont as dowry when she married the English duke of Clarence, as his second wife, in 1368, while Bernabo's nephew Giangaleazzo's daughter Valentina married Louis Duke of Orléans in 1389. In 1533 Henry (II) of France married Catherine de Medici. But marriage for the purposes of power politics and indeed for local estate consolidation was the lot of only a small elite.

Women en masse were more affected by economic than political developments in this period, and economic developments were driven by demographic changes. In 1200 Europe was coming to the end of a period of good climate and population expansion. The early fourteenth century saw a downturn for both. Widespread cold wet weather in the teens of the century led to crop failure and animal disease and in turn to famine and increased human mortality. Just over 30 years later came that most fearsome of epidemics, known to history as the Black Death (1347–51) which affected Europe generally, though less severely in the Low Countries and Denmark. It is estimated that at least a third of the population died.

Owing to the recurrence of plagues, more localized but still severe, population recovery was slow to regenerate, but by the early sixteenth century increase was definitely underway. The demographic downturn brought improved living standards in the fifteenth century to those who worked their own land and to those who hired out their own labour. Despite late fourteenth-century efforts to peg wage rates and prices in the interests of employers and consumers, men and women employed in towns and countryside, for example as weavers or reapers, could secure higher wages and take advantage of opportunities for greater mobility. The unfree characteristics of the peasant/villein/serf were widely reduced. As economic conditions opened up in the fifteenth century, towns offered comparatively greater opportunities of employment for women, but by the end of the century technical developments (the introduction of heavier machinery needing male handlers and considerable capital investment) and population growth (providing plenty of male workers) was swinging the employment market away from women. Even domestic service was taking on more males, as can be seen in Florence.

Women were throughout the period disadvantaged by customs of training and professional qualification. Educating girls had never been institutionalized. Latin, the universal language not only of the western church but also of international communication in philosophy, law and diplomacy, was picked up to a limited extent by choir*boys* and studied more seriously in grammar schools and at higher levels in universities, all male institutions. The recovery of Latin elegance and style associated with renaissance humanism touched only girls of high family with literary tastes. It is not particularly noteworthy that Boccaccio should dedicate his *Famous Women* to Andrea Acciaiuoli, praising her powers of intellect and urging her to read the work, but it is surprising that he should comment about his ninety-third illustrious woman, Epicharis, honoured for hanging herself to ensure she did not reveal the secrets of a conspiracy against Nero, that she was a freedwoman, but more shameful was the fact that she lacked any taste for good literature. Was Boccaccio serious? It was true of most women, and came from their lack of exposure to literature of any 'good' quality. Women truly did not have much of a renaissance: the superiority of men was upheld by renaissance writers in the realms of theology, medicine and law.

In religious history, the time had long passed when Christian princesses, through marriage to pagan kings, were credited with converting whole peoples, but the Reformation was to bring conditions where difference in religion, that is in denomination, was to enter the world of matrimonial politics once more. In the early years of the Reformation couples who had married when orthodoxy was the norm could find themselves pulled in different directions and some marriages came under strain – see Chapter 6. Later the tendency was to marry on denominational lines. In normal conditions women could get less far in the late medieval church than they had in earlier times, when deaconesses had realistic roles and there were powerful abbesses of double houses. Barred from priestly orders and preaching, religious women in the period acquired fame mostly as mystics, prophets and ascetics, who could be listened to with approval if the church was satisfied they were divinely inspired, for this overrode birth, intellect and education. Neither birth nor education destined Margery Kempe, daughter of a burgess of Lynn, or Catherine of Siena, daughter of a dyer, for a distinguished career, but they drove themselves with an inner conviction. It is not surprising that historians should have found persuasive the supposition that given the generally gender-prejudiced attitude of the established church, the heresies of the late middle ages must have attracted women and offered them more equality, but the tide has recently turned against such optimistic interpretation. The Reformation also disappoints those who approach it expecting to see it introduce a freer society. Truly, the companionable aspect of marriage was developed, which was some 'improvement' for the wife's standing in it, but she was still expected to be subordinate, respectful of her husband's wishes, to be protected rather than given her head. The Protestant making of divorce fairer for women was an achievement, but one should not imagine that opportunities for separating were easily made available within our period.

The Evidence

Compared with earlier times the later medieval period has left an enormous amount of evidence, widely spread in terms of chronology and geography. The great expansion is in the survival of the written word. Marked improvement in quality in written evidence comes from so much of it being in near contemporary form.

Where archaeology was highly significant for the dark ages, excavation is less prominent in studying the later period from which much concrete evidence survives above ground. Sites still isolated on Umbrian hill tops, or clinging to Pyrenean gorges, convey a sense of small community security amid the less tamed countryside. Scattered, small, almost casual, settlements which grew and shrank with natural population developments look like places where the rhythm of life, largely dictated by surrounding agriculture, would change little unless forced by the passage of armies. By contrast the more formally designed imposed plantations, usually defensive, look unnatural, demanding some sort of imposed response from their inhabitants. Aigues-Mortes, crammed into its four-square defences, still shows the 'clean break' created by strictly containing walls. Restored medieval fortifications at Carcassonne show the impenetrable verticality besiegers faced. Avila is another well-walled town. The very need for the walls, and their long protracted maintenance, demonstrates how alarming raids and sieges were. Walls convey the prevalent insecurity, and the need to shut out hostile forces, human or lupine. With a few famous exceptions, medieval women were not famed for their activities on scaling ladders but they knew all about needing protection, and the suffering of hardships in a town under siege.

The civic layout and architecture of the big flourishing cities such as Venice and Florence, though visually complicated by later structures, show the flaunting wealth of the palazzo families in the last century of the period and the civic dignity of the city as a corporate body. North European guildhalls and town halls dominating, with cathedrals, the central squares, have a less flamboyant and more functional aura hinting at stolid burghers engrossed in business, that great bustling activity with its own rhythms of supply and demand. The higgledy-piggledy confusion of blind alleys and dog-leg streets within city walls of towns such as York and Norwich, along with the impressive number of parish churches, gives insight into the close habitation of comparatively rich and poor, and indicates how these characteristics created conditions favourable to doorstep charity on the one hand and indiscriminate spread of fire or disease on the other.

Urban sites, smaller market towns and even villages illustrate medieval people living together, drawing attention to the aspects which demanded co-operation and/or inspired community spirit. In the countryside too, running together for cover was the main survival strategy, as the architecture of *maisons-fortes* and pele towers reflects. By contrast the architecture of residential monasticism set a group of people apart, stressing withdrawal from the habits of the world, although still, in urban settings, open to fire, flood and disease, like their neighbours. Even more 'apart' is the architecture of the castle, where many examples of cone-topped stone towers of immense strength as portrayed in artwork such as the Duke of Berry's *Très Riches Heures* still stand on the continent. The mid-fourteenth-century massively solid royal castle of Vincennes, coupled with Charles V's inventory of 1379–80 detailing many contents, gives a rich insight into royal castle life. The additions to the chateau of Blois from Louis XII's time look much more residential. High-perched riverside castles in Germany were solid but look more ethereal because of their impressive height, as at Eltz on the Moselle. Both Eltz and Marksburg on the Rhine originated before our period but were added to and lived in through it. Residential castles may have been assuringly secure to live in, but from outside they were menacing indicators of ruling dominance, such as the count of Flanders' twelfth-century castle Gravensteen at Ghent. In *The Flowering of the Middle Ages* a diagram of Goodrich Castle in Herefordshire, built for the de Valences between 1300 and 1350, shows the domestic arrangements of the castle.[3] Castle architecture gives reality to literary motifs – the keeping of a woman in a tower by a jealous husband or possessive father, banqueting scenes, and courtyard arrivals or departures of heroes on horseback, watched, welcomed or waved off by ladies.

Regional features of architectural design and structural materials make more sensible zoning than politics or even language. People naturally built with the locally available materials, be they flint, limestone or timber. They built structures suited to heavy rainfall or blinding sunlight or exposed winds, and for the purposes of defence, devotion, local husbandry or trade. Sarah Rees Jones has attempted to identify women's influence on the design of housing, but offers more about women homeowners and tenants than about their proven input into the design of houses or of rooms within.[4] Rather more convincingly, in *Gender and Material Culture: the Archaeology of Religious Women* (1994), Roberta Gilchrist outlined an architecture associable with women religious, generally speaking 'suitably' smaller, less sturdy, and less advantageously sited than houses for men. Cathedral architecture is the main structural glory of the middle ages, but these buildings were commissioned, designed and built almost entirely by men. Women might commission commemorative chapels and of course they entered the churches as parishioners and pilgrims. The working farmstead structure, usually adapted over the centuries, is the easiest to repeople imaginatively with medieval inhabitants. The buildings underline the obvious farm use, but written sources are needed to eavesdrop on the kitchen conversations of Montaillou or, in a town context, to appreciate the dangerous opportunities presented in the Ménagier's house at Paris if maidservants were allowed to occupy rooms with street-facing windows.

The more that is already known about a person from documentation, the less important words and images chiselled on stone or incised on brass seem, though upper-class effigies do begin to be more lifelike (with faces based on death masks) and informative (about civilian dress and armour). Graves and inscriptions are not particularly significant source material for the later middle ages, but exhumation seems capable of providing new information in the future from biological testing of the remains, which will supply more data on specific conditions such as arthritis and on 'tell-tale' analyses of the bones which can reveal where – or at least in what geological conditions – the deceased was brought up, eating and drinking and absorbing the mineral print of a district. Believed identified skeletons may be examined for specific family genetic conditions, and anonymous skeletons in significant numbers in a cemetery may be examined for the incidence of disease in a population. DNA testing could reveal who was not his father's son, and throw new light on wives' fidelity or otherwise. Researchers were thrown back on skeletons to estimate average heights in the early middle ages; for the later period measurements can be taken from surviving armour, and this can include women's armour. Tomalin, in *The Fortunes of the Warrior Heroine in Italian Literature* (1982), cites the armour in Bologna identified with Catherine Sforza, which was made for a tall, plump woman, designed for ease of movement and comfort, and probably worn under a dress. Whether Catherine's or not, it belongs to her time. Discovery of alleged armour of Joan of Arc is heralded from time to time; a bascinet in New York Metropolitan Museum might have belonged to her.

Midway between material evidence and documentation comes representational art, materially visible and touchable, but a product of artistic interpretation. The quality of representation improved immeasurably between 1200 and 1550. The artist's was mainly a male profession (though Christine de Pizan knew a woman illuminator) but women were both commissioners and subjects of artistic representation. Noteworthy representations include the statue of Jeanne Duchess of Berry from the Great Hall of the duke's palace at Poitiers (c.1385), and the famous Van Eyck double portrait of 1434, placed in artistic and social context in Edwin Hall's *The Arnolfini Betrothal: Medieval Marriage and the Enigma of Van Eyck's Double Portrait* (1994). Illuminated manuscripts are particularly good sources of illustrations of women. Books of Hours form the largest single category of surviving illuminated manuscript. Created for wealthy patrons, the luxury volumes beautifully illustrated at great expense, Books of Hours normally begin with a calendar which sets out the saints' days of the liturgical year, reconciling the church and zodiac calendars and featuring illustrated seasonal occupations. These are the illustrations which interest social historians, in preference to portraits of owners or commissioners of manuscripts and churches. The activities normally chosen for the calendar are feasting (January, Twelfth Night), sitting indoors by a fire (February), pruning (March), a garden scene (April), hawking or boating (May), hay harvesting (June), corn reaping (July), threshing (August), treading grapes

(September), ploughing and sowing (October), gathering acorns for pigs (November), and pig killing or baking bread (December). The May hawking or boating scenes look fairly aristocratic and the feasting scenes often show an upper-class company being served by menials. The agricultural scenes presumably illustrate farming practices, although it must be remarked that the peasants tend to look clean and well dressed and rather well fed. The Hours of Charles of Angoulême, a late fifteenth-century text, has a happy scene of peasants dancing round a tree looking extremely clean though not exactly jolly. (The expressions on the faces of women reapers in the Luttrell Psalter, an English work of the early fourteenth century, are much sourer; one woman holding a pitcher on her head looks particularly down in the mouth, and a man and a woman are shown breaking up clods with mallets. They all look a rather more churlish lot. Incidentally women are also portrayed in this manuscript spinning with a wheel and carding wool.)

Moving to documentary evidence, from the class of impersonal administrative record there is a positive plethora of texts of canon, civil and common law and customs, for realms, towns and manors. As far as women's interests are concerned, widely applied canon law has been studied largely in relation to marriage and the family. It is a church legal source, the register of Jacques Fournier, Bishop of Pamiers and inquisitor, which provided the information analysed in E. Le Roy Ladurie's famed study of Montaillou and is also the starting point of Shahar's work on Waldensian women. Secular laws of regional application have been probed mainly for inheritance customs. Town legislation has been studied for women's civil rights on a broader scale – inheritance, marriage and separation, widows' rights, trading capabilities, rentier activities. Douai's archives are the base of Howell's *The Marriage Exchange: Property, Social Place and Gender in the Cities of the Low Countries 1300–1550* (1998). Tax records, where the most common unit is the household answered for by its head, can be informative about households headed by women, as well as (sometimes) counting women in male-headed households. The dominant text here is the Florentine *catasto* of 1427 analysed by David Herlihy and Christiane Klapisch-Zuber, and interpreted in a variety of sociological surveys. Florence then controlled nearly all the northern half of today's Tuscany, embracing its own city and *contado* (which formed only 40 per cent of its territory), lesser towns and more distant countryside. The *catasto* covered around 60,000 households and over 260,000 persons, the overall sex ratio working out at 110 men for every 100 women. Of less impersonal nature, charter material and notarial records make it possible to see the incidence of female involvement in land transactions, with or without male donors being involved. There is much there to flesh out the workings of dowry (from the bride's family) and dower (from the groom's).

Moving on to contemporary historical writing, where there is more input of authorial opinion, there is a continuation of chronicling, and under humanist influence the historical writing begins to become more deliberately interpreted history. The texts are naturally most interested in the doers and shakers, and as these were rarely women historical writing is not a particularly rich source. Joan of Arc received a certain amount of attention from contemporaries, which proves that silence about women can be due to their failure to draw writers' notice rather than antifeminist disregard. Female religious houses were never as strong on historical writing as men's, but the Dominican convents established the 'sisterbook' (*schwesternbucher*) as a genre, containing in-house history, obituaries and anecdotes. Sister Bartolomea Riccoboni's compilation from Corpus Domini Venice is drawn on in Chapter 6. Local and personal family memoranda offer good material, in which class come the *Journal d'un Bourgeois de Paris* translated by Janet Shirley in 1968 as *A Parisian Journal 1405–1449*, and the *ricordanze* of Italian merchants. Iris Origo's *The Merchant of Prato* (1963) drew on Francesco Datini's astonishing archive containing 140,000 letters, 11,000 of them private.

More imaginative literature, in Latin and the vernacular tongues, burgeoned in this period. The thirteenth century inherited from the late twelfth a well-rooted Arthurian canon which inspired translators and imitators throughout the period. The problem with using this as 'evidence' about women is that no one can be certain quite when an episode, comment or description entered the chain of texts, and therefore in what period it was originally authored. At best one may have a date for a given manuscript and the implication that its content was deemed acceptable to an audience at that time – be it as plausible, or nostalgic, or satirical. In the thirteenth-century '*cantefable*' *Aucassin and Nicolette*, the heroine takes the initiative with regard to her dreamy lover, reversing the more normal literary pattern of the male ennobled and inspired by love for his characterless lady. (This inversion is seen earlier in some of Marie de France's *Lais*.) Three thirteenth-century romances, two by Jean Renart, will be commented on in Chapter 2. Also inherited from the twelfth century was the lyrically expressed courtly love first voiced by troubadours. This was refined into polite literature (in contrast with the earthy fabliaux). Joan Ferrante showed how Dante developed the allegory and courtly love streams in the *Divine Comedy*, elevating the once human Beatrice into his own spiritual guide, playing for him the role widely ascribed to the Virgin, but this is not sacrilegious because it is the Virgin who sends Beatrice to save him. The prolific French poet Eustace Deschamps portrayed women across the board, sometimes misogynistically, sometimes sympathetically. His incomplete *Mirror of Marriage* (1380s) runs through the traditional antifeminist canon, deterring Franc Vouloir from matrimony.

People read, or listened to others read, literature for pleasure, but the serious writers were inclined to include a didactic element and even the fabliaux had an element of 'the moral of this story is...' about them. An interesting feature of the period is the collecting together of brief tales centred on women. Boccaccio's *Famous Women* (*De Mulieribus Claris*), a Latin work written in 1361–2, was the first of this kind in the period. It was soon followed by Chaucer's much briefer *Legend of Good Women* (c. 1386, whether this was inspired by Boccaccio or not is disputed) and Christine de Pizan's *The Book of the City of Ladies* (1405), which draws heavily on Boccaccio for source material. Boccaccio dedicated his book to Andrea Acciauoli in a rather unflattering preface wherein he decided not to aim as high as Queen Joanna of Naples as dedicatee. Chaucer's book, of ladies martyred for love, was, according to the 'F' prologue, to be sent to the queen at Eltham or Sheen (Richard II's first queen, Anne of Bohemia). Christine's sequel, *The Book of the Three Virtues,* was written for Marguerite of Nevers (Margaret of Burgundy) around the time of her marriage (1405) to the dauphin. The implication is that it was appropriate to dedicate a work about women to a woman. Would it have been inappropriate to dedicate such a work to a man? Boccaccio stated that he compiled his 'slim volume in praise of women' more for his friends' pleasure than for a wider public, but promptly added that he pondered where to direct it to have a better chance of reaching the public. Would dedicating a book to a woman further it more strongly than dedicating it to a man? It seems unlikely. Anne of Bohemia and Margaret of Burgundy were well-born and well-married; Andrea, married to the count of Altavilla, was the sister of an old friend of Boccaccio's who was powerful at Joanna of Naples' court. Were these ladies' husbands or Andrea's brother the real target, with a dainty compliment to their women? Was it imagined only women would be interested? If men were expected to read these works, concentrating on women, it marks a change of taste. Yet the friends of Boccaccio's dedication were unlikely to have been an all-female circle; on the other hand most of Boccaccio's moralizing in the work was to improve the behaviour of contemporary women, not men, although possibly fathers could have learnt a thing or two from the warnings.

There is unquestionably more known female authorship from the later middle ages, and on serious subjects. Women themselves wrote letters, biographies (not only of women), sisterbooks, mystical and visionary literature, lyric and other poetry, short tales, tracts and treatises in the period. Letters range from official, such as Joan of Arc's letters to Reims, to the private, such as Perchta of Rožmberk's letters to her father about her unhappy marriage to John of Lichtenstein. Famed mystical writers from successive periods within the timescale will be discussed in Chapter 6. One development which enabled women to communicate more easily was the increasing use of the vernacular for literary expression. Not much of their work, however, really offers evidence from which conclusions may be drawn about women in general. Mystical works show the heights of the mystic's spiritual experience but essentially theirs was a rarefied world quite out of the ordinary. These works were quite often written by a male confessor or secretary and Catherine Mooney has raised the significance of male mediation of a woman's communication in *Gendered Voices: Medieval Saints and their Interpreters* (1999). A well-reputed holy woman might risk criticizing the worldly church, or offer advice to its male clergy and even to secular rulers, but her daring (always presented as not hers as such but divine inspiration using her as an instrument) and their listening (based on the same presumption) both derived from her acceptance as a woman elevated by divine grace above her natural position. By contrast the involvement in Catholic reform of Marguerite of Navarre (d 1549) has to be understood to appreciate the context of her *Heptameron*'s vicious and scatological handling of monks and friars in particular. Christine de Pizan (d c.1430), a laywoman, was the most outstanding female writer of the middle ages, and is treated more fully below in Chapter 7.

The Historiography of the Subject

Eileen Power's wide-ranging pioneering essay on 'The Position of Women' was published in 1926 in *The Legacy of the Middle Ages*, edited by C. G. Crump and E. F. Jacob, and was hardly improved upon when her widower, M. M. Postan, published what he saw as her more popular output on the subject as *Medieval Women* in 1975. At that date there was still surprisingly little directly published on women in the Middle Ages, and general histories paid them little attention. Thirty years on, the general reader has a good choice of survey books on medieval women from the end of antiquity to the Renaissance or Reformation, or over a shorter time span, or for a particular region. Narrowing the focus, there are more specialized studies of women, sometimes women considered in the context of the family, and for smaller areas or for shorter periods. Narrowing further, there are studies, usually in articles or papers, on classes of women in particular locations. The professionally religious women, such as nuns in convents, increasingly confined tertiaries, and more loosely tethered beguines, as groups, and the individual mystics who might be part of such groupings, or recluses, or who simply defy any stable categorization, have attracted much study but the average laywoman's religious practice is a subject which could do with more attention. There are also studies of women specifically in the context of changes in economy or religion.

Areas of more abstract classification, notably physical sexual difference (as perceived but not of course accurately understood by contemporaries) and more especially the concept of gender, that is the cultural (including educational) consequences of sexual difference, have become more recent focuses of attention. As the twentieth century became more open about sexual practices and orientation, such aspects as abortion and contraception, prostitution, homosexuality and lesbianism in the middle ages have been taken up.

The traditional historical source material – chronicles, more opinionated histories, laws and judicial records, tax records, and private memoranda and letters – tends to give most information on elite women, queens, noblewomen, leading merchants' wives, abbesses and other religious women often of high birth with highly placed ecclesiastical relatives. To penetrate more ordinary levels of society one needs particularly the tax records based on household units, which is where the Florentine *catasto* of 1427 has been so immensely important. Bishop Fournier's Register also illuminates lower-class society: both have already been referred to above in discussion of the evidence. A huge collection of studies has been based deliberately on fiction, particularly on the vernacular romances of the period. The literary representation of women (and these figures' intended reception by readers or hearers) is a matter of image, nuance, interpretation. More imaginative theories can be floated and argued with varying degrees of plausibility about literary sources than, say, about municipal records. The literary source material is a pleasurable read and its use for historical interpretation can be tied in with other types of source – obviously the perspective of the lover's lady as his superior and an ennobling influence on him calls for comparison with the Virgin's portrayal by the church to the faithful. There is a further body of serious treatises and commentaries which can be combed for insight into the authors' views on women. One of the most valuable achievements of the last few decades has been the publication of translated editions of the works of medieval women writers, making them very much more widely available. With the arrival of women's studies in the academic curriculum has come the publication of useful sourcebooks for teaching purposes.

The outcome of research has been presented in all possible forms. There are single-authored books, books of collected essays from one author or several (the latter sometimes conference papers from a particular gathering of specialists in a field) and isolated contributions to journals and websites. Well-established journals receptive to articles on medieval women, such as the *Journal of Medieval and Renaissance Studies, Past & Present, Renaissance Quarterly, Speculum,* and *Viator,* have been joined by specialists such as *Feminist Studies, Gender and History,* the *Journal of Women's History, Signs* and *Women's Studies.* What follows is a discussion of works of the various kinds indicated above, arranged by themes. Arbitrarily, many works on specifically English women have been left out to avoid overweighting one area, but the discussion is restricted to works available in English since these are so much easier for readers in Britain and the United States to obtain and absorb.

Of the general books, S. Shahar's *The Fourth Estate: a History of Women in the Middle Ages,* translated into English by C. Galai in 1983, was pioneering. Concentrating on the period from the early twelfth to mid-fifteenth century it covers western Europe, expressly excluding Scandinavia, Scotland and Ireland. (Many works which do not admit to excluding these territories virtually do so by finding nothing to say about them.) Shahar began with the framework of public and legal rights, then dealt with nuns, then with married women, then the three classes of society in hierarchical order – noblewomen, townswomen and peasantwomen – and ended with the outsider categories of witches and heretics. This sectionalizing has been very influential. Three years later came M. W. Labarge's *Women in Medieval Life.* The 1986 edition was subtitled 'A Small Sound of the Trumpet', which has been (wisely) dropped from the 2001 edition. The study limited itself to France, England, the Low Countries and southern Germany, and apart from an earlier background chapter, to the period 1100–1500. Instead of fixing her framework in public and private rights, Labarge ranged more widely over physical conditions and social patterns, and theories and teaching as well as laws. Her next five chapters run through queens, noble ladies, nuns and beguines, recluses and mystics, and townswomen and peasants. Then follow chapters on women as healers and nurses, and on women on the fringe, who include prostitutes, criminals, heretics and sorcerers. The final chapter assesses women's contribution to medieval culture, moving through nuns to mystics and then through women's participation in music, embroidery, book collecting, and writing, culminating with Christine de Pizan. The book is an orderly survey and an attractive read, but it merely tells readers how things were, with little inspiring of curiosity to locate and try to fill gaps. E. Ennen's *The Medieval Woman*, translated by E. Jephcott (1989) has more about it. Ambitiously, it copes with 500–1500, subdividing at 1050 and 1250. It includes statistically based interpretation such as variant sex ratios in various places at different times. Throughout the work there is a strong awareness of development which is brought to a flourish in a conclusion looking at constants and variables and continuity in change. In short, this is not just a book of information about women, drawing illustration from Germany, France, Italy, Spain, the Low Countries and England, but a book with perspective. A multi-authored general book is *Women in Medieval Western European Culture*, edited by L. E. Mitchell (1999), an excellent work covering 500–1500.

Recently, survey writers have tended to tackle either the earlier or the later period. J. Ward's *Women in Medieval Europe 1200–1500* (2002) is comprehensive, clearly set out and provided with excellent notes and further reading. Establishing the framework provided by church and law, the book is arranged with four chapters on domestic circumstances, two on women and work, two on aspects of women and power and patronage, then five on women in the context of religion, including one on laywomen and charity and another on lay beliefs and religious practice. The book ends with heresy and witchcraft.

Studies selecting a particular geographical area for study are relieved of the responsibility to consider all aspects of the general scene since some may not locally apply. Not surprisingly, therefore, such works often read with more pace. Two which excel are H. Dillard's *Daughters of the Reconquest: Women in Castilian Town Society 1100–1300* (1984), and D. Nicholas's *The Domestic Life of a Medieval City: Women, Children and the Family in Fourteenth-Century Ghent* (1985). In a class apart are the massive analyses and interpretations based on the Florentine *catasto* of 1427. D. Herlihy and C. Klapisch-Zuber first produced their monumental *Les Toscans et leur familles* in 1978; it was translated into English, apparently condensed by half but still hefty, as *Tuscans and their Families* in 1985. Women emerge from this household-assessed taxation record in their thousands: *Tuscans and their Families* is a book of immense significance, and though certain chapters have greater relevance to the study of women than others, the whole needs to be read to gain a proper context for the statistics and an understanding of the record and the procedures which produced it. Those daunted by the size of the book could profit from reading Klapisch-Zuber's essay on 'State and Family in a Renaissance Society: the Florentine *Catasto* of 1427', in her *Women, Family and Ritual in Renaissance Italy* (1985). This translated collection of 14 essays (previously published between 1972 and 1983 in French or Italian journals and books) draws on the *catasto* and other tax surveys, family *ricordanze*, bequests, art and laws. Klapisch-Zuber contributed an article on 'Women Servants in Florence during the Fourteenth and Fifteenth Centuries' to *Women and Work in Preindustrial Europe*, edited by B. A. Hanawalt (1986), a wide-ranging book within its theme, including contributions by Otis on municipal wet-nurses in Montpellier, Wiesner on early modern midwifery (in Nuremberg), Reyerson on businesswomen in Montpellier, Davies on women in the crafts in sixteenth-century Lyons and M. Howell on 'Women, Family Economy and the Structure of Market Production in North European Cities', a subject more fully treated in her *Women, Production and Patriarchy in Late Medieval Cities* (1986) focusing on Leiden and Cologne. On a higher social level, *Aristocratic Women in Medieval France* edited by T. Evergates (1999) is mainly pre-1200 but does run through the thirteenth century with the hereditary countesses of Champagne and Flanders, treated by Evergates and Karen Nicholas respectively.

Ennen's survey was mentioned above as particularly conscious of change, and some studies have been deliberately focused on changing conditions. The most obvious changes in the period were demographic and religious. The falling-off of population expansion early in the fourteenth century caused by bad climate in the teens of the century affecting overpopulated economies, followed by the ravages of the Black Death and subsequent plagues, had immediate consequences for the sorrowing and shaken survivors, and long-term consequences for employment and production for over a century. The late fourteenth-century population crash is considered in *Tuscans and their Families*, and in terms of opening employment possibilities for women it is handled by P. J. P. Goldberg in *Women, Work and Life Cycle in York and Yorkshire c.1300–1520* (1992). The big religious change was the Reformation, which has been treated in various ways in terms of women. R. H. Bainton tackled *Women of the Reformation in Germany and Italy* in 1971, and carried the study through France and England (1973) and from Spain to Scandinavia (1977). A more purposeful method was applied by Lyndal Roper in *The Holy Household: Women and Morals in Reformation Augsburg* (1989). Writing on the gender aspect of the Reformation tends naturally to be pulled into the early modern period. The contribution 'Women, Gender and Sexuality' by Wiesner-Hanks in *Palgrave Advances in the European Reformations*, edited by A. Ryrie (2006), is a good survey.

The intrinsic interests of keen religionists meant that women famous in the religious sphere, such as St Clare and St Catherine of Siena, were subjects for study long before women's studies as such burst on the scene, but often publications prove to be of religious orientation rather than historical analysis. As a good brisk overall view, P. Ranft's *Women and the Religious Life in Premodern Europe* (1996) cannot be bettered. L. P. Hindsley's *The Mystics of Engelthal* (1998) is doubly useful, for it not only studies the writings of a group of women mystics but accounts for the whole spiritual context of a particular Dominican monastery. On the beguines, E. W. McDonnell, *The Beguines and Beghards in Medieval Culture* (1954) is still cited everywhere, but there is now W. Simons, *Cities of Ladies: Beguine Communities in the Medieval Low Countries 1200–1565* (2001). M. Warner's *Alone of All her Sex: the Myth and Cult of the Virgin Mary* (1976) was a ground-breaking study and is particularly valuable for non-Catholics who may not realize, until they read it, the gaps in their own understanding of the development of dogma and the practical impact of church teaching especially on women. K. L. Jansen's *The Making of the Magdalen: Preaching and Popular Devotion in the Later Middle Ages* (2000) is more directly historical in approach. *Women in the Church*, edited by W. J. Sheils and D. Wood (*Studies in Church History*, 27, 1990), offers wide-ranging papers from the 1989–90 meetings of the Ecclesiastical History Society. For heresy and other religions, recent works include Shahar's *Women in a Late Medieval Sect* (2001), E. Baumgarten's *Mothers and Children: Jewish Family Life in Medieval Europe* (2004) and R. L. Melamed's *Heretics or Daughters of Israel? The Crypto-Jewish Women of Castile* (1999).

To concentrate on a particular convent, order, saint or sect is comparatively straightforward. C. W. Bynum touched on something altogether more insubstantial when she wrote *Holy Feast and Holy Fast: the Religious Significance of Food to Medieval Women* (1987). It seems doubtful that such a topic would have been undertaken, and certainly not in such a way, before the modern psychological interest in eating disorders. With Bynum's guidance, female dietary excesses and fervid outbursts connected with the Eucharist seem totally explicable. *Holy Feast and Holy Fast* was a gender-conscious book. It separated male and female attitudes to eating, and to nurturing others. *Gendered Voices: Medieval Saints and their Interpreters*, edited by C. M. Mooney (1999), also focuses on subtleties of gender in the religious context, in the particular area of male interpretation of female saints and visionaries. *Gender and Society in Renaissance Italy*, edited by J. C. Brown and R. C. Davis in 1998, has a good introduction to the development of the gender perspective. *Gender and Difference in the Middle Ages*, edited by S. Farmer and C. B. Pasternack (2003), is not as satisfying, probably because it tackles widely varied times and places. *Gender in Debate from the Early Middle Ages to the Renaissance*, edited by T. S. Fenster and C. A. Lees (2002), has a good balance of French, German, Italian and Spanish material. One of the big areas of gender discrimination in the medieval period was in education. *Beyond their Sex: Learned Women of the European Past*, edited by P. Labalme in 1980, contains useful articles on this topic.

Medieval physiology was inherited from the ancients and the Arabs and only in the last century or so of the period was much actual observation feeding into the sum of knowledge. J. Cadden's *The Meaning of Sex Difference in the Middle Ages: Medicine, Science and Culture* (1993) is largely about the earlier medieval period when the transmission of knowledge was in full swing. For the later period and moving into early modern times, I. McLean's *The Renaissance Notion of Woman: a Study of the Fortunes of Medical Science in European Intellectual Life* (1980) is stimulating. For the most part the anatomical differences between the male and female body were interpreted in the man's favour, leaving the woman as defective. Where she was most strikingly different was in her reproductive organs, and the constant need for birthing assistance produced some experts – or at least specialist practitioners – in the midwives, whose study by Wiesner was noted above. S. Ozment's *When Fathers Ruled: Family Life in Reformation Europe* (1983) is actually the unlikely sounding source of a good critique of Eucharius Rösslin's *Rosengarten* of 1513, the first printed manual for midwives. The *Handbook of Medieval Sexuality*, edited by V. L. Bullough and J. A. Brundage (1996), is an excellent introduction to many aspects, with notes and guides to sources attached to the contributions which are grouped under the headings of sexual norms, variance from norms, and cultural issues. The chapter on prostitution was written by R. M. Karras, who wrote *Common Women: Prostitution and Sexuality in Medieval England* (1996); L. Otis had already produced *Prostitution in Medieval Society: the History of an Urban Institution in Languedoc* (1985) and contributed an article on prostitution in Perpignan to *Women in the Medieval World* (1985), edited by J. Kirshner and S. F. Wemple. J. Rossiaud's *Medieval Prostitution* (1988) centres on activity down the Rhône valley from Burgundy to Provence.

Throughout the last thirty years a constant feature has been the historical study of women through literature of the period. J. Ferrante's *Women as Image in Medieval Literature from the Twelfth Century to Dante* (1975) remains a good clear introduction to certain prevalent types of writing – exegesis, allegory, lyric and romance – and their respective handling of women culminating with Dante (d 1321). L. Sponsler's *Women in the Medieval Spanish Epic and Lyric Traditions* (1975) tracks the softening of attitude to women in later versions of the epics and the emerging ballads and lyrics. M. Tomalin's *The Features of the Warrior Heroine in Italian Literature* is significantly subtitled 'An Index of Emancipation' and convincingly links the literature to contemporary times and attitudes. Though not specifically focused on women, L. Muir's *Literature and Society in Medieval France: the Mirror and the Image 1100–1500* (1985) contributes to the understanding of how that society saw itself, women included. (Muir's comments on *Aucassin and Nicolette*, for example, are helpful to the reader approaching the text for the first time.) A good deal more startling is E. J. Burns's *Bodytalk: When Women Speak in Old French Literature* (1993). The romances Burns deals with are pre-1200 in origin, but the fabliaux she handles are thirteenth- and fourteenth-century compositions. With more specific focus, S. Severin examined *Witchcraft in Celestina* (1995).

Bringing the sources to wider public knowledge took off as medieval women's history became more widely taught. E. Amt's *Women's Lives in Medieval Europe: a Sourcebook* (1993) is one of the best sourcebooks, but is open to criticism for its heavy use of material from England, which forms half the sources illustrating the noble life and more than half those illustrating the working life. Among the religious sources included are the rule of St Clare from 1253, and a description of the beguines of St Elizabeth's, Ghent, from 1328. The book ends with practical housekeeping extracts from the Parisian Ménagier's book from 1392, previously only available in English in E. Power's 1928 translation *The Goodman of Paris*, which is not easily accessible. Amt includes evidence from official sources and male commentators, as does J. Murray in *Love, Marriage and Family in the Middle Ages: A Reader* (2001), which contains a good selection of material but some readers may find its comprehension questions after the texts annoying. C. Larrington's *Women and Writing in Medieval Europe: a Sourcebook* (1995) selects from writings by, for and about women. There are seven sections, each with a thematic introduction followed by texts. The extracts, with the exception of two Montaillou items from Fournier's register, are all from constructed writing, that is literary, historical, theological, narrative and imaginative writing. It has a really good spread from Iceland to Byzantium and brings to light some rarely publicized writing such as salacious verse by the Welsh female poet Gwerful Mechain (d c.1500), and the play *Marika of Nijmeghen* attributed to a fourteenth–fifteenth-century writer Anna Bijns from Antwerp. Where M. Thiébaux's *The Writings of Medieval Women* (2nd edition 1994) is mostly pre-1200, E. Spearing's *Medieval Writings on Female Spirituality* (2002) has a broad collection of extracts, including women writers and mostly post-1200. Two volumes from the Manchester Medieval

Sources series can be recommended to readers with interests confined to England: *Women in England c. 1275–1525* (1995) translated and edited by P. J. P. Goldberg, and *Women of the English Nobility and Gentry 1066–1500* (1995) translated and edited by J. Ward.

Medieval Women Writers, edited by K. Wilson (1983), covers 15 women writers. Each is interpreted by a different author, with a footnoted essay, a sample of their writing, and a bibliography. The later writers included are Mechthild of Magdeburg, Hadewijch of Brabant, St Bridget of Sweden, St Catherine of Siena, Julian of Norwich, Margery Kempe, Florencia Pinar and Christine de Pizan. This is a tremendously useful volume for giving an overall grasp of the variety of women's writing in different times and places, a sample larger than a few quotations from their work, and guidance for further reading. P. Dronke, who contributed on Castelloza the Provençal trobairitz, published his own *Women Writers of the Middle Ages: a Critical Study of Texts from Perpetua († 203) to Marguerite Porete († 1310)* in 1984, but this does not have much to offer for the period after 1200 since only the last chapter is relevant, running from Hildegard to Marguerite, but questionably paying quite a lot of attention to Grazide Lizier of Montaillou, whose words are known to us through her testimony at the Cathar inquisitions but who can hardly be considered a woman writer in the sense of a purposeful author.

Appetites whetted by samples of women's writing have been increasingly well supplied by modern editions of whole works. It is surprising that Christine de Pizan's extremely valuable *Book of the Treasure of the City of Ladies or Book of the Three Virtues* was only first translated into English, by S. Lawson, in 1985. Christine's rather less useful *Book of the City of Ladies* was rendered into modern English by E. J. Richards in 1982 (after previous translation in 1521). The importance of both books is indicated in Chapter 7 below. (For clarity the former book will henceforth be referred to by its alternative *Three Virtues* title – by which it is sometimes identified anyway – because otherwise its title's similarity with the *Book of the City of Ladies* is confusing. The *Three Virtues* was a sequel to the *Book of the City of Ladies*, and there is further confusion, since some translations use 'Treasure' and others 'Treasury' for the French *Trésor*.) Christine's *The Book of the Body Politic* was first translated into modern English in 1994. The American scholar C. C. Willard edited and/or translated several of Christine's works for publication. She edited the *Livre de la Paix*, in French, in 1958, based on her own doctoral thesis of 1940; translated *The Book of the Three Virtues* under the title *A Medieval Woman's Mirror of Honor: the Treasury of the City of Ladies* in 1989; and in 1999 edited *The Book of Deeds of Arms and Chivalry*, translated by her husband S. Willard. She produced a selection of Pizan extracts including poems in *The Writings of Christine de Pizan* in 1993. As a critical commentator, she contributed an examination of the *Livre des Trois Virtus* as a fifteenth-century view of women's role in society to R. Morewedge's *The Role of Women in the Middle Ages*, published as early as 1975 and originating as a conference paper in 1972, and also supplied the Pizan contribution to Wilson's *Medieval Women Writers*. Her delightful biography *Christine de Pizan, her Life and Works* was published in 1984. The 'discovery' of Christine has led to a shelf-sagging mass of publications, editions, commentaries, biographies and festschrift offerings and conference papers.

The mystical writers have had their longer works published as well as featuring in extracts in anthologies. Mechthild of Magdeburg's *Flowing Light of the Divinity* was published in 1991, Gertrude of Helfta's *Herald of Divine Love* in 1993. Julian of Norwich's *Revelations of Divine Love* has been edited several times under slightly varying titles. Finally, the growing Library of Medieval Women is a series to watch. It includes from the later medieval period J. B. Holloway's *Saint Bride and her Book: Birgitta of Sweden's Revelations* (1992/2000), R. Blumenfeld-Kosinski's *The Writings of Margaret of Oingt Medieval Prioress and Mystic* (1990), M. B. Williamson's *The Memoirs of Helene Kottaner* (1998) and J. M. Klassen's *The Letters of the Rožmberk sisters* (2001).

Readers should also bear in mind that there is much on medieval women to be found in books on such topics as canon law, marriage, household, private life, and demography. Works on queens and power wielded by women seem less significant in the historiography of this later period than they were for earlier times, although P. Matarasso's *Queen's Mate: Three Women of Power in France on the Eve of the Renaissance* (2001) is exceptional, and two books edited by M. C. Erler and M. Kowaleski, *Women and Power in the Middle Ages* (1988) and *Gendering the Master Narrative: Women and Power in the Middle Ages* (2003) are stimulating. K. M. Wilson and N. Margolis, *Women in the Middle Ages, an Encyclopedia* (2004) is a useful reference work.

2

Contemporary Gender Theory and Society's Expectations of Women

The framework of gender relations inherited from Greek and Roman theories and Judeo-Christian and barbarian practices had been handed down through the centuries to the start of our period. With classical ideas and Roman law revitalized in the twelfth-century renaissance, and most of what western Europe learned from the Arabs already absorbed by 1200, there was little cause for substantial rethinking of social frameworks in the next centuries. The Renaissance of the fifteenth and sixteenth centuries again placed emphasis on the formal, civilized societies of the ancient world, and although humanism tends to be associated with more liberated thought, doubts have been rightly cast on whether women enjoyed a renaissance alongside men. The Protestant Reformers liked to see themselves as freeing women from the tyranny of nunneries, but the freedom they offered them was still patriarchally dominated. What does emerge in the period on the theoretical side is a more conscious discussion of the subject, with more public airing of the women's side of the case.

Developments from Judeo-Christian Tradition, Canon Law and Ancient Medicine

The main features of the Judeo-Christian inheritance, transmitted particularly in the Bible and canon law, were upheld and indeed developed by (largely male) writers and preachers through the period up to 1200. In the Old Testament male babies were clearly preferred, daughters were expected to be virginal until marriage, wives' prime function was procreational, and they were kept busy with household responsibilities. The New Testament added the massively influential pronouncements of St Paul, subordinating women to their husbands, and silencing them in church, and Christ and Paul took a much more uncompromising attitude to divorce than the Old Testament had. Further developed by the Church Fathers, the sometimes contradictory gender dynamics of the Bible continued to be influential, and the massive codifying of canon law especially in the twelfth century made it easier to identify the sources, and supporters, of particular behavioural regulations. The papacy's grip on the west strengthened, reaching a high point with the pontificate of Innocent III, and the Fourth Lateran council of 1215.

Nothing shook women's position in western Christianity fundamentally after 1200. Their souls were already established as equal to men's, marriage was already subject to discipline as monogamous and ideally lifelong, concubinage was disapproved, and Christian laywomen merged into gender-neutral parishioners in terms of required church attendance, confession and communion. Women had long been allowed to enter professional religious communities, and had never in normal circumstances been allowed to practise sacerdotal ministry, both of which conditions pertained throughout the period. In the context of Judeo-Christian inheritance, opportunities for women changed little. To the conventual life, previously dominated by the Benedictines, were added the new openings of the Dominican and Franciscan orders, but the difference between a Dominican or Franciscan nun and a Benedictine one was far less striking than that between a mendicant friar and a member of an older regular order because the women were soon, for the most part, more tightly cloistered than the essentially extramural friars, and even the worldlier tertiaries tended to get reined in. Women in orders resisted strict claustration, both openly as in the struggles of St Clare to keep her order as close to the male Franciscans as possible, and more subversively by keeping imposed rules badly, letting visitors in and allowing visits out, as in the notoriously lax Benedictine St Zaccaria in Venice in the late fifteenth and early sixteenth centuries. At the end of the period stricter enforcement of claustration was one of the measures of the Council of Trent.

The development of the cults of two women over the period, the Virgin Mary and Mary Magdalen, shows that much could be constructed on quite slender textual tradition and slanted to the church's purpose. Marina Warner's *Alone of All Her Sex: the Myth and Cult of the Virgin Mary* claims that Mary represented a central theme in the history of western attitudes to women. The Gospels really offer little about Mary; apocryphal writings extended interest back to her own conception, birth and infancy, and the focus subsequently widened (into her family) and deepened (into the arguments around perpetual virginity, immaculate conception and assumption). Her feast days multiplied from the seventh century, and artistic representation in mosaics, stone- and woodcarving, ivories, painting and manuscript illumination testifies to the widespread enthusiasm for her cult and its development over the centuries. Leading churchmen of the eleventh and twelfth centuries promoted her cult and indeed the Cistercians customarily dedicated their abbeys to her. Hymns were composed in her honour. At the same period that the Virgin's status was consolidated, the literary cult of the lady celebrated in troubadour poetry became fashionable; it is now argued that these were independent developments even though coincidental in time, and should not be seen as indicative of a positive movement in the standing of women at large. In the thirteenth century the streams came together with Mary increasingly seen as 'Our Lady', and attracting poets' attention. Much anonymous poetry defies categorization as secular or religious because it cannot be known whether the poet was addressing his corporal mistress or his chaste inspirational lady, the Queen of Heaven. Paradoxically, Mary the *Virgin* had a dimension beyond that of worldly women as objects of poetic adoration because she was celebrated as a *mother*, which they were not. Lovers wrote of the thrill of courtship, especially illicit stolen kisses, and of ecstasy if the affair reached consummation, but they did not revel in the calmer deep constancy enjoyed by long-established couples, giving life and rejoicing in their children. Yet the essence of motherhood, with its pains of pregnancy and labour and the selflessness required in coping with the messiness of infancy and the responsibility of child rearing, was well enough identified and appreciated, and this is often found expressed in writings discussing the motherly qualities of Christ. In art, the Virgin and Child became more natural and affectionate figures, less hieratic than earlier representations, while the image of Mary as the grieving mother at the Crucifixion also became popular in western Europe. Statues, paintings and manuscript illumination show the changing styles of representation which in turn reflect the prevalent religious atmosphere. Youthful Virgins straddling bouncing babe on hip, and tender ones seated with lifelike baby at the breast reflect the more intimate affective religion of the later middle ages, by contrast with the rigid authoritative unbending figures of the first millennium, and the impractically classically draped elegant and distant Virgins of the Renaissance. Mary's mothering attributes could be sympathized with by ordinary women (and men), but her role as the great intercessor for mankind was beyond human emulation, even if the mother's role in a family with a stern father had similarities, and her role as Queen of Heaven was occasionally paralleled with an earthly queen's.

When Christians thought of Mary as Queen of Heaven she was positioned well above the human race, and her bodily assumption kept her from the indignity of having corporal relics handled. When they thought of her as the mother of the holy child, they were grasping a more familiar image and bringing her down closer to the normality of family life as they knew it. To check any disrespect implicit in this homeliness, distance could be reasserted through the miraculous elements of virgin birth, and the virgin's own immaculate conception. Still believers yearned to domesticize the holy family. Mary certainly attracted a lot more attention than Joseph, and it was Mary's mother St Anne and her cousin St Elizabeth who provided the extensions. (Considering that the beholders lived in patrilineal societies this interest in Christ's mother's side rather bucks the secular trend.) Joseph, whose standing increased in the fifteenth century, was more than just the chance foster father of the son of God, since his 14-generation descent from David, differently listed in Matthew 1 and Luke 3, slotted Christ into place as 'son of David, son of Abraham' and Isaiah's 'root of Jesse' (David's father). The period took some homely liberties with Joseph which have relevance for gender studies: in nativity plays he could be naïve and bumbling, a cradle-rocker and baby feeder, and in art the 'housefather' preparing the baby's bath, or after he became a more vigorous authoritative household head, the craft head of household teaching the young Christ carpentry as in the misericord at St Sulpice de Favières.[1]

To refocus on Mary, she was essentially too perfect to be a role model for women with all their faults. Women could not emulate her, and they could only hope for her intercession out of her grace and mercy. No comfort for penitent sinners came from her example, but such was offered by Mary Magdalen. Another construction from slight textual tradition, the Magdalen was in her western form a medieval 'invention' created by Gregory the Great's conflation of three biblical figures: Mary of Bethany, sister of Lazarus, Mary of Magdala to whom the risen Christ first appeared, a woman from whom he had earlier cast out devils and who had been at the Crucifixion, and the unnamed forgiven sinner of Luke 7:37–8. Later legends had her, with her sister Martha and Lazarus and others, washed up in a rudderless boat on the coast of Provence, where her body was 'discovered' at St Maximin (Aix) in 1279 (though Vézelay's relics of her, supposedly stolen from Provence to rescue her from Saracen invasion in the eighth century, had been displayed as recently as 1265). Even more than the figure of the Virgin, the figure of the Magdalen illustrates the western church's ability to develop an identification to suit its purpose over the centuries. Gregory's Magdalen created from one, two or three persons was only part of the manipulation. There is nothing in the biblical references to make it beyond doubt that the nature of the penitent woman's many sins was harlotry, nor is the beauty of any of the women cited stressed, but the medieval western image of the Magdalen was of a beautiful penitent harlot, which made painting her a pleasurable proposition. She was famed for her hair (this derived from the episode of the sinner bathing Christ's feet with tears and drying them with her hair) and artists flung themselves into depicting a luxuriance of hair, sometimes clothing her in wavy tresses hanging down to her feet. Houses for repentant prostitutes were regularly dedicated to her, and because of the Lazarus episode, itself conflated with the leprous beggar of Luke 16:20, she became patron of leper hospitals. Because of her assumed past she became patron of many luxury crafts – perfumiers, apothecaries, glovemakers, hairdressers and cosmeticians. Mary Magdalen fulfilled many needs with her versatility. Jansen's *The Making of the Magdalen* concentrates on the period of the height of her cult in Provence and Italy, tying it in with the penitential preaching of the mendicant orders in particular. Both sexes could repent, but the penitent prostitute figure of the Middle Ages was characteristically female, so the Magdalen image was especially targeted at conscience-stricken women. But the Magdalen was not only a saint for women. As one of Christ's circle, honoured by his appearing first to her after resurrection, Mary Magdalen was worthy of men's devotion, and this particular revelationary favour could be held up to the most abject sinner to show divine forgiveness could still be hoped for by the truly penitent. Mary Magdalen was a symbol of hope for medieval sinners and more approachable than the Virgin.

The church's use of the Virgin and saints as mediators through whom human beings might less awesomely approach the Almighty showed the friendlier face of medieval religion. Familiarity with the saints was encouraged through the linking of patron saints to cities, churches, chapels, religious guilds and crafts. By their symbols – Mary Magdalen's was an ointment jar – their images were as decipherable to the initiated illiterate as by any written label to a reader. Their feast days were regulated in the recurring ecclesiastical calendar. Miracles were performed at their shrines and by their relics. There were more men saints than women, but women were well represented, and individual women saints were as respected as men; they were not second class because of their sex.

By contrast with this human face, canon law was dry and unappealing, full of contentious interpretation, redefined in particulars, always growing. Women mostly came into contact with its matrimonial jurisdiction. The Fourth Lateran tried to reduce causes for matrimonial litigation by meeting some of the problems in advance. It redefined the degrees of consanguinity and affinity, reducing the prohibited relationships to four degrees. It sought to strengthen the publicity of marriage, forbidding priests' presence at clandestine weddings, and instituted publication of banns before marriage, providing opportunity for knowledge of impediments to be raised before the event took place. It tightened up the reliability of evidence allowable in matrimonial cases, ruling out hearsay. However, clandestine marriage, though sinful, remained valid until the Council of Trent, and papal dispensation could be obtained for marriages within four degrees.

Marriage for Christians was ideally lifelong and monogamous. There was no medieval facility for modern-style divorce, freeing the parties to contract marriage again. Marriages could only be annulled (when proven in effect to have been non-marriages despite appearances), in which case the parties were as free to marry other spouses as if the marriage had not taken place, or ended by separation ('from bed and board') in which case the parties were released from living together but remained legally married to each other and therefore unable to marry anyone else. By the later middle ages grounds for annulment included forced marriage lacking free consent, previous undisclosed valid marriage to a partner still alive, non-consummation/impotence and subsequently discovered prohibited kinship or affinity. Grounds for separation included a partner's adultery, heresy or violence to the other. Annulment was essential if either party wished to have legitimate heirs with a subsequent partner. Separation was only convenience, not change of status. Church courts had established their right of jurisdiction over matrimonial business by the start of the period, but in some cities secular officials handled some matrimonial matters. Courts of both jurisdictions tended to try to preserve marriages, and sometimes this meant sending couples back home to resume cohabitation. In the late 1360s a separated Venetian wife, claiming that court-awarded maintenance from her husband was too small, appealed against the award. The doge and small council ordered her to return home, where she was physically battered by her husband with the added insult 'Take that for the lord doge!' After this, higher maintenance was awarded to her. However, 14 years later, in 1382, she was living with the man and named him as executor of her will. At that date she had two sons under 18.[2] Wife beating (wifely chastisement being not viewed askance) was no doubt commoner than husband battering.

Within marriages and within matrimonial law imbalances usually caused more trouble to women than men because women were the more dependent. The man generally set the family's status. If he succeeded in extricating himself from what his wife had believed a proper marriage, he remained a king, aristocrat, landowner, craftsman or trader, but she lost security and standing. His sexual relations with her barely dented his subsequent matrimonial prospects, but hers with him might reduce her chances of future matrimony. Within her marriage a barren wife had a sense of failure and foreboding. The merchant of Prato's wife was childless; he sired bastards and adopted a natural daughter, bringing her into the home for his wife to bring up. This behaviour was not exceptional – neither the fathering of bastards nor their acknowledgement and sometimes incorporation into the family circle. In Florence bastard boys tended to be luckier than girls in this respect. Bastardy appears quite widespread in Bruges, where testamentary evidence suggests boys and girls received similar treatment. The mothering of bastards was not so tolerable, though it must have occurred more often than was known.

Many marital cases hung on circumstances obscured by time. Marriage was easily entered into: the validity of clandestine marriage made a marriage out of two freely marriageable people saying, unwitnessed, in the present tense that they took each other as husband or wife. Saying it in future tense left it conditional, but then subsequent intercourse confirmed it. Even with witnesses, informal marriages, contracted say during a drinking session, were unwise – and more so for the women than the man, for he might have made his proposal to make her pliant for intercourse and she might be left holding the baby if he later denied the event altogether, or chose to remember that he was already married. Given the rules, it is surprising how many people with possessions, even realms, at stake selected marriage partners of dubious marriageability.

The scientific, medical legacy of Antiquity remained largely unchallenged. Greek medical ideas, all holding women as inferior, less perfect in physical body and mental capacity, moist on the scale of humours, and contributing less to the embryo, continued to hold sway with important Arabic contributions, both streams being translated into Latin. Towards the end of the period empirical science was pushing back the boundaries of anatomical knowledge but it was dangerous work disapproved of by the church. For women the main practical advances came in application to midwifery. Da Vinci left anatomical drawings which included a foetus in the womb. Rösslin's *Rosengarten* published in 1513 (by Frankfurt's city physician) was a manual for midwives which had illustrated instruction on turning babies in the womb and discussed many possible foetal positions and the safest delivery from each, and showed good understanding of natural childbirth although the bizarre crops up among the sensible. Rösslin also dealt with care of the newborn and childhood diseases. Midwifery had apparently advanced through observation and practice to the benefit of some mothers at least. It was one of the few areas where there were attempts to professionalize the practitioners, at least in some towns. Women were kept out of the universities and prevented thereby from qualifying conventionally as physicians; a few appear in records in process of being hounded and barred from practising. Nursing was a vocation recruiting from those religiously inspired to it, or a manual employment like any other job, or the amateur caring of family members. The Third Order Franciscan Hospitallers, an active religious community of women who ran hostels but also provided home nursing (in pairs to avoid scandal), had about 100 houses in France and the Low Countries by 1500. City councils, for example Strasbourg in 1532, employed nurses to care for patients at home but did not recruit single women except widows.

Developments in Secular Law

The legacy of Roman written law persisted in southern Europe in contrast to the unwritten customary law of the north. The twelfth-century Renaissance increased the study of civil law (by men) and the later Renaissance extended scholarship in the same field. The different laws and customs within Europe rubbed against each other and borrowed from each other. Two fields of particular relevance to women will be illustrated here: the giving and management of dower and dowry and related marriage payments, and the effect of feudal law on women.

Payments associated with marriage arose from acknowledgement of responsibility to support a woman after her marriage. Who paid what, into whose management, and for what purpose, must be considered, and also whether there were any controls on the amounts changing hands and over the descent of any residue after the wife's death. Unfortunately the most appalling confusion has been created between 'dower' and 'dowry', from the variant meanings of the Latin *dos*, the obscurities of other terminology, and errors made by translators and historians. It is comparatively simple to start from the modern distinction between the dowry, given by the bride's family at the time of the marriage, and the dower, a part of the husband's estate granted to support his widow, an allocation which could be assigned at the time of the marriage. This clarifies from which family each provision came. Furthermore, it helps distinguish the separable uses and descent of the two entities. The dowry was given to the husband to assist the new couple's establishment, but ideally remained to support the widow and pass to her descendants, or return to her family if she was childless, and return with her to her natal family if the couple divorced through fault of the husband. (She forfeited her dowry if she had been adulterous.) Women can be seen giving parts of their own dowries to daughters. The widow had only life usufruct of the dower, which would pass to the deceased husband's heir(s). Unhelpfully, *dos* was used for the bridal gift to the husband in Roman law, and the husband's gift to the bride in Germanic law (the Roman law's *donatio ante nuptias*). The situation is further complicated by the balancing of what are sometimes termed 'dowry' and 'counter-dowry' (or reverse dowry), and the use of terms such as *maritagium* (marriage portion). Also, there were different procedures for the treatment of landed and movable property in different areas. Further confusion has arisen from editors and writers treating dower and dowry as the same, or failing to clarify which they are describing. Nevertheless, some rulings are clear and straightforward and Amt has collected useful ones from thirteenth-century Normandy, Sicily and Magdeburg in *Women's Lives in Medieval Europe*, including some showing the involvement of feudal obligations. Cautiously, therefore, we may look for the mechanics of the marital gift systems.

The primitive brideprice had dropped from use by 1200, but the *morgengabe* (morning gift) is still found, originally payment in exchange for the bride's surrender of her virginity, and acknowledging the groom's acceptance of his wife. More substantial was the groom's long-term dowering of his wife, the *donatio propter nuptias*, providing for her widowhood. Some landholders chose to identify certain estates and reserve them for the wife's dower, but dowering was so widespread and normal a practice that it was often simply a matter of assigning to her after his death the locally customary proportion of a husband's estates reserved for dower – most commonly a third, sometimes a half. The estates might be calculated on the total properties held by the husband at the time of his death, or on property held at any time during the marriage, or be a specified dower agreed at the church door at the time of the wedding. Where the middle pattern prevailed, any property alienated at some point during the marriage would remain liable for the earlier holder's wife's dower, but if she agreed to the alienation this liability would be removed. The dower principle applied to feudal tenants, non-military freeholders and some peasantry. Just as proportions varied, so did the terms of the widow's entitlement.

Some systems allowed the widow usufruct for life, even if she married again. (This made marrying widows tempting in those societies.) Under other regimes, remarriage ended the first husband's responsibility and the widow lost the rights. With widely ranging death ages, some of the larger estates we know most about carried a cumulative dower burden. The English Clifford estates in 1391–3 were supporting the widows of the fourth, fifth and sixth lords. In the top echelons, dowers could be enormous – the English queen's was worth about £4500 a year in the fourteenth century.

The old Roman *dos* from the bride's family developed in a more rogue way, in some places being restricted to a token payment, in others inflating to alarming proportions. Severe dowry inflation is particularly associated with Italian city states, causing the fathers of newborn daughters alarm at the prospect of the expense. Florence instituted a state savings/insurance scheme, the *monte delle doti*, in 1425, for parents to make deposits after a girl's birth to grow into a dowry by her late teens. The average patrician dowry in Florence was 600 florins in 1427, but in 1466 Alessandra Strozzi dismissed 1000 florins as fit for an artisan. Venice put a 1600 ducat ceiling on dowries in 1420, but was forced to raise the figure repeatedly. At these times of legislative interference the arguments put forward tell of girls unable to marry because of the high costs of dowries, and thus of men deprived of the chance to marry them, and families overstretched and impoverished. Keepers of family *ricordanze* noted sums paid out for daughters marrying out and sums gained from wives marrying in. The dowry was paid over initially to the husband, who had care of the wife's property while he lived. When Venice imposed the dowry ceiling in 1420 an exception to 2000 ducats was made for daughters of rich non-nobles marrying into the old nobility. This class-partial exception indicates that the old nobility, politically influential but financially hard up, expected to benefit from the infusion of funds, but two-thirds of the payment was protected for the bride's benefit. In Florence the dowry's original purpose of supporting the household, and hopefully, the widow, and still leaving some residue for her descendants, was endangered by fifteenth-century grooms who were spending large parts of it on the wedding, including costly outfits for the bride (though her trousseau proper came from her side of the family) and decoration of the bridal chamber, instant gratification no doubt, but hazarding the bride's future security, especially where the husbands were selling off these luxuries within a year or two. In such a situation the bride and her family seem to be being had. Her family's interest in the dowry did not end with its handing over because in well-off families it ensured the daughter some status and security. It should have accompanied her in the event of her husband's death and her return from his house, in which situation she was entitled to recover her dowry from her late husband's family whatever the cash flow problems this caused. As a consequence, his and her children often tried to retain her in her late husband's home, to prevent loss of the dowry, and her own family tried to fetch her back to recover control of it, especially if she was under 40 and potentially remarriageable. (The money could be used for a second dowry if the widow remarried.) Where women did not inherit from their parents on equal terms with brothers, as in Florence, the dowry was their inheritance, paid in advance at the time of the marriage. In places where daughters shared inheritance rights with brothers, as in Ghent, the woman could chose between keeping the dowry she had received and returning it to the family pot to have it replaced by an equal share-out with her siblings.

In the Castilian towns studied by Dillard, a woman received *arras* from her husband, which could be from a tenth to a half of his property or expected inheritance and could be received as lands, livestock, slaves and clothing up to the twelfth century. Then it began to be limited according to the status of the bride. In Madrid in 1235, 50 *maravedis* was the top limit for a town virgin. Up to a third of the *arras* could be spent on the wedding feasting, which reduced its worth to the widow and children (who had been expected to inherit three-quarters of it). This *arras*, confusingly, is also termed *dos*, but *dos* as dowry or marriage portion from the bride's side did not exist in Castilian towns. Wedding gifts from the parents were taken into account as advance shares of the inheritance when the parents died. (Castile's Visigothic past gave females inheritance rights equal to those of brothers.) A married couple's property was separable as his, hers and theirs (the latter being acquisitions and accretions during the marriage) and these were expected to follow the line of origin or be shared. In setting Douai's customs in context in *The Marriage Exchange*, Howell contrasted the favouring of the conjugal unit in the Picard–Walloon area with the dotal regimes of the south where no conjugal property was created, and each spouse's contribution to the marriage remained distinct. There the bride's family's *dot* was in the husband's hands during the marriage but reclaimed by the widow as the survivor, sometimes with an increase, or with usufruct of some part of the husband's property as at death as well. If he survived her he could have usufruct of her property but children or the natal family would inherit residually. In the north, in Walloon territory, the husband managed all the property during his lifetime but at a death the survivor took all, absolutely. In Picardy this survivor's taking all only happened automatically if there had been a live birth to the couple. Otherwise half the property went to the survivor and half to the deceased's kin, unless a document had been created giving the survivor all despite childlessness. In Flanders property was shared between surviving spouse and lineal kin. In Douai over the later middle ages the townsfolk swung over from their customary practice of survivor taking all to regulation by marriage contract. This gave the widow her original contribution plus an increase unless she chose to remain where she was with just the usufruct of the appropriate property. This latter situation was the *douaire coutumier* of Paris too. Husbands could override the prevalent local practice by leaving wills directing all or part of their property to their widows for life, or only for part of it (for example until remarriage). Wills were also used from the thirteenth century to override custom in Castile. Until widowhood no married woman had herself untrammelled testamentary bestowal. She could only make a will with her husband's permission. In England from the late thirteenth century it became common for the husband's family to settle lands jointly on a married couple and the widow held on to such 'jointure'. Dower and jointure lands escaped royal custody during heirs' minority, but were trapped with the dowager until her death.

All this shows something of the variety of marital endowment and inheritance in the medieval west. At root is one common premise – that a woman marrying needed an assured financial future beyond the marriage and in legal systems dower and dowry rights were well protected. Most systems expected both sides to the match to contribute in some way. All expected the wife's part to be managed by the husband while he lived. After widowhood, a woman might have absolute possession or only lifetime usufruct, or until she remarried. Throughout the period it was the practice to give quasi-dowries with daughters entering convents too, but usually this was a less expensive level. The daughter who neither married nor took the veil lost out. Only in areas where daughters and sons shared equal inheritance did such a daughter get a share and only when the parents had died, perhaps 10 or 20 years after her married sisters had taken their dowries. Occasionally historians mention this as an unfairness, but it did not rouse much comment at the time. The married daughter was the norm, moreover she attracted attention because it was with her absorption into another kin, and mothering of children carrying the father's name, that the descent of her property began slipping away from the natal kin, making some safeguards seem to them desirable. It is noticeable that in some places such as Picardy, mentioned above, the birth of a living child automatically changed the conditions. These marriage exchanges were not gifts bringing marriage arrangements to a close, but resources placed with an eye on future eventualities, viewed differently from spear and distaff side. In practice the widow might have considerable trouble upholding her rights.

The classical age of feudalism was over by the thirteenth century but its influence on laws and property was still felt. Feudalism had been most highly developed in north France and Burgundy: it had been exported by the Normans to south Italy and England, and was operative also in Germany, north Italy and north-east Spain, but did not penetrate Scandinavia or Ireland. It originated in the world of military service and was characterized by bonds of interdependence between men, and as a consequence has often been interpreted as a malign environment for women, condemning them to passivity. Much recent work has correctively shown the vigour of individual aristocratic women, especially in France, but it is still clear that feudalism must be credited with an adverse influence on women's rights of succession.

The originally military nature of feudal service made it desirable to treat the fief as indivisible. With an indivisible fee, in many areas male primogeniture was resorted to as the mechanism for producing a single successor to take responsibility for performing the service due. Where partition among brothers was practised (as *parage* or *frèrage*) the younger ones held their portions from the eldest, who was treated as the single vassal. It took time for fiefs to become heritable at all, and longer, overall, for them to be accepted as heritable by women, which occurred on a varied timescale, earlier in France and the Low Countries than in Germany. Invariably a woman only inherited outright in default of a male heir. A further disadvantage for her was that as it was expected that her husband would perform the service, her overlord acquired an acute and interfering interest in her marriage, particularly in France and England. The husband would frequently be the one to swear fealty and perform homage for the fee. Where women did inherit fiefs, and particularly larger baronies, honours and higher titles, they had vassals of their own and did in person take their fealty and homage and hold jurisdiction over them. Evergates's research suggests about a fifth of feudal tenants were women in the thirteenth century, but many of these were widows who had performed homage to take up dower lands. Flanders had two successive hereditary countesses in the thirteenth century, both daughters of Count Baldwin (d 1205). When the first, Jeanne, died in 1244 her daughter had predeceased her so the county passed to her younger sister Marguerite, who abdicated in 1278 in favour of her son. Jeanne's rule in particular has recently been praised by Karen Nicholas, who points out, however, that most of the barons disliked women's rule and rallied less willingly to their support.[3]

In England, when the earl of Hereford, Essex and Northampton died without male heirs in 1373 the earldoms were divided between his two daughters and co-heiresses. The elder was married, within Edward III's lifetime, to his youngest son Thomas of Woodstock who became earl of Essex. John of Gaunt forewent 5000 marks due to him from Richard II as war service wages to purchase the marriage of the younger, who was married to his son, later Henry IV, who took Hereford and Northampton. However, it was 1421 before there was settlement of this estate with Woodstock's daughter Anne who had styled herself countess of Hereford without recognition. Royal families were particularly well placed to grab heiresses for sons, and indeed to use female succession to bring territories into closer control. When the count of Champagne died in 1274 leaving a year-old daughter, the child Jeanne was taken to the French royal court to be reared as the fiancée of one of Philip III's sons. At her marriage in 1284 her father-in-law assumed the comital title in her name. At his death in 1285 she became Philip IV's queen. Champagne kept its institutions and identity but its independence was on the way to being lost. The same happened to Brittany when Charles VIII and Louis XII in turn married the Duchess Anne. A case where the successive husbands of a sole heiress did not take over was the English earldom of Norfolk. After the death of Roger Bigod in 1306 the earldom lapsed until created for Edward I's son Thomas of Brotherton in 1312 on terms which eventually allowed his daughter Margaret to succeed in 1338, though she was never styled countess until 1377, and neither of her two husbands were known as earls. Uniquely, Margaret was created duchess in 1397 when her grandson Thomas Mowbray was created duke; on her death in 1399 he succeeded to the earldom.

In areas where partible inheritance was practised, the separate treatment of different types of property within a family shows the pernicious effect of feudalism on women's rights. In Champagne around 1290 allodial property was shared equally among all siblings, but the feudal property was divided unequally so that brothers received twice as much as sisters, and women could not inherit fiefs collaterally. The different rules governing allods and fiefs underline that feudalism was not gender neutral, reinforcing the conclusion that the aristocratic women who proved active in the feudal chain did so when males had failed, and in effect operated as honorary lords.

The Continuation of Misogyny and Response to it

The misogynistic forces of Greek medicine and Judeo-Christian tradition combined to keep women in an inferior position through the earlier middle ages, physiologically a failed male, morally weaker, and menstrually unclean. For centuries there was little to promote any disturbing of this perspective. It was preserved and handed on in written texts, mostly male-authored as the most educated people were men, and indeed were increasingly segregated churchmen, for whom entanglement with women could be regarded as disastrous. So misogyny throve and writings against women continued, some deep, some comparatively playful. Christine de Pizan's train of thought in *The City of Ladies* began (she said) from reading Mathéolus, whose standard misogynist *Book of the Lamentations of Mathéolus* of c.1300 was translated from Latin into French about 80 years later by Jean le Fevre de Ressons, who also offered a defensive response in his somewhat facetious *Livre de Leësce.* However, there was always an alternative perspective, traced in Blamire's *The Case for Women in Medieval Culture* (1997).

By the fourteenth century some of the grounding of misogyny was at least out in the open. By the end of the century Chaucer put into the Wife of Bath's prologue the remark that if women had written stories, as clerics had, they would have written of more male wickedness than all the sex could redress. Christine de Pizan agreed: in *L'Épistre au Dieu d'Amours* (1399) she noted if women had written the books they would read differently. In the *City of Ladies* she put her finger on their lack of education as the root cause of women's lack of fulfilment.

Christine de Pizan, treated further in Chapter 7 below, gives us the best entry point into late medieval misogyny because she was herself a woman, and thus a true, if far from typical, female speaker, unlike the female voices imaginatively created by male writers, whether hostile or sympathetic to women. Her first defence of women was *L'Épistre au Dieu d'Amours,* in which she wrote as a royal secretary at the court of Cupid, reading a letter banishing disloyal lovers in response to purported complaint of women being betrayed by them. The work was inspired as a protest against the peddling of misogyny in the *Roman de la Rose,* and shows familiarity with many misogynist arguments while offering refutations. Christine kept up the attack on de Meun in her verse *Le Dit de la Rose* (1402) and in her prose contributions to the debate on the *Roman de la Rose.* Her fuller treatment in the *City of Ladies* Blamires considers the most powerful profeminine work of the middle ages, indeed one not exceeded as a comprehensive profeminine statement until the sixteenth century.[4] The follow-up *Book of the Three Virtues* offered advice on a more practical plane, and this was the more widely disseminated of the two works. Her last work was a profeminist celebration of Joan of Arc written in July 1429 at the height of Joan's success. Another literary debate was sparked off by Alain Chartier's *Belle Dame Sans Merci* (c.1424), in which the lady's mercilessness is accompanied by cool detachment, and in the 1440s Martin le Franc's *Le Champion des Dames* spoke out again against Meun's misogyny.

Women in Literature

The literature of Europe after 1200 is vast and varied, both vernacular and Latin. To begin to understand its treatment of women one must remember that it was the outcome of a wide range of purposes. The courtly literature was to engage and amuse the leisured classes, and at its most philosophical, to delve into woman's moral probity, especially her sexual propensities. The lowbrow tales from tradition (cropping up in different guises in many different areas) in fabliaux or stage farce, have less literate origins but pass into 'quality' writing incorporated by literary giants such as Boccaccio and Chaucer. In the middle came the homespun but aspirational literature designed to entertain but educatively, like the *Book of the Knight of the Tower*, compiled for his daughters.

The Arthurian literature dominated at the end of the twelfth century by French writers, particularly Chrétien de Troyes, continued to inspire rehandling and translation into many European vernaculars, the resulting texts sitting awkwardly between the social cultures where the stories originated and those in which later readers found them pleasurable. The roles assigned to women, or comments made about them, in later versions cannot be assumed to be reflective of opinions of the writers' times. Malory's c.1470 'Death of Arthur' veils Lancelot and Guinevere on the verge of discovery saying, with reference to the earlier French source, love at that time was not as it is now, so whether they were in bed or at other 'disports' will be passed over. Compared with the widespread passivity and unresponsive personalities of female characters in Arthurian literature, some of the early thirteenth-century French non-Arthurian romances show more interesting female character development. Jean Renart's heroines Aélis (from *L'Escoufle*, c.1202), and Lienor (from *Roman de la Rose ou de Guillaume de Dole*, c.1210), and Frêne (from *Galeran de Bretagne*, c.1216, a retelling of Marie de France's story) are presented as young women let down by men, who react resourcefully to the removal of protection or prospects, and end up with their men and high status. As Aélis and Frêne join up with other women outside their own class in the course of their adventures, introducing poor women textile workers and a rich bourgeois widow and her daughter into their stories, R. L. Krueger cites these romances for their remarkably fully realized portrayals of active women.[5] Nicolette is also the resourceful one of her pairing, but no one could call the delightful parodic romp *Aucassin and Nicolette* in any way realistic. The late thirteenth-century *Romance of Silence* has a heroine reared as a boy in order to forestall failure of a male heir, a fairly 'extreme' remedy for an inheritance problem which was real enough.

Le Roman de la Rose, which Muir calls the best known and least read work of medieval French literature, presents something rather different. The first 4058 lines were composed around 1225–30 by Guillaume de Lorris as a dream allegory of courtly love: set in the walled garden of the god of love the poet/lover, aided and impeded by personifications such as Fair Welcome and Danger, strives to pick his desired rose. The poem, claiming to encompass 'all the Art of Love' breaks off apparently unfinished and was continued in very different tone by Jean de Meun around 1275. He added 17,622 lines treating love and other matters in the encyclopaedic fashion of the period, with many long argumentative speeches from the allegorical characters, including much antifeminism. The older-fashioned chivalry of Lorris's part is supplanted by harder-headed realism and the use of strong language. The whole poem remained extraordinarily influential, as over 300 manuscripts of it testify. Over a century later a high literary debate *la querelle de la rose* engaged the leaders of the Paris literary world as the first round in the *querelle des femmes.* Christine de Pizan and Jean Gerson weighed in against the impropriety of the language and the moral implications of Meun's poem, and the slander of women (especially by the loathsome Old Woman). This is proof, if such is needed, that literature may not only reflect attitudes but also further them and inspire counteraction.

On a pleasanter note, Dante's love for his Beatrice (generally identified as the real Beatrice dei Portinari, who married Simone de Bardi), and Petrarch's for his (unidentified) Laura, reflect the idea of love for a woman ennobling a man. Dante's *Vita Nuova*, from the early 1290s (Beatrice died in 1290), and the role he gives Beatrice as his guide in the Paradiso of the *Divina Commedia* (completed by 1321) cast Beatrice as his spiritual saviour. However, it is a third Italian, Giovanni Boccaccio (d 1375) who may best repay attention here, for the form of his *Decameron*, and the content of his Latin *De Mulieribus Claris*, translated into French in the early fifteenth century. Both were famous and influential works. The framework of storytelling in a mixed-sex group gathered in a contrived situation may have become more fashionable due to Boccaccio. In the *Decameron* the 10 tellers are refugees from plague-stricken Florence, in Chaucer's *The Canterbury Tales* a group of pilgrims on a short journey; in Marguerite of Navarre's *Heptameron* returning spa visitors delayed by severe rains and flooding. All three collections show women in a rich variety of situations.

Among the *Decameron* tales is the dire story of the sufferings of patient Griselda, first apparently written down by Boccaccio, and picked up by Chaucer, via Petrarch's Latin translation, for the Clerk's Tale. In this story a noble husband who has married a pure but poor wife decides to test her, firstly by removing her two children (whom she imagines killed) and then by sending her back to her father in order to marry a new wife, recalling her to organize the receiving of the bride. All this she bears with forbearance and dignity, though she does let slip her own perspective on the matter when she urges the husband not to torment his new young wife in the same way. The new 'bride' proves to be Griselda's daughter, safely reared, along with Griselda's son, by then 7 years old, by the husband's sister in Bologna, and the husband explains his experiment and the couple settle down in wedded contentment. Extreme as the story is, it is not the only indication in literature that husbands felt entitled to set tests of their wives' fidelity, steadfastness or obedience. A shorter lasting experiment, wherein two out of three merchants' wives failed a test thought up by their husbands on returning from a business trip, while the third misunderstood an instruction with hilarious consequences, can be found in the Knight of La Tour Landry's book, written around 1371 and printed in English translation by Caxton in 1484.[6]

While literature has plentiful examples of ideally submissive wives, and Christine de Pizan admits women had to put up with tyrannical husbands, there were subversive alternatives. There can be no better comment on the portrayal of women in medieval literature than Eileen Power's mischievous remark that the man whose ideal was to be married to Griselda found himself wed to the Wife of Bath.[7]

The Influence of the Renaissance and the Reformation

It is a common assumption that the middle ages were unsophisticated and barbaric, from which interpretation the Renaissance and Reformation moving towards our own (questionably) more enlightened times may be expected to prove 'progressive'. It comes as an unpleasant shock to those with this perspective to be told that the high middle ages eroded women's earlier rights, that women's options contracted as the Renaissance flourished, and that the Reformation strengthened patriarchal ideology and ushered in at the very end of our period an appalling phase of witch-hunting (largely of females). Why do these periods of apparently general progress disappoint when viewed in the context of women's gender?

The Renaissance made humanism fashionable, though only in the upper social classes. It established the cultured gentleman's pattern of education for the next 300 years and made this available in local grammar schools to an enlarged social grouping, but these institutions were almost exclusively for boys. Exceptionally, girls of the ruling classes throughout Europe were exposed to the new humanist education, either taught by their fathers or by usually male tutors at home, tutors not infrequently engaged originally to teach their brothers. They became proficient, indeed precocious, classical scholars. But in numbers they remained small, and the scholarship they acquired was the standard male-orientated learning. They were thus trapped between being taught to think like men, and adopt the same abstract humanist standards, and being required to behave like women in polite society – modest, self-effacing and docile. The motives of the educators were not as liberating as they might seem – providing a husband with a more interesting wife for him to converse with still orbits the woman round the man. Women had no prospect of being able to train for the professions. So the Renaissance was hardly liberating for women.

As for the Reformation, the reformed religion was still a repressive force. In some ways its thought policing was more restrictive because, especially within the confines of German and Swiss reformed cities, with their control freak tendencies, it was more efficient. The obsession with sexual morality was applied heavy-handedly on women, but the new regulations permitting divorce were more sympathetic to remarriage. The reformed religion was patriarchal and Reformation Europe is characterized as the heyday of the patriarchal nuclear family. With the forces of classical culture and reformed religion clamping down on them, economic forces offered no way out, with the guild concept of the working household described by Roper as a 'male vision'.[8] Society was still firmly dominated by rules made and administered by men and reflective of their interest. However in the following chapters much female resilience and plenty of cooperative partnerships between the sexes will be seen in practice, when opportunity arose.

3

The Practical Situation: Women's Function in Rural Communities

Medieval countryfolk, people of the communities productively engaged in agriculture, lived in villages or hamlets, and, often, on land which was part of someone else's manor, though freely farmed allods existed everywhere except England. Each of these factors conditioned aspects of their lives. They mainly belonged to a household, physically identifiable by its plot, hearth, walls and roof, in and around which they slept, ate and worked. The household unit, nuclear or extended, embraced members of a family related to one another by birth, or marriage, and live-in servants who might be poor relations or totally unrelated. The members of the unit were identified by relationship to the household head – mother, wife, brother or sister, brother- or sister-in-law, child, nephew, niece or servant. As inhabitants of the village or hamlet, people belonged to an economic community in which some degree of co-operative activity was the norm. Especially in arable villages with scattered strips in fields, co-operation with ploughing, harrowing, sowing and harvesting crops and controlling animals was a structural framework for work, seasonally cyclical. In regions where pastoral activities prevailed, and hamlet or even more isolated living was the common pattern, the employment opportunities for women were different. As the rural inhabitants worked at their tasks in these conditions they were in many cases also tenants of an overlord, and this relationship imposed constraints on their freedom of action. Free tenants of manors were less burdened than bond tenants, even though they might hold less land, and bond tenants were of varying degrees of unfreedom down to serfdom. This chapter will look in turn at the role of women in the agricultural cycle of the arable estates, and in pastoral economies, then at the characteristic ways in which manorial obligation weighed noticeably on the tenantry, and how this affected women. The domestic roles of countrywomen will be considered; finally the rural woman's life cycle will be summarized in a section which forms an appropriate recapitulation of her functions rearranged by the progress of her life.

The three and a half centuries from 1200 progressed unevenly for rural inhabitants. Twelfth-century expansion continued in the thirteenth-century countryside which became rather fuller of people, and arable cultivation was pushed to, or indeed beyond, the limits of sustainable recurrent cropping. In nine villages in the *viguerie* of Nice 440 hearths enumerated in 1263 had become 722 in 1315, and in the early fourteenth century the densest rural population level was 19 hearths per square kilometre in the French plain.[1] Already by 1300 there were signs that the demographic peak had been reached or passed, except east of the Elbe where colonizing development went on for another few decades but still peaked before 1350. The famines in the teens of the fourteenth century led into a couple of centuries which saw, for example, eleven periods of dearth recorded in Languedoc. The population was in decline widely in Europe even before the Black Death. Plague refugees' flight from close-packed towns to the countryside suggests the latter was thought by contemporaries to be healthier and safer but manorial records testify to high death rates – vacant holdings, and a surge of tenancy changes and death dues. In the short term crops spoiled for lack of cultivators, and considerable dislocation occurred. Recurrent plagues continued to decrease the rural population, and people deserted poorer land for better, and moved to towns. It took a long time for the population to begin to advance again. Montaillou's population, estimated at 200–250 around 1320, was only around 100 by the end of the century and this was a normal drop for southern France in the later fourteenth century (due to war as well as disease). As late as around 1470 most European villages had only half the households they had had in the early fourteenth century.

In the aftermath of plagues, natural conditions favoured the survivors: with more land to go round, tenants could increase their holdings above subsistence margins, and labourers, with fewer hands available for hire, could press for wage increases. But in such conditions the seigniorial system had legal powers to protect its interests: bondage to the soil could be utilized by lords to keep tenants in place and prevent them moving to better conditions. Moreover, faced with rising wages and lower rents, the lords had another reserve to fall back on if they could extort the maximum from their feudal rights, see below. Peasantry, having sensed some freedom, resented repression (backed by state attempts at wage control from Spain to Norway) and civil disobedience and full-scale revolts took place, generally with little success. Using evidence from Thornbury, Gloucestershire, Peter Franklin suggested women were among the leaders of the civil disobedience in some places.[2] The condition of the peasantry in western Europe generally improved. Less labour service was owed and more cash rent paid (less degrading and often falling in real terms). Demesnes were farmed out widely in fourteenth-century France, and métayage (sharecropping) spread in Italy, Provence and Aquitaine. Better off peasants consolidated holdings, so a more prosperous peasantry came into being in the fifteenth century. Wages rose, and the prices of commodities and land fell. But not all was rosy. Less labour-intensive livestock rearing expanded, reducing employment opportunities. Taxation increased. Poorer peasants fell into debt. Villages shrank and some were wholly deserted: some 25 per cent of those existing in Germany in 1300 subsequently disappeared.

A newly significant feature of this overall period was a closer relationship between town and countryside. The impact of the towns on their hinterlands was much greater than before, especially in Italy (the most urbanized part of Europe) where the city actually controlled its immediate surrounding countryside (the *contado*) and legislated for it, and taxed it. Elsewhere the bond was not so constitutional but the laws of supply and demand made for a close relationship, the countryside providing the town with immigrants, food and wool, the town supplying manufactured goods. The balance of power usually favoured the town – the fixing of prices was to the consumers' not the producers' benefit.

In looking at rural women in this period we must acknowledge differences based not only on terrain and climate, but also on politics (the Spanish peninsular reconquest, the Hundred Years' War's ravages in France and the rampages of the great companies in Italy), demographic changes (the end of the great upsurge in the thirteenth century, cataclysmic fall in the fourteenth, slow upturn beginning in the fifteenth and taking off in the early sixteenth) and inheritance customs. The variety of inheritance customs in peasant societies was huge, embracing primogeniture, ultimogeniture, impartible inheritance, and partible inheritance either descending to all or only to sons. As summarized in Shahar's *The Fourth Estate*, in some societies the land was impartible but held and cultivated jointly by all the offspring (as in Mâconnais), in others divided among the offspring remaining in the village (as around Orléans and Paris, in Switzerland and parts of Germany), or divided only among males (in Brittany, Normandy, Maine and Anjou). Whatever the custom, within it, sons usually had preference over daughters, but daughters did receive dowries, and moved off to husbands' homes for the most part.

From this period a good deal of evidence has survived, though unevenly distributed over time and place. From the estate administration come custumals, rentals, leases and métayage contracts, and accounts, revealing the estate as a working farm unit. Court rolls are a good source of information about rural women but they are an English phenomenon (though manorial jurisdiction was not). Manorial court rolls registered three types of business: land transactions, civil business between tenants (unfulfilled contracts for example) and minor criminal affairs; offences against the lord such as theft of his wood or handgrinding grain and thus not using his mill; and offences against the community such as brewing weak ale or baking shortweight loaves. Women were the principal brewers until ale began to be replaced by beer, brewed with hops, giving rise to a larger scale industry taken over by men.

Two of the richest sources for this period are the register of Bishop Fournier of Pamiers dating from the inquisition against Cathars in the south of France in the 1320s, and the 1427 Florentine *catasto* relevant in this chapter for its statistics on rural households' size, occupation, mobility and sharecropping. There are descriptions of peasant sufferings observed in war-torn France, such as Thomas Basin's report that peasants had been slain or put to flight between the Loire and the Seine during the reign of Charles VII. Of course women suffered alongside men in these conditions. There is also, for the first time in quantity and detail, contemporary pictorial illustration, especially in the Books of Hours discussed in the Introduction, wherein the surprisingly mud-free agriculturalists may portray the Arcadian view of simple country life which is often held by those who have not experienced it.

Medieval Agriculture and Cyclical Demands

The medieval new year began at various dates in different places but the agricultural cycle will be considered here using the modern January to December calendar. At the end of the Twelve Days of Christmas, which could be celebrated in the northern hemisphere without good weather for outdoor working being lost, things moved rapidly into routine. Besides ploughing, in anticipation of spring planting, January was a good month for felling trees, both men's occupations. Harrowing could be done following ploughing and was a male occupation when done with a heavy metal frame, but with both ploughing and harrowing women could be out in the field goading the oxen. By early February the natural world begins to stir out of hibernation, and the Scandinavian countries celebrate the return of the sun. The calendar illustrations for February or March often show woodcutting and pruning, with people sitting inside warming themselves by the fire. March was also a good time of year for grafting, gardening and mending fences. Shepherds were busy with lambing, in these early spring months, though lambs were born earlier in the south, around Christmas at Montaillou. It is likely womenfolk helped at the lambing peak and tried to rear the tiniest and orphans. Women were also to be found weeding in the spring: Thierry d'Hireçon, cited in Duby, was paying 4–6 deniers a day to women weeding the corn on his demesnes in Artois in the first decades of the fourteenth century. April was a weeding month; however, a Flemish Book of Hours to be described in the next section has a busy rural scene for April, and the April calendar picture is often more leisurely, reflecting the sweet delights of disporting in a well-tended upper-class garden. In a Dutch version of Christine de Pizan's *City of Ladies* (British Library MS Add 20698) a steeple-hatted lady stands over a rather well-dressed young woman with a spade and some interesting looking overshoes tied to her feet: if these are not gardeners' galoshes the poor girl has very large feet. The May calendar picture is also usually upper class, hawking or boating. May was popular with the countryfolk who sallied out a-Maying to fetch flowering hawthorn into their houses and dance round a maypole or tree. May was also a weeding month. June brought haymaking and herb gathering and the midsummer festivities, often celebrated with bonfires. Hay was cut green with the scythe, a man's implement. July saw both sexes out in the field with their sickles reaping the golden corn, and harvesting continued in August which is often illustrated by threshing or winnowing. (The autumn- or winter-sown grains were harvested in the early summer, the spring-sown grain in late summer.) Gleaning, the collecting of loose grain from the stubble after the harvesting, was particularly associated with old and poor women, who appeared before manorial courts for doing it illegally. Bread from the new grain could now be baked, and berries and soft fruits picked. In Alpine districts cattle were brought down from summer pastures at the end of the month. At Frocester in the 1260s the heavy burdens on Margery the widow illustrated in Duby's documents included, for a half virgate described as 24 acres, 3 days a week of manual service worth 3 farthings (¾d) a day from 24 June 'until August' while on the fourth day she was to carry on her back to Gloucester or elsewhere at the bailiff's will, a service worth 1½d. From 1 August until 29 September she owed manual service with a man 5 days a week, worth 1½d a day, also a day's carrying service alternate weeks, and 8 boonworks with a man in autumn worth altogether 12d. In vine-growing regions, September was the month of the grape harvest which occupied both sexes. Treading the grapes would follow, and both harvesting and treading are featured on calendars. The end of the month brought Michaelmas, the date from which and to which English manorial accounts ran, and it was a common date for rents and debts to be due, hopefully when people were flush with funds after the harvests and extra opportunities for paid work in the harvest period. At Frocester Margery owed 2s at this date, and entered a new period of obligations, owing plough service of half an acre a week, valued at 3d a day, right through until the following 1 August.[3] October saw ploughing ready for overwintering crops, and the late harvesting of apples (by both sexes). Martinmas (12 November) was the traditional time for killing animals, especially pigs, and salting the meat for winter consumption, although this also features on some December calendars (leaving the victims being fattened on acorns in the woods for the November scene). With Christmas came another common date for rent payment (Margery at Frocester owed 12d at Christmas), the Twelve Days of festivities taking us back to the start of another year.

There is some truth in the long-established division of labour which accords house and garden to the women and arable fields and pasture to the men. Shahar plays the distinction down, arguing that although truly men did not demean themselves with women's work, women did perform men's tasks. Where women did the same job, men's rates of pay were generally higher. (Walter of Henley's *Husbandry* actually recommends employing women to sift and winnow for this reason.) Gender division of labour at Montaillou is summarized by Ladurie as for men ploughing, harvesting cereals and turnips, hunting and fishing, for women tending the garden and fire, cooking, fetching water and washing pots, gathering kindling, weeding the corn, tying sheaves, cutting cabbages, mending the winnowing fan and joining the migrant harvesters. At night they sat spinning by the fire. Ladurie concluded the women had a hard time, especially in their youth. On some estates the old weaving labour service by bondmen's wives was still being exacted at the start of the fourteenth century: cloth woven from manorial wool was required from women on the dependent manses of St Emmeram at Ratisbon (Regensburg) in 1301.[4]

Many of the tasks women performed everywhere in the agricultural year were done without recorded payment and most probably without payment at all. It was simply custom and economic good sense for the able-bodied members of a family, including wives and growing children, to weigh in to complete the work which had to be done and sometimes their attendance was enforced at the harvest boonworks. Women would not have billed their husbands for weeding, or feeding the chickens, though the more astute of them might have realized that by contributing to the household economy in this way they were saving the household head expenditure on wages to others to do the work, or freeing up the working men's time to allow them to hire themselves out. However, there was some hiring of women at wage in their own right, as by Thierry de Hireçon. The rolls of the English justices of labourers and justices of the peace who enforced the mid-fourteenth-century labour laws have plenty of instances of women reapers being in court for taking excessive wages and food for their employment. Piecework rates were normally paid to women hired as extra hands at harvest time, and not only for harvesting itself: temporaries were needed to prepare food for the extra workers.

Variant Specializations

Grain was needed for bread, the staff of life in most societies, and for the pot meals that varied from thin gruel to thick pottage, and barley was needed for brewing. Wheat was a luxury grain for the fine bread of the upper classes; where peasants grew it, it might be as a crop to serve as rent or sell for rent money or profit. For food they grew maslin, oats or rye. Where climate and terrain permitted the arable option was generally taken, and as a crisis of the Malthusian kind developed at the start of the period, this option was pushed into unsuitable soils. Where mixed farming was practised – the best natural balance for producing grains, dairy products and manure for the land – the part allowed for animal husbandry tended to be expanded less than the area given over to arable when new land was taken in. So there was not enough animal manure to service the arable acreage and medieval fields became very poorly fertilized. Many of the job opportunities in arable farming are normally for men. Ploughing, harrowing, deep digging, carting and threshing are all tasks requiring physical strengths, as are tree felling and fencing. Women weeded and reaped, but not exclusively. Nor were they totally excluded from the men's activities in a supportive role. Viewed as a ploughman's apprentice, we expect the ploughman's assistant to be a ploughboy, but the ploughman could have his wife goading the ox team as a matter of course, not as part of training. *Pierce the Ploughman's Crede*, a late fourteenth-century English alliterative poem, has a sorry description of a poor ploughman with his toes through his shoes, ankle-deep in mud, driving four scraggy oxen with his wife walking beside him with the ox goad, in a ragged coat cut short to the knee and wearing a winnowing sheet on top against the weather. Their children cry piteously at the edge of the field. It is a very plausible picture. Both parents were out in the field when a house-fire recorded in an extract from coroners' rolls in Amt's *Women's Lives in Medieval Europe* killed a nearly 3-year-old child, left with her nearly 6-year-old sister. In vine-growing areas women worked in the vineyards.

In pastoral regions, however, there were more opportunities for women, primarily in the animal husbandry itself, and secondarily arising from the by-products. Right through from the earlier period, dairying was a female speciality, and it continued to be women's work through this period and beyond. The work included milking, separating curds and whey, and making butter and cheese. Care of poultry and gathering of eggs often appear within the dairywoman's brief. An unusual slant is provided in the c.1290 legal text *Fleta*, from England, which deals with dairy administration rather than the mechanics of the job. After listing the moral rectitude necessary in a dairymaid, the text says she should not have visitors in the dairy who might remove anything, thereby leading to a deficit in her account. She had to receive the utensils of her job from the reeve with a written indenture dated on the commencement of her work and return them with the same indenture. Could she be expected to read the indenture at this date? Probably not, for she had to account for the gallons of milk she received by tally (a notched stick marked to show the quantity), and she had to make butter and cheese, take charge of the poultry and frequently render account and answer to the bailiff (superior to the reeve) for the resulting produce. These accounts were audited higher up and there is a warning that some auditors would not allow a smaller yearly yield than 12d for a goose and 4d for a hen. Medieval accounting was on the charge/discharge principle, not profit and loss as we know it. So the dairymaid would be charged with having received so many gallons of milk and had to discharge herself of responsibility for it by showing how much butter or cheese she had turned it into. The same number of hens had to be handed over at the end of the accounting period as had been received at the start, with an increase for the appropriate number of chickens hatched, eggs or capons sent up to the manor house or sold, and an explanation of any shortfall, such as hens killed by foxes or escaping. There was a 'going rate' for reproduction, anything below which aroused the auditors' suspicions. This kind of accounting is most often an all-male affair at the level of bailiffs, reeves and stockmen, but *Fleta* shows the dairymaid also was caught up in it. The text goes on that when the dairymaid can reasonably find the leisure (!) she should winnow, cover the fire and do similar odd jobs. *Fleta* shows us the administrative side of the dairywoman's work, and the illuminated manuscripts show us the physical side. Two Flemish Books of Hours from the early sixteenth century show the same activities but in a different landscape. In the Fitzwilliam Museum MS 1058–1975 mentioned above a woman is milking an amenable looking cow into a pail while two men and a dog drive a procession of sheep out through a gate. An open doorway into a building behind the milkmaid shows a large jug on a table within. The da Costa Hours (Pierpont Morgan Library MS 399) has a picture showing a woman milking a cow while two men and a boy drive a stream of sheep from a building towards a gate. A larger building is in the background, and from one opening in it a woman is driving a large horned beast out. Through another doorway into the building a woman can be seen standing at a waist-high churn, agitating the contents with a long-handled implement requiring both hands. Women are not often portrayed manhandling cattle, but the smaller farm animals such as sheep and pigs were easier to manage. The shepherdess is a traditional figure but nevertheless women's role with regard to sheep and pigs seems a more casual activity than it was for men. The common practices of keeping women's work near the home and giving to men the more distant activity restricted women's herding. Thus the itinerant shepherds of Montaillou were men, and the swine in the forest feeding on mast and acorns were the responsibility of men. Where a peasant family had only a few domestic animals women seem to have been able to manage them. Chaucer's elderly impoverished widow in 'The Nun's Priest's Tale' had three large sows, three cattle and a sheep, and a cock and seven hens kept in an enclosed yard fenced with sticks. She kept herself and two daughters by this animal husbandry. But where animal husbandry was the regional speciality the scale was different. A tax inquisition of 1471, cited in Duby, shows that eight parishes near Vence had 28,000 sheep and 1100 cattle, every country family having 100–200 animals.

In northern Europe practically all animals had to be put indoors for the winter, and when they were out of doors they might be moved up the valley sides in the summer. But some owners had great herds and flocks and moved them on a large scale, especially in Italy and Spain and Alpine areas. Tens of thousands of animals came down from the mountains in Provence to winter pastures in the Arles region in the thirteenth century. Sheep bred for wool and beef cattle would present no problems, but where cows and sheep needed milking, their movement in large numbers far from the home village must have been more troublesome. In the early middle ages women went up to the Icelandic shielings to milk cows, and separated the curds and whey up there, the curds being taken back to the base farm for cheese making. The Alpine herdsmen apparently returned down to the villages at the end of August and presented the first new cheese to the priest, but who had made it and where? Duby tells of 50–100 cattle (cows or sheep) being entrusted to the families of herdsmen in the thirteenth-century Tyrolean and Bavarian Alps, for rents of several hundred cheeses and 40 pounds or so of butter a year, the families tilling the homestead tofts and a few fields taken from the pasture, but living mainly on milk and wild foods and a little grain supplied by their masters. He writes further of whole communities spending the summer months grazing cattle up the Alps. At Montaillou there was a pattern of wintering sheep in Catalonia and spending the summer months in the Pyrenees mountain pastures. The shepherds, all men, made cheese from ewes' milk in their *cabanes.*[5]

Manorial Women

The medieval serfs, at the bottom of the social heap, were better off than slaves but because they were tied to the soil they lacked the freedom to take advantage of situations otherwise favourable to them. The conditions of countrymen and women in this period shaded more or less imperceptibly from abject serfdom to low-level freedom with a lot of overlap, there being free peasants poorer than bond tenants. Those classed as bondmen/women, dependants, men subject to taille, serfs or villeins were all subject to degrees of unfreedom. Chevage (payment for permission to live away from the manor), mortmain or heriot (death duty), formariage or merchet (payment to marry) and *taille à merci* or tallage were characteristic dues exacted by their lords, with, at any rate in England, leyrwite for extra-marital sex/pregnancy. Lords could enforce monopolies of ovens or mills. Some lords were willing to enfranchise their dependants at least to some extent, for a price.

Women felt the force of manorialism in a variety of ways. As wives and widows of peasant tenants, they were expected to weigh in with the performance of the labour services due for the holding. As widows and heiresses they were disadvantaged. Duby documents the 1291 custom at St Ouen of Rouen, which awarded the male heir the first choice animal of the deceased and the abbot the second choice, but if the heir was female, the abbot had first choice and she second, and where there was only one animal, the abbot had it. Two charges fell on women as a seigniorial due: leyrwite, the fine due to the lord from a bondwoman who committed fornication/and or bore a child out of wedlock, and merchet/formariage, the fine due on a bondwoman's marriage, especially to a man of another manorial lord. Leyrwite and merchet were degrading gender-specific reflections of personal unfreedom. They singled out women's sexual misbehaviour, in the case of leyrwite, and made a taxable event out of a normal moment in her life cycle in the case of merchet. The charges were commonly paid by the woman's father or husband-to-be, but on manors of the abbey of Ramsey between 1398 and 1458 the merchet was paid by the woman herself in a third of the 426 cases. The significance of this is that so many of the brides were sufficiently self-resourced to pay their own merchet fee, which in turn suggests women had more financial independence than is often imagined.[6] It was customary in most of Germany for the sum to be larger if the woman was marrying off the manor (and so being lost to its lord's resources). At the worst, half the offspring of such a 'mixed' marriage might be reclaimed by the mother's lord. Marriage out of class was also a risk to the lord's interests. Enfranchisement of men, wives and heirs on six villages of the abbey of Saint-Denis in 1248 stipulated that any of the men who married a woman of the lord's household should be demoted to her status, privilege notwithstanding. Merchet applied to widows' remarriages too, and pro rata there were similar constraints on the widows of peasant tenants as on those of feudal vassals, that is pressure from their lords to remarry, fines for remarrying without permission, and fines for permission to remarry a man of their own choice. At Halesowen, studied by Zvi Razi in *Life, Marriage and Death in a Medieval Parish* (1980) the incidence of leyrwite fell markedly after the Black Death, suggesting that the earlier cohabiting was not so much by choice but through inability to marry when entry fines were high and young couples could not establish new legitimate households.

The notorious seigniorial right *'droit de seigneur'* or *'ius primae noctis'*, the supposed entitlement of the lord to sleep with villein girls on their wedding night, is totally denied legal existence in the medieval west in *Women in the Middle Ages: An Encyclopedia,* but legal rights aside, it must have been almost impossible for a young woman who attracted her lord's unwelcome attention to escape him, and his attention might not have been that unwelcome to the family if it was thought the lord might promote the girl's interests when he tired of her by marrying her off to another servant, or supporting any illegitimate child. Village girls were also prey of unscrupulous local priests, nowhere more so than at Montaillou.

Women in the Household

Tuscan farmhouses have been sized at 33–39 feet by 16–20 feet, crude huts there 13–16 feet by 26–33. Peasant housing remained cramped. Many homes were impermanent structures, commonly rebuilt on the same site but with different alignments. Much building was timber framed, either rooted into the ground with posts driven into holes, or mounted on stone foundations of two or three courses clearing the superstructure from the ground. Montaillou houses, worth 40 livres tournois, had stone kitchens but the rest was wood and daub. A common construction was the cruck bay, with a pair of curved posts stretching from the lower edge of the building to the apex of the roof, a single bay house having two pairs of crucks rising from the four corners, a double bay six pairs, treble eight. Timber crucks bore the weight of the thatched or shingle roofs, so needed only lightweight walling infill of mud and wattle or lath and plaster. The longhouse was widespread, inherited from earlier times, usually having a cross-passage dividing it into two: to one side went animals – oxen, cows, sheep or pigs – to the other human inhabitants. The human part was often larger, had a hearth in the middle of the only or main room, with in the latter case a smaller room beyond it which served as a bedroom or a specialist area such as a dairy. The housewives swept their floors so continuously that the floor levels were hollowed down. The upper parts of these homes, smoke blackened and sooty, were not well constructed. At Montaillou the roofs were tiled with shingles and it was possible for a curious person outside to push up the edge of the roof and look in. Partition walling was so thin that conversations could be heard through walls, and on the Wakefield manor a case was brought alleging burglary achieved by breaking through a party wall. From the various depositions from Montaillou Ladurie brought out the central importance of the kitchen. The hearth had no chimney, and was covered up at night against the risk of fire. Round the hearth were pots, pans, cauldrons, jugs and basins, and people sat on benches round the fire or at a table. People slept in the kitchen sometimes, but more often in other rooms alongside or in a first floor solier with beds and benches, and in some Montaillou houses there was a cellar. However, single-storey construction was more common for rural housing – upper storeys were upper class. At Montaillou women baked bread at home, for Montaillou did not have that manorial monopoly the communal oven (a feature for example in the Île de France), but not every house had an oven, which was a sign of wealth. The poorer housewives would have to take their dough to a richer neighbour to bake it. Much cooking was done on the hearth in large cauldrons and this was dangerous. Fatal scaldings from cauldrons toppling over were not uncommon occurrences in the English coroners' rolls. The damped-down fires under Montaillou's wooden shingles were just as potentially dangerous as under England's thatched roofs and night-time was a hazardous period for the start of fires from exploding embers and lit candles. Analysis from coroners' inquests showed Barbara Hanawalt not only where women were most at risk, being liable to drown fetching water from wells, and washing clothes in streams, and to be scalded in cooking and laundry accidents, but also the time of day most of the investigated fatalities occurred – for women laundering in the morning, and (especially) at times when they were preparing meals, and for both sexes when they were asleep, exposed to fire at night.[7]

Thus women swept the floors, did the laundry, washed the cooking utensils, and prepared and cooked the family's food. Some of this food they scavenged from the hedgerows, collected from their hens, even butchered if one of the family pigs had been killed, hanging hams and bacon in the kitchen roof as at Montaillou. Depending on local resources they combed and spun wool, or dressed flax, especially in winter evenings (by firelight or candlelight). Duby cites a woolcomb, a spool and two pounds of spinning wool recorded in a widow's house in a Sologne village after her death in 1377. In the plot, garden, garth or croft adjacent to the house women tended vegetables and herbs and kept hens. Around the home almost all of the time, they looked after their children, kept the fires in and burglars out, and were on hand in local emergencies such as penned animals getting out. Their routines usually penetrate written record only when something untoward happened. Amt's selection from the Bedfordshire coroners' rolls tells how a servant digging under the walls of his mistress's old dovecote was killed when the wall fell on him. He was found by his wife, who came with his breakfast, looked for him, found his surcoat, cap and spade, and then 'his whole body broken'. Women may be seen in the background of the calendar illustrations carrying water in pitchers on their heads, and at Montaillou they went out to join the harvesting carrying a loaf likewise. The pattern of work which gave rise to the saying 'women's work is never done' is clear enough in these rural households, for where the men went 'out to work' at clearly defined tasks and stopped when the day's work was finished, the women had their work all round them and just took up one thing after another, even, in the Luttrell Psalter, carrying the distaff under one arm when feeding the hens. At night it would be the woman who got up to nurse sick children or ailing adults in the house. This is not just imaginative reconstruction. *Piers Plowman* contains a plaintive passage about the countrywoman's woe, rising to rock the cradle and up before dawn to card and comb wool, wash and scrape and wind yarn and peel rushes for lighting, and at Montaillou women stayed by their husbands' sickbeds, and women sat in vigil with corpses. This distinctive work pattern was openly recognized. Gill, the wife of Mak the sheep stealer in the Wakefield Second Shepherds' Pageant of the late fifteenth century, on being broken off her spinning by her returning husband wanting to be let in, complained about housewives being continually interrupted. No doubt the play had a male author, but the words he assigned to this non-biblical character would have rung true in the audience.

Life Cycle

In societies with little contraceptive knowledge, uncertain and dangerous abortion techniques, no welfare state to cushion the desperately poor, and a degree of shame in bearing a bastard child, infanticide must have occurred even though society at large condemned it. Shahar points out that letters of remission granted to peasant mothers guilty of murder in France in the fourteenth and fifteenth centuries throw up disgrace and terror as their motivation, rather than economic hardship.[8] Savage penalties for infanticide included burning and burial alive in Germany and eastern France. Countrywomen breastfed their own babies for one to two years, in contrast to aristocratic mothers, but circumstances could dictate otherwise, as in an instance highlighted by Ladurie. Raymonde Arsen, originating from Prades d'Aillon, was working in Pamiers when Raymond Belot, her first cousin, approached her, at Easter, about working at his house. She said she was under contract to her current employer until 24 June, and she gave him notice then. Fetching her illegitimate daughter Alazais from a nurse at Saint-Victor, she took the child to Prades, where she put her to another nurse, who took her to Aston. Raymonde then went harvesting, first in the Arques valley, and then back upland to Prades d'Aillon, where the harvest was later. Only after that did she enter the Belots' service, sleeping in the barn. A single parent, needing work and taking advantage of the seasons to get it, Raymonde had to make such arrangements to have her infant fed and minded.

Small girls played around in the family home until they became old enough to be put to useful practices in an informal apprenticeship, perhaps tending geese or a few pigs or sheep at about 7 years old, running errands and carrying food to farm workers. When older and more responsible and skilful they could be trusted with feeding animals, weeding, picking vegetables, helping with harvesting and so on; they were also left as babysitters, although the little girl minding her sister in Bedfordshire was not yet 6 herself. Girls were far from safe even at home. Grazide Rives, later Lizier, was deflowered by Pierre Clergue at 14 or 15, in the barn while her mother was out harvesting. He continued sexual relations with her at her mother's ostal with her mother's knowledge and consent, until he arranged her marriage the following January. For the 4 years of her husband's life, and with his knowledge, but when he was out, the priest went on having frequent sex with her.

Girls were usually brought up to work with other women and girls, boys with the men and boys. From an early age the pattern of risks run differed between the sexes. In the coroners' rolls studied by Hanawalt girls were victims of accidents about the house, scalded by cooking pots knocked over on the hearth and burned in house fires, but boys were fatally injured in the fields or woodcutting. Nevertheless, there were cross-gender experiences. Joan of Arc said she had spun and sewn at home, like any girl, but later it was remembered that she had gone ploughing with her father and had taken animals to graze. In her own lifetime Christine de Pizan called her a shepherdess. Joan had been taught the rudiments of the faith by her mother. Children were taken in as servants by better off families – girls especially – and some might end up as servants in towns; in either setting they worked to save capital towards marriage.

The age at which peasant girls married, and the size of household they ended up in, were features much influenced by the inheritance customs of the locality. The commonest pattern was the west or north-west European nuclear family, although there were also nuclear families in the south. In northern Europe, and also in Austria, the ageing peasant couple often handed over the holding to one son as they grew too old to cope with it. In southern Europe the peasant head of household more often remained head until death, causing his son(s) to have to wait for the succession. Sons who married before their father's death either piled into the extended household under his jurisdiction, or left the estate: this applied in Tuscany. In Languedoc even after the father's death, his widow might head the household, further delaying the next generation's takeover. In Languedoc brothers lived together and cultivated jointly; this was known as frèrèche, and this extended family pattern became common after the Black Death on both sides of the Rhône. In Haute Ariège, the peasant father chose one heir – usually male – and in Béarn a female elder daughter succeeded over younger brothers, but this was exceptional. Peasant girls married at

Montaillou as early as 14 or 15, though others were 17 or 18. The rural girls in Pisa were marrying at an average age of just over 17 in the early fifteenth century. At Halesowen before the plague peasant girls married at 18 to 22. Their husbands were often older, by two to four years at Halesowen, anything from two to ten years at Montaillou, nine to ten years in the Pisan countryside. Within communities, the daughters of richer peasantry married younger than those of poorer. These marriages were the outcome of family negotiation in many instances. A peasant heiress was a good catch, as was a widow in those areas where she did not lose dower from an earlier husband if she remarried. Providing a daughter with a dowry was common practice but among the poor it was very little. Duby cited the cases of two peasant fathers in upper Provence in 1330, where the richer gave his daughter 75 livres, a tunic of Chalons cloth, a robe of Ypres cloth trimmed with fur and a chest and two sets of bedding, the poorer only two pieces of cloth and a coverlet, and the groom had to pay for the tunic and robe of cloth the bride was customarily expected to wear. But a few rich peasants could give dowries of 50 gold florins. Duby also shows early evidence of what we might call the compensation culture of modern times: a tenant of a vineyard of the prior of the Portes Charterhouse, sued in 1263 because he had neglected it and not paid the service for over 30 years, asked for the vineyard to be ceded to his daughter as her dowry, and although the father, daughter and son-in-law had to accept the refusal, the daughter was given 45 sous for her renunciation.[9]

As a wife, the peasant woman embarked on the mixture of care of family, house and animals indicated in the previous section. Using figures extracted from the Florentine *catasto* of 1427, Herlihy drew conclusions about male-headed households in the rural quarter of Sancto Spirito, stretching from Florence into the Chianti hills. Households with access to a farm, by lease, sharecropping or inheritance, were bigger than those of artisans and persons of unknown occupation, averaging nearly 6 compared with 4.5 for artisans and just over 4 for the unknowns.[10] Since she and her husband constituted two of these household members, the rural wife here did not have a large number of people to care for, or a large number of children. Halesowen couples before the plague had only 2.8 children, averaging 2.9 in the middling level, 5.1 in the prosperous and 1.8 in the very poor. Births at Montaillou are estimated at 4.5 per family. Law and custom made the husband the ruler of the roost, but at this social level, with neither partner elevated above the other by formal education, and probably little class difference between the couple, their lives may have been more of an equality and partnership than in other classes of society. If initially marriage brought the husband enhanced status, confirming his maturity after bachelorhood and entry into the 'respectable married man' class, his wife gained respect as she grew older. The Montaillou mothers generally enjoyed respect from their children in their old age. Childbirth in poorer conditions was hazardous but if she survived the peasant mother did bring up her own children, and on the Montaillou evidence Ladurie suggests peasants were loving parents before the higher classes took up a closer and more affectionate relationship with their own offspring.

If peasant wives survived their husbands they might have a customary amount of dower, generally between a third and a half of the husband's landed property, and commonly for life. This the widow might cultivate, perhaps with hired help, or she might remarry (easier done when population pressure was high and land desirable). After the Black Death it was not so easy for a widow to find wage labour she could afford, and men could get land without having to marry a widow to get hers, so remarriage rates fell. Many widows stayed on in the family house, now headed by the heir. Here the luckiest were as warm and dry as, and fed as well as, the rest of the family, if the son and his wife were comfortably placed and kind hearted or even only conscientious. Probably more lived with a son and his family with a certain amount of tension between the generations but generally tolerable relations. Some fell out. Shahar draws attention to French wills which expected the widow to live with a son but required the son to set his mother up in her separate cottage if conditions became intolerable.[11] An agreement made at Cranfield in February 1294 bound a couple's son to provide them with food and drink for the rest of their lives, living with him in the principal messuage, but if the parties fell out, making remaining in peace in the same house impossible, the son was to provide the parents (or the surviving one) with a house with a curtilage where they could live honourably, and yearly at Michaelmas 3 quarters of wheat, 1½ quarters of barley, 1 quarter of oats and ½ a quarter of peas and beans. The parents had the chattels of the house as at the date of giving up the land.[12] Impoverished old women living alone were at most risk of being accused of witchcraft. When peasant women died, they were doubtless mourned by their families but their funerals have left little mark, unlike the showy obsequies of the aristocracy and civic rich. A 'decent Christian burial' was the proper end for most. Then the deceased's affairs had to be tidied up. Duby supplies the inventory of the property of a bondswoman at Fraguignes who died without heirs in the early fourteenth century, valuing grain owed to her, cash in her purse, small debts owed to her and an even smaller one she owed her master.[13]

4

The Practical Situation: Women's Function in Urban Communities

By 1200, towns and cities were a well-established feature of the European scene. Certain areas were more urbanized than others, and the main concentrations were in north Italy and the Low Countries, especially Flanders. Urban population on the continent is thought to have doubled between 1200 and 1300, but in most places it clearly declined, sharply, in the fourteenth century. Places considered as towns varied from 800–1000 people to 100,000, and in a few cases more. Clearly the Italian cities included some of the most populous – pre-plague estimates include c.100,000 for Venice, c.95–96,000 for Florence, 75,000 for Milan (taking lower estimates where there are differences of opinion). Pre-plague Genoa is variously rated at 60–65--70–100,000. Estimates for Ghent vary from c.55,000 to c.75,000, Bruges seems more agreed at 30–35,000. The pre-plague population of Paris has been variously estimated at anything from 80,000 to 200,000 (even 200–300,000). Following famine and disease in the teens of the century, the Black Death arrived at Genoa in 1347 and spread rapidly. Florence is thought to have lost half its population, and at Avignon, then home to the papacy, 11,000 are said to have died in six weeks. The plague was not confined to cities, but gradually it became a predominantly urban phenomenon.

Work on the populations of Florence and Pisa has shown how recurrent plagues damaged the age profile of the communities in the early fifteenth century. Children, with no resistance derived from surviving an earlier outbreak, were particularly vulnerable, checking the population's ability to recover for several generations. There was a particularly lethal outbreak at Florence in 1400, and a moderately severe one in 1424, in which 70 per cent of the plague deaths were children or dependants; these epidemics explain some of the age profile imbalance revealed in the 1427 *catasto*. Troubling though these events were, war was another destructive force. In campaigns towns were besieged and sacked or burned in raids. The ruthless sack of Limoges by the Black Prince in 1370 was notorious. The *Parisian Journal* reveals how the strangling of communications created food shortages and price rises for townsfolk. In 1420 the descent of the English and French newly intermarried royals on to Paris was quickly followed by a rise in corn prices and the writer's sympathy went out particularly to the women. There was such scarcity that people were queuing at the bakeries before dawn and bribing the bakers and their assistants with drink, besides having to pay twice the normal price for a loaf. 'Poor creatures', says the writer, 'trying to get bread for their poor husbands away in the fields or for their children dying of hunger at home.'[1]

Despite the shrinkage of urban population which was largely due to plague, more of the European population, proportionately, lived in towns and cities in the mid-fifteenth century than they had around 1300. As in the years before 1200, the more encompassing lines of their datable town walling let us trace the physical expansion of certain towns or cities, for example Florence. The Italian cities were the most sophisticated as civic entities and already had control over large areas of the adjacent countryside, which they manipulated to provide food supplies and raw materials in the interests of the urban community. There were already in 1200 city states with advanced methods of taxation and public debt finance, and expansionist foreign policies in terms of trade and colonization. Although northern cities did not have the constitutional connection with their hinterlands as demonstrated in the Italian *contadi*, they did have close relations. Parisians were still well aware of the rural agricultural cycle in the fifteenth century: the *Journal* notes disruptions to the harvesting, commenting for example in September 1417 that no one dared to leave the city to harvest the grapes anywhere on the Porte St Jacques side, and in August 1430 noting that around 50–60 carters from Paris and its neighbourhood fetching corn belonging to the citizens of Paris, newly harvested near Bourget, ran into their enemies the Armagnacs and suffered loss of life and burning of crop and carts. Another impact of the countryside on the city of Paris was the periodic intrusion of wolves into the city. In 1439, according to the *Journal*, wolves killed and ate 14 people between Montmartre and the Porte St Antoine, both in the vineyards and in the Marais, the last week in September. On 16 December wolves appeared suddenly and killed 4 housewives, and the next Friday they wounded 16 more people in the Paris neighbourhood, 11 of whom died of their bites.

What such vastly different communities had in common was that they did not survive primarily by the working of the land. Yet all these towns and cities, even the greatest, were closely tied to the countryside around them, and conscious of the agricultural routine and the seasonality of foodstuffs. Most suffered devastation by epidemics in the period, and recurrently. Many endured sieges or disruption due to troop movements. In wars, economic sanctions such as the removal of a staple to another town could cause acute distress. Even large towns varied hugely in the level of autonomy they exercised over municipal affairs. Paris was surprisingly lacking in independence for its size, due to close crown control. Italian city communes were much more self-governing but even they surrendered to 'foreign' rulers in pressing circumstances. From the many published studies and editions and analyses of source material, selection is made in this chapter to illustrate women in urban communities over the whole period, the whole geographical area, and a wide range of types of urban experience.

Variant Opportunities for Women

Towns varied visibly in size, quality of buildings, and density of habitation; they existed by meeting a variety of economic and administrative needs, and were themselves administered in a variety of ways, dominated by crown, ecclesiastical lord, duke or count or by usually oligarchic councils of various descriptions. Over this period there was a small increase of democratic opportunity, most generally taking the form of the admission of some representatives of leading guilds to some levels of governing bodies, but this was not an emancipation of the wage-earning employees, and still less an adult franchise. Women had no roles in these town governments, but the constitutions of their cities and towns were relevant to the urban woman's situation and its variety. In the big prospering Italian city states the women born into the patriciate had as secure an upbringing as can be imagined for the time, infant mortality and plague epidemics aside. Patrician families often lived in the same neighbourhood and rallied to the support of the 'house'. Within a kin poor relations might get some support from richer, and orphans be taken into service with wealthier relatives. The daughters' marriages were of dynastic significance, and the rate of dowries rose so high that some city states felt the need to intervene, as mentioned above at Venice and Florence in the 1420s. Such developments, touching deep into private lives, emerged as products of certain types of patrician-controlled city state. Completely different conditions pertained in the chartered frontier towns of Castile, where the city fathers were anxious to protect daughters from adventurers in a mobile society and to tie down into settlement as many married couples as possible. Different again were the trading towns and cities of the Low Countries, where the burghers wanted to keep capital flowing. In both these last areas inheritance customs gave equal shares to the children of both sexes, though the 'pot' they shared was readjusted for each marriage's offspring in the case of serial marriage, whereas the Italian custom was for sons alone to share the inheritance, daughters being dowried instead.

Towns, however small, were more densely populated than the countryside, the comparatively cramped layouts forced rich and poor into closer contact, and the employment opportunities were very much wider than the largely agricultural occupations of the countryside. In *Medieval Regions and their Cities* (1972), J. C. Russell calculated size and population densities of particular cities at certain dates, showing many at 100–150–200 per hectare pre-plague – Reims at 100, Paris at 182 (taking the 80,000 estimate for its 439 hectares). The *Parisian Journal* in 1423 estimated 24,000 houses empty, which seems barely credible. Some cities had room to expand, but others were constrained. Genoa's site limited its expansion, wedged between mountains and sea. Some figures are more reliable than others but the greater density of population compared with rural areas is clear. It would have been physically obvious to the visitor, seeing close packed often three- or four-storey housing compared to the detached cottages in crofts in typical villages and isolated farmsteads. In towns too, physically one house might contain more than one household, in apartment type arrangements. Moreover, the building was often multi-purpose: storehouse, workshop and home.

The most vigorous cities and towns contained many parishes, and tax records show that there were richer and poorer areas within the urban space. The population and wealth in late fourteenth-century Venice concentrated near the Rialto commercial centre of the city. Here Queller counted more than half of 19 rich noble households (assessed at 20,001 *lire a grossi* or more) living at the time of the *estimo* of 1379.[2] At Ghent in the fourteenth century the central parish of St Nicklaas was the wealthiest zone and contained the big markets. The tax records are not, however, forthcoming about those too poor to be taxed. An urban underclass, possibly half the population of a large city, they seem to have congregated in alleys, dead ends and courtyards. 'Spinster clustering' is a term coined for concentrations of usually impoverished single women, often including migrants from the countryside, some scraping by on earnings from low-status jobs such as spinning, some dependent on prostitution, some engaged in both. Medieval towns and cities had their classier districts and their grottier zones but the overall density of population brought the two into fairly close contact, and spread hazards such as fire and disease fairly indiscriminately among the inhabitants. Airborne or waterborne infections were no respecter of class, and though the living conditions of the better off were slightly more sanitary, and their houses more likely to be constructed of less flammable materials, these advantages were only marginal and applied to only normal conditions of infection and very localized fire. An epidemic or large conflagration meant serious disaster for all classes. The only advantage the rich townsfolk might have had could have been a refuge on a country estate.

Town life was unhealthy and urban population expansion, when it occurred, relied on immigration for constant replenishment. Women seem to have been particularly attracted into towns. The Florentine *catasto* of 1427 suggests that widowed women were drawn into the city because on the whole it was safer to live alone there and easier to make a living or tap into urban charities. The outcome of women's attraction into towns was an unbalanced sex ratio, with women exceeding men by around 10 per cent. For those close to destitution and truly alone, the towns and cities offered the possibility of cheaper accommodation in a rented room, and paid work as a live-out servant, shop assistant, pedlar, and so on (or better still for the migrant female singleton, live-in domestic service). However, female domestic servants were vulnerable to exploitation, as will be shown below.

For those born in the urban centres as for those attracted from outside, towns offered a wide range of employment, varying according to the place's size, location and resources. Coastal and river transportation of goods created specialist ports in suitable sites. These varied from centres specializing in luxury imports or bulk wool exports to localized shipments distributing local grain or wine, and the seasonal argosies and types of warehouse varied with the specialities. Although wool clothmaking was a rural craft, much was done in towns and cities, which came to dominate especially the luxury, better finished end of the textile market, and also developed silk manufacturing, which was frequently monopolized by women. Local supplies of iron led to the speciality of metalworking in towns such as Nuremberg. Although hides came from rurally reared animals, leather trades also seem to have become a speciality of towns. Variety spiced up urban life: the Paris *taille* records of 1292 show women in 172 occupations. Women were generally in lower status work and menial jobs, the main exception being in silk manufacture. Even where guilds allowed women to help with home-based crafts or to carry them on after a husband's death, they generally lacked the chance to receive full professional training. In terms of being trained, tested and licensed to practise, a normal qualifying pattern for the more prestigious male careers, women seem to have come nearest to achieving it in midwifery.

Compared with the countryside, where they were more or less bound to spend their day in contact with a small circle of neighbourhood acquaintances, in the urban environment women could expect to be more exposed to strangers, work more often for a wage (as distinct from helping the family discharge the labour which either formed, or paid, the rural rent) and could at times participate in something out of the ordinary such as taking part in a mass procession, watching the entry of a king to the city, or the execution of a criminal. While many women of the working classes in town and country simply looked after the family and helped their husbands, there were more independent employment opportunities for women in towns – that is jobs where they were not simply helping out in the home-based workshop, where most industry was conducted into the sixteenth century. Many entered household service, both married and unmarried and widowed. This was the occupation where they appear most numerous in the Paris *taille* rolls of 1292. Their second main occupation there was peddling. Neither are prestigious occupations, and nor was work at the inns and taverns which flourished in medieval cities: Avignon had 66 taverns in the fourteenth century, Bruges 54 in 1441. Brewers' and innkeepers' wives were involved in their businesses but extra females were employed for barmaid/tapster work. Thus the towns and cities, with richer families employing youngsters and older women in their households, and drinking places and residential inns employing female staff, mopped up female labour in a big way not possible in villages and hamlets.

Agricultural work was seasonal and these seasons still impinged on even the largest cities, as already shown in the case of Paris. Long-distance trading centres also had their seasons, of fleet sailings and returns, and fairs. But another of the differences between town and country was the more even tempo of the work pattern in town industries. Truly the wool clip was effectively seasonal but textile manufacturing could go on smoothly round the year. The metal industries had no seasons. This does not mean to say that employment was steady all the year round, nor a job for life. Winter weather and short daylight imposed constraints. The craftsmen with their own workshops could usually keep going, solo, in tough times, and hire extra labour in good: the trouble came for the labourers who faced being laid off in circumstances totally beyond their own control. The rise and fall of female employment in cities such as Cologne and York in the fifteenth century and Lyons in the sixteenth reflects the flexibility of medieval employment, economically practical from the employers' standpoint, catastrophically unreliable from the wage-earners' point of view. When times were harsh, male protectionism set up barriers to restrict women workers in trades, and these can be seen in guild regulations.

Women in Trading and Craft

The Master Book of Nuremberg of 1363 reveals a quarter of them were bakers, butchers, tailors and shoemakers and another quarter metalworkers. At Ghent in 1358, over half the masters were in textile-related work. At Tours in the mid-fifteenth century the breakdown of employment was a quarter in cloth and clothing, a fifth in leather and hides, a tenth in victualling, and 18 per cent in construction and 11 per cent in metalwork (the last two being high due to the presence of the royal court).[3] Trade practices and organizations were designed for and by male participants. Masters trained apprentices who mostly stayed at journeymen level. The degree of apprenticeship open to women is difficult to assess as it seems to be very different in different times and places, but emerges most clearly in silk manufacture. In Montpellier before the plague women were apprenticed but in what Reyerson classes as 'women's work' not prestigious male occupations.[4] Most guilds let widows continue their husbands' business, at least for a time, but not usually as masters, and some pressured the widow to remarry within the craft. The work of wives and daughters in the household shop is rarely specified but its understood contribution to the workforce can be seen at York where regulations limited a married master's apprentices because he had his wife's assistance. Wives are known to have helped husbands in leatherworking and metalworking in Cologne and York. Their years of involvement stood them in good stead if they kept up the business as widows. The Paris *taille* records show widows as butchers, fishmongers, bakers, cordwainers, cutlers, glass grinders, tailors and dyers as well as in daintier crafts of making bags, hats and belts and rosaries. But by the early fourteenth century women were being restricted, and this was the dominant direction of affairs in the fifteenth century.

Women everywhere were pedlars, hucksters and petty moneylenders but they did sometimes hold their own at more prestigious merchant levels. Their early involvement in *commenda* contracts in Genoa and Venice continued at both places into this period. Many kept the accounts in family businesses everywhere. Cologne merchant wives generally ran the home office in their husbands' absence. Notarial documents from fourteenth-century Genoa have many instances of women conducting business in their husband's absence, or without a husband. Aristocratic women in Ghent were involved on their own and in partnerships in wine, cloth and mercery. Remarkably, a woman handled 24 per cent of Cologne's sugar imports between 1460 and 1468, and even more remarkably, given the nature of the business, one handled 5.8 per cent of Cologne's sheet metal trade and 1.4 per cent of its copper market between 1452 and 1459. Nearly a third of the city's cloth trade was in female control 1419–28.[5] In London Richard Hill's widow Johanna carried on his bell foundry for the year she survived him, 1440–1, and seven of her bells survive, with his mark of a cross and circle within a shield, but the shield is surmounted by a widow's lozenge-shaped shield containing a floret.[6] There are many indications of individual enterprise in profiting from by-products in certain trades, and in forming alliances. Butchers' wives made and sold sausages as well as candles made from tallow. In *The Later Medieval City* Nicholas noticed that tanners married into butchers' families, and brewers married each others' daughters.

Brewing is an interesting subject because in this period it was in different places undergoing some change of practice. In the English countryside much ale brewing was done by women, but this was not the case in towns. In Winchester a quarter of the brewers were women in the late fourteenth century but this proportion declined in the fifteenth. On the continent hops began being used in the thirteenth century, but only penetrated the London trade after the 1420s, pushed then by the Flemish colony. As late as 1470 brewers in Norwich were forbidden to use hops. But hops made beer keep longer than ale and so made way for brewing in larger quantities with longer shelf-life. Thus domestic brewing in comparatively small quantities – in England very much a women's sideline requiring little capital investment – declined in face of the more economic larger scale enterprise monopolized by men.

Only a few cities are known to have had separate women's guilds. At Cologne they were for yarn makers, spinners of gold thread and silk throwers and silk weavers. Silk work was the craft where women were most commonly organized on similar lines to men. The silk mistresses could have formal apprentices and supervise the production, but most were married women with their husbands dealing in the raw materials and finished silk. Moreover the silkwomen's guilds were not politically powerful in their cities, and men had almost all the administrative roles in the women's guilds visible in Cologne, Paris and Rouen. It is widely agreed that the catastrophic fall in population had a liberating effect on the work available to women in towns, but conditions were not encouraging over the whole period for women in trades and crafts. They were let into jobs in urban craft production during the population decline and while the sex ratio made recruitment of male workers difficult, but by c.1450, with population recovery beginning, exclusion was coming in to protect male jobs. Women returned to low-status work, often working part-time, and many engaged in the family business without wage as such. Where women were employed in their own individual capacities their wages were less than men's. Nicholas cites casual unskilled labouring by women on construction sites in Wurzburg in the fifteenth century for two-thirds of the male wage, and 58 women working securing roof tiles at Parma Charterhouse in 1396 at half the male rate, and Dillard shows that women worked on construction projects in thirteenth-century Navarre and in fourteenth-century Seville, where they were also at lower pay rates than men.

Ghent seems to have been a reasonably encouraging environment for women. In his book on domestic life there Nicholas has a chapter subtitled 'the independent businesswoman' no less. They included innkeepers and cloth wholesalers. The most remarkable woman in his book was Celie Amelakens née Rebbe, who had male business partners and became one of only two women in fourteenth-century Ghent to engage in tax farming. She was a moneychanger and hosteller. Alice van den Plassche in Ghent was described by her heirs as 'her own woman, free businesswoman, keeping an inn'. Alice, the wife of Gillis van der Pale, was intermediary when her husband, in Rome, received a loan from the Bardi on behalf of the government of Ghent in 1350. 'Merchantwoman' was a legal status that allowed married women to act independently and thus relieved their husbands of liability for their wives' business dealings – like *feme sole* in England. Nicholas's more prosaic examples include a woman delivering pastries for a male employer, daughters of barbers and spicers entering their fathers' guilds, wives of master trousermakers being subject to the guild court in contexts suggesting involvement in the business, and women being members of the doublet makers' guild by special permission of the *scepenen*. In Ghent women could not be master weavers but they could own looms. Guilds became more restrictive of women in the fifteenth century. In both Leiden and Cologne the work of Martha Howell shows that higher status employment seems to have been gained by women through their families and particularly their husbands. The town businesswoman seems to have been only rarely 'her own woman', and even where she was, her type lost out in production and trade as the male-dominated guilds got more political and the family unit declined in market production.

Women and Service Functions

The Ménagier of Paris classified serving folk in three categories: those hired ad hoc for work for a fixed time – either to do a specific piece of work, or for a day or two, or a seasonal spell, such as reapers, mowers, threshers and wine-pressers; those hired for a specific purpose by the piece, such as dressmakers, furriers, bakers, butchers and shoemakers; and those hired as domestic servants, taken on by the year and living in the house. It is these latter who will receive most attention here, followed by a number of specialist services including wet-nursing and midwifery.

The Paris 1292 *taille* rolls show domestic service as a large employer of women and this remained true right through the period. The Florentine census of 1552 showed 16.7 per cent of the population in service, 70 per cent of these being female, and this after a trend to the greater employment of male servants began in the 1490s. Perhaps more significant is the statistic that 42 per cent of the households in the 1552 census had at least one servant. More startling, to the modern reader, is a slavery statistic from Genoa a century earlier, counting 2005 female slaves and 54 males in 1458. Epstein describes the female slaves' work as cooking, cleaning, carrying water, going to ovens, digging latrines, and serving their masters' sexual appetites.[7] Slavery was more widespread in Genoa than elsewhere, but it is also evidenced in wealthy urban Italian households in other places in the fifteenth century. The 1427 *catasto*, which did not count salaried household employees but treated slaves as properties, recorded them in 261 households in Florence. Nearly a quarter of the abandoned children admitted to the San Gallo hospital in the 1430s, and more than a third of those admitted to the Innocenti in 1445 were described as children of slavewomen. Female slaves had to suffer the sexual demands of their masters, extending to the masters' sons and friends. If a child resulted, it could be abandoned to the foundlings' institutions and the mother's milk put to use either to feed the master's legitimate child, or to nourish someone else's child by hiring out the lactating mother to its parents. Though technically free, in-dwelling servant girls were little better placed with regard to such exploitation.

A good employer could, by contrast, be a poor young girl's salvation. Where all went well, a girl could be taken into a richer household at 8 or

9 years of age. She might work for food and clothes, as in a case in Genoa in 1256 where Epstein found a woman placing her daughter as a servant for 14 years on these terms. She might serve for about 10 years for a promised dowry, only leaving to be married. If she was paid wages, they were likely to be rolled up until the end of the service period. In these latter instances she emerged from service with a lump sum, the skills she had learned during the years of service, and the benefits of the sexually protective security of a 'good' household. Klapisch-Zuber waxes rather lyrical about the possibilities of such an arrangement guaranteeing the girl's virtue and guarding her savings,[8] but the cynic might question both suppositions. Guarding an employee's savings is one way to describe not paying them for years. What some of the employed thought about it can be seen in their recourse to leaving service after a short period, obliging the employer to pay up. One wonders about interest arising especially over the longer terms, and whether the dowries mentioned were as generous as they might appear considering they were really pre-earned. But as the master did usually provide board and lodging, whether in lieu of or on top of wages, service did offer some security. Wage rates themselves took little note of inflation. In Florence the fifteenth-century average was 8.5 *fiorini* per annum, though the statutory recommendation was 9, and in the late fifteenth century these rates fell – to 7 *fiorini* in the 1490s, but the price of wheat had risen. While the imagination stretches to doughty old retainers provided for in old age and hard-working girls patiently amassing a bottom drawer, the reality was, judging from the *ricordanze*, that 60 out of 100 female servants left the household within a year, and 19 within a month. Klapisch-Zuber suggests the married and widowed women often took on a job for a specific purpose and left when they had earned enough, for example to pay a debt, a rent, or a nurse. This suggests a more calculated sale of labour, which bought no loyalty from the employer's point of view. The younger girls, aspiring to marriage after an adolescence in domestic service, tended to stay longer. The arrangements carried risks for both sides: the employee might find herself financially and sexually exploited and generally ill-treated, the employer might find he had admitted to his household a thieving idler who became pregnant through her own activities and not employer's abuse. However, there were some long harmonious relations and bequests from either party to the other must sometimes be testimony to regard, and not just death-bed reparation offered by an employer conscious of meanness or worse, or an employee feeling guilty about concealed sharp practice. Clerical wills sometimes testify to long associations where the housekeepers were probably established

sexual partners. In Ghent, where maintenance was often a servant's only gain until the master died and accumulated wages could be recovered from his estate, the priest Thomas Uten Berge left his house to a maid who had served him without pay for 30 years and apparently loaned him money. It was not unknown for the servant woman to marry the master of the household. When Celie Amelakens, widow of Godevard, died in 1382, while living with her eldest son Jan, a wine merchant, in his share of Godevard's house, he had married, between 1375 and 1382, Mergriet Mabels, who had been at least 16 years in the household. When Jan died this 'elevated' widow coped with the dispute between her late husband and his brother Jacob over Celie's estate.

Much domestic service was not particularly skilled. Where only one servant was employed, it would be a case of 'maid of all work'. The dividing line between house and shop was indistinct and maids might be found serving customers or delivering goods. A wealthy household like the Ménagier's might have a small staff, and some specialization and pecking order within it. The Ménagier's establishment at Paris had a couple of head servants in charge. The housekeeper set the chambermaids to sweep out the hall and reception area first thing and to dust and shake cushions and covers of the benches before cleaning and tidying other rooms daily. Clothes, furs and coverlets were aired in the summer sun, shaken and beaten and grease spots treated. At night the house was closed and locked up by the butler or housekeeper and one of them kept the keys so there was no coming and going without permission, and before the household retired to bed one of these two went round with a candle inspecting the wines, verjuice and vinegar against theft, and ensured that fires were damped down. The live-in staff were taught to extinguish candles on going to bed, and they retired at night knowing what they would have to do next day. The Ménagier advised his wife, if she had girls or chambermaids of 15–20 years of age, to have them sleep in a closet or chamber near the mistress, one where there was no dormer window or low window on to the road, 'since they are foolish at that age and have seen nothing of the world'.[9]

One specialist service was wet-nursing, for the upper and middle classes who could afford it. It is particularly well recorded among the Florentines, where Klapisch-Zuber has studied it through *ricordanze* from the period 1300–1530. During this time, it was a widening practice in Florence, spreading from almost exclusively prominent families in the fourteenth century down to those of skilled craftsmen and small merchants. One of the ways it spread downwards was through the knock-on effect when a couple sent their own child out to nurse in order to sell the wife's milk to a higher bidder. Klapisch-Zuber published extracts from Piero di Francesco Puro da Vicchio's journal, booking children in and out with their swaddling cloths and cradles, and recording agreed rates of pay. Although this may seem a cold mercenary approach, practically using his wife as a human cow, it is emotionally warming to note his comments on a grocer's son accepted in 1428: 'they had let him get so weak that we nearly lost him. With the grace of God and my wife, we saved him'.[10]

Wet-nurses could be fetched in to live in the baby's home, in which case their life styles and diet could be under some control and this was the practice in Dillard's Castilian towns, but it was much more common in Florence, unless a household slave was available to suckle, to send the baby to the nurse's home, and increasingly this was in the countryside. In over 400 nurses in the Florentine sample, each nurse resident in the employer's home was outnumbered by over four taking the child home with them. Wet-nurses operating from their own homes in the city, like Piero's wife, were much less common and seem to have specialized in short-term, almost emergency nursing, in between other arrangements. The baby boy saved by the couple in June 1428 could only be kept until the anticipated delivery of another baby prudently booked in before birth for Piero's wife's sole attention. However, even in the short extracts cited by Klapisch-Zuber some babies were kept for longer terms, one for 23 months. One of the short-stay infants was from the hospital of Santa Maria della Scala, and kept just from 7 to 31 May 1428. The foundling institutions needed wet-nurses (and here they suckled children from the lowest rungs of society). In fifteenth-century Montpellier 275 wet-nurses paid by the municipality were mainly wives of craftsmen and agricultural workers.

Wet-nurses who moved in to private homes were paid more: in the late fourteenth century 100 *soldi* a month compared with a peasant nurse's average of 62. The live-in wet-nurse was the highest paid category of domestic worker in Florence from 1400 to 1480, but she was expected to pay her own living expenses. There is a sociology of wet-nursing – how far parents were willing to send children, for how long they were willing to pay for them, and how the child's treatment varied with its sex and birth position in the family. However, the concern here is with the lactating mother not her charges. Obviously she had to bear a child of her own to start the process, and it is clear she was not expected to continue sneakily suckling her own baby alongside the paying guest. The hiring parents expected full monopoly of the breasts. A recently delivered mother whose own child had died at birth or within days was highly desirable – parents did not seem to worry about what had caused that child's death. Although medical texts went into details about matching the nurse physically as much as possible with the true mother, again parents (this means fathers, who apparently took the decisions and supervised the arrangements) did not agitate themselves about this, nor about other class or moral distinctions – slaves, sharecroppers' wives and unmarried mothers were employed alongside wives of sturdier substance. The medical texts recommended various controls of the nurse's environment and diet for the child's benefit, but children put out to nurse were beyond supervision by the rule book. Nor did nursing in this period last as long as the experts recommended. The one thing that worried the employing parents was that the quality of the milk would deteriorate if the nurse became pregnant herself, and it was required that she own up to this and let the parents remove the child. Where a pregnancy was concealed for a time, the employers kept a watch for the nurse's eventual delivery, so that they could calculate the period in which their offspring had been cheated and deduct pay accordingly. Since it would have been difficult to recover payments already made in good faith, presumably this meant the pregnant nurse had to wait until her own delivery to be paid for services ended some months before.

The outside nurses could expect inspection visits to view the child's progress, or would take the child to visit its family to display it periodically. As there was usually some pre-existing connection between the families (for example the nurse was from a sharecropping family on the employer's land, or lived in a village where the family had some presence) reports could be made by mutual contacts in the normal course of events. Between 17 and 18 per cent of the babies put out to nurse in the sample died, 85 per cent of these by what was accepted to be illness, but some 14 per cent by suffocation when asleep. Even where the birth family had had the forethought to send a strong cradle with the child, suffocation could happen, most commonly caused by being laid on by an adult the baby was sleeping with. The church preached against the dangers of overlying, but it was, paradoxically, sometimes the outcome of kindly intention.

In normal circumstances medieval women in labour were helped by other women who had been through the experience. Assisting at a birth could become a practice some women got called on to do more often than others, and individuals might get a reputation for being more successful than others, keeping calm and observant in a crisis, being patient and encouraging with the mother, dextrous at the actual birth, and knowledgeable about handling the newborn and the exhausted mother. This was how Margaret of Cortona became a favourite with patrician families. Midwifery was eminently practical. It was an advantage for a populous centre providing sufficient demand to have a cadre of midwives, trained to be more informed than the average well-meaning 'old wife', and answerable in a professional manner for maintaining proper care and attention. Towns were where midwifery as a qualified profession emerged and Nuremberg has been studied in this context as it was in the fifteenth and sixteenth centuries advanced in terms of public health and hygiene.[11] Here midwives served a 4-year apprenticeship and had to train apprentices in turn. Their services were free to the poor but graded fees were charged to others. Rösslin's *Rosengarten* (1513) for midwives and pregnant women was for midwives who were literate and could benefit professionally from reading as a method of instruction. Widows and older unmarried women were preferred for the job. They had to be of impeccable reputation because they were relied on to examine suspected aborters and suspected victims of infanticide, to report illegitimate births, and to baptize in emergencies. They were thus involved in mechanisms of social control as well as the non-judgemental aspect of easing birth. After the birth the midwife washed the child, rubbed its limbs with salt and honey and wrapped it. Some paintings of the birth of Christ show contemporary practice fairly well.

A less skilled special service was laundrywork, and if we connect this with the more dubious employment at bath-houses, we may move on to a more contentious type of service, prostitution.

Prostitution

Prostitution was viewed differently according to the prevalent social and religious mores of place and time. St Louis of France ordered the expulsion from his kingdom of 'women of evil life' in the 1250s, and by the 1520s cities were beginning a repression of prostitution which outlasted our period. But between 1350 and 1450, a municipal institutionalization of prostitution spread widely in southern Europe, in Italy – Lucca, Venice, Florence, Siena – and in Provence, Burgundy and Languedoc.

Prostitution could occur anywhere, but it was in more populous places that it became a larger scale business, attracting more attention. So it is urban prostitution that is most visible to the researcher, and it was in towns and cities that it flourished and indeed in some became institutionalized. Some towns tried to repress it, or perhaps merely drive it underground. P. J. P. Goldberg, in *Women in England c.1275–1525* (1995) publishes ordinances from York from 1301 which awarded the arresting bailiff the doors and roof timbers of prostitutes' lodgings, and at Bristol in 1344 the mayor's servants took their doors and windows. Places frequented by prostitutes such as niches in the town walls were the focus of attention in Ghent in 1350 and efforts made to ban women going there and sitting in them. In other places women at large in the community were known to be prostitutes and were either banned from wearing certain clothing (flaunting their attractiveness and success?) or ordered to wear particular garments (to prevent ordinary women being mistakenly approached by clients). Such sumptuary legislation is especially associated with Mediterranean municipalities after 1300. In law, prostitutes at the start of the period were mainly outstanding for their subhuman rights. As they were available for sex, it was argued that the offence of rape could not be committed against them, so they could make no claim for redress. Late thirteenth-century royal decrees instructed the authorities in Seville and Murcia to punish men for beating or raping prostitutes. Church teaching disapproved of prostitution, but Christianity is a religion holding out penitence and forgiveness and unwilling to make hopeless outcasts of sinners. (The woman taken in adultery was an episode of Christ's ministry enacted in miracle plays.) Furthermore, churchmen, as professional celibates, and as institutional landowners in towns and cities, are known to have availed themselves of the individuals, and provided and taken rent for the premises.

Some towns took a practical approach to the problem, building municipal brothels with ratepayers' money and leasing them to management. The purpose-built facilities described in J. Rossiaud's *Medieval Prostitution* included gardens, courtyards, common rooms, kitchens and private individual bedchambers. At Tarascon the town brothel had only 4 bedchambers, at Dijon, after enlargement in 1447, there were 20. In some places prostitutes were obliged to live in the brothel, in others they might live at large in the town and be free to solicit in taverns and public spaces, but were supposed to take their clients back to the municipal brothel for their services. Prostitution also concentrated round public baths. These stews, according to Rossiaud, 'everywhere' where they can be studied in operation, were offering both innocent bathing and purposeful prostitution. Attempts were made to keep the two apart, mainly by designating respectable hours and more or less implying that being there at other times was asking for trouble, which was also the attitude in Castilian towns. Some baths, however, seem to have been wholly covers for other activities – Rossiaud cites an inventory from an Avignon bathhouse listing beds everywhere but no bathing apparatus. Still less regulated were small bordelages run by procuresses with two or three girls and others who could be called in, and freelancing women soliciting where opportunity allowed.

It is generally agreed that prostitution was more commonly found in districts with a mobile population, and that it concentrated in poorer districts and that prostitution and criminality kept close company. This is not to say that the prostitutes or the clients were mainly recent migrants or short-term residents, nor that the prostitutes themselves were thieves and vagabonds. Two-thirds of the Dijon prostitutes in Rossiaud's study came from the city or nearby, and most had lived there more than a year. Girls mainly began the life style around 17, mostly occasionally at first. The municipal brothels had the most foreign girls working at them, indeed some towns forbade daughters of the citizenry working at the municipal brothel. A noticeable contingent in the Rhône valley came from Flanders, Artois, Picardy, Hainaut and Barrois. In Florence in 1436 over 70 per cent of the municipal brothel women came from northern Europe – and over half of these from the Low Countries – but by 1481–91 north Italy provided over three-quarters of the city's public prostitutes and by 1511–21 the figure was 96 per cent. The organized city prostitutes had a client for half an hour and in fifteenth-century Dijon were paid one blanc, the equivalent of half a day's work in the vineyards. Before the Reformation the city fathers' attitude to prostitution was inclined to be tolerant. With late marriage for men, some outlet had to be found for youthful male sexuality, and better prostitution than abuse of wives and daughters or sodomy, and better organized municipal prostitution than disorderly bawdy houses. The women's viewpoint is as usual more obscure. Some had been sold into it by their own relatives, others lured into it by unscrupulous males they fell in with. Some started haphazardly when in urgent need, and either found the life preferable to hard slog in the vineyards or perpetual spinning, or soon found themselves unable to get other work. A woman being sexually abused regularly by a master and his sons and friends while nominally in honest domestic service might think prostitution could offer little worse and had some perks such as attractive working clothes and the socialization of the tavern. However, it was a risky occupation, exposing the women to physical injury and sometimes theft – of their fee, or their clothes, even their life – with less than standard protection from the law. Moreover it was an occupation for the young and reasonably attractive, whom clients preferred. Older ones had eventually to become madams, or enter institutions as penitents and then put up with the restrictions, or manage to get themselves married. Many of the prostitutes in Dijon apparently ended up quite respectably married, but this was a place where most were native and indeed local. The chances of achieving marriage in a place where one was a conspicuous foreigner might have been fewer.

Domestic Life

The obvious source for illustration here is the Ménagier of Paris's handbook for his young wife, written around 1392. The Ménagier was a well-off citizen and his wife, gentler born than he, was only 15 when he married her; he expected her to survive him and remarry and wrote partly to set out what he wanted done for his own comfort and partly so that she would reflect well on him when she catered for a second husband and reared her own daughters. The ménage was large and the Ménagier wanted his wife to know how to choose menservants, doorkeepers, handymen and other hefties and to select tradesmen, tailors, shoemakers, bakers and so on. She had to know how to set the household menservants and chambermaids to work, and how, as 'sovereign mistress' of the house, to order dinners, suppers, dishes and courses, and know enough to make sure she got the best out of butchers and poulterers and understood spices. Indeed, she had to understand cookery including invalid fare. His text even includes suitable pastimes for her.

The directions take us to the heart of home life. Care of the husband had pride of place – he had to be kept in clean linen, welcomed home with a footbath before the fire and clean shoes and hose, good food and drink, and a good bedding with white sheets and nightcaps and next day fresh shirts and garments. In winter he was to have a good and smokeless fire, and the Ménagier further advised 'and let him rest well and be well covered between your breasts, and thus bewitch him'. Six different ways of keeping fleas at bay were discussed, and the use of a mosquito net. Other flies were also a pest and ways of controlling them were set down. The Ménagier was clearly a man of experience. He had a lot to teach his wife, and fortunately she had the help of two mature servants, Master Jehan the Dispenser, a sort of butler/major domo, and Dame Agnes the Beguine, the (head) housekeeper, to keep the staff in order on her behalf. The Ménagier warned his wife in effect to get a contract price out of temporary workers before letting them start on the job, and to take soundings as to how they had performed for others before employing them. As to the regular staff, no chambermaids were to be taken on without sending to their last place of employment to ascertain how long they had stayed, why they left, and any propensity to gossip or drink. When a girl was taken on it was all to be registered in Master Jehan's account book, along with her parentage, next of kin and so on. But though Master Jehan and Dame Agnes were on hand to act as interface between mistress and staff, she was mistress after her husband, laying down the rules and correcting wrongdoing. She had to be knowledgeable enough to know what the staff ought to be doing and select the menus they had to prepare.

A very similar picture comes from the section on 'The system and control that a woman of rank ought to maintain in her household' in Christine de Pizan's *The Book of the Three Virtues*. Christine saw it as the man's job to acquire the provisions and get them delivered to the house but the woman's to manage and allocate them; she had to be familiar with food preparation to know how to organize it and what orders to give. She had to see that the house was clean and orderly and the husband well groomed and the children controlled so they were not heard whining or making a lot of noise. Christine had a strict sense of social hierarchy and stated that wives of country labourers should not enjoy the same rank as the wife of a Paris artisan, nor she as the wife of a merchant, nor she as an unmarried lady, nor she as a married one, nor she as a countess and thus up to the queen. Christine lamented that each should keep to her station but this was not prevalent practice. A recent over-the-top lying-in of a merchant's wife taking up three finely furnished chambers with no expense spared was cited with disapproval, and a rather tart comment about the appellation of merchant being taken by those who in Lombardy would only be called retailers as they sold in small amounts. After this swipe at social pretensions in Paris, Christine went on to the wives of artisans in cities and fine towns – separating goldsmiths, embroiderers, armourers and tapestry makers and others as more respectable than masons and shoemakers and such like. However, all artisan wives received the same advice: to be painstaking and diligent and encourage their husbands and workmen to go to work early in the morning and work till late. The wives should involve themselves in their husbands' work sufficiently to oversee the workers in his absence and reprove their wrongdoing. Interestingly, Christine thought it the wife's role to warn her husband to take care not to make a bad deal when customers were driving a hard bargain, and to advise him against giving too much credit too lightly. To keep her husband happily at home she should stay there and not go out gadding and gossiping like 'slovenly housewives roaming about the town in groups'.

Though the Ménagier's house was large, with reception areas and chambers, solar, kitchen and so on, and well furnished with cushioned benches and beds with sheets and apparently costly apparel, the daily round had some aspects common to humbler households – for example the advice to remove burning pottage from the fire and put it in another pot. But neither of these writers was engaging with the much poorer urban housewife whose life was more hand to mouth. The *Paris Journal* reference to the early morning queues at the bakers as the housewives tried to get bread for their husbands and children comes down to a harsher level.

The housing stock in a late medieval town varied from a Medici palace or Jacques Coeur's house at Bourges to lean-to shacks. Town housing of the more normal kind (that is, excluding merchant princes) was two-, three- or even four-storey. Stone or brick houses were definitely the luxury end of the market, but some places set up fire regulations which at least ordered non-flammable roofing such as tiles. Another possibility was for a timber and plaster house to stand on a stone undercroft. It is mostly the stonework, the better quality building, which has survived. The density of urban population dictated that houses had narrow frontages (to pack more into the street) and ran back on their plots, which in thirteenth-century Florence were 4–6 metres wide and 10–15 metres deep. With cellars and ground floors often taken up with storage, craft and trade, the residential part had to be above, and any expansion had to take the form of extension at the rear or upwards. Houses were entered from the street so it is no wonder the Ménagier's maids were set to sweep the entrance(s) first thing. His house had its own kitchen, but in the York Goodramgate Lady Row terraced housing, built in 1316 (offering, in the most basic units, one bay up and one bay down, 13 feet by 16 below with a slightly larger jettied upper floor) the residents are thought to have kept warm by brazier and to have taken their food to the York bakeries to heat. The plethora of food purveyors in medieval towns – bakers, cooks, pastrycooks, piemen and so on – is part explained by the difficulties of home baking. Other domestic facilities also varied. Few houses had a piped water supply. Public wells, fountains and conduits had to be visited to fetch water: consequently even if the supply was copious people would use the least possible to minimize the frequency of visits. The water supply was far from free from contamination, and sanitation and sewerage were big problems in densely populated areas. The latrines dug by slavewomen in Italian urban households were presumably for private use. Towns did set up public ones but one cannot imagine that these were anything like adequate for a residential population, though they might have alleviated the problem on market and fair days for short-stay visitors. Medieval people complained about bad smells, but they did not appreciate the health risks of untreated sewage. According to Nicholas in *The Later Medieval City* the archbishop of Reims had to forbid urinating inside the bread hall in 1370, while in Nuremberg the Tucher and Behain houses had

30-metre cess pits but they were cleaned only every 30 years. Presumably there was a great deal of slopping out into open drains and one can guess that the women of the house did most of this unsavoury work.

Nicholas also throws into focus the sharing of houses in Ghent, which must have complicated life within. The practice was derived from the inheritance customs. Celie Amelakens owned a fifth share of the de Rebbe house on the Vismarkt, the financial centre, but lived with her older son in his share of his father's house, as noted above. Marital separations in the city created further complexities. One couple settled for dividing their two sons, each taking one child and living alternate years in the family home, a musical chairs experience which can hardly have been stable. In another case it was – reasonably – settled that neither party could occupy the house without the other's consent, but it could be rented out for joint profit. In Italy the better off clans in towns acquired properties close together in a particular neighbourhood and were loth to let these escape the kin's control. Lapo di Giovanni Niccolini dei Sirigatti took advantage of rights to repurchase family houses, rights left to him in the wills of a woman in one case and a man in the other, and only exercised by him some 20 years later.[12] What all this tells us is that few urban housewives chose their living conditions. All over Europe they tended to move to join the husband. They might have to live for a time with his parents. They might be put into a vacant house owned by the kin or an apartment in one. The incoming bride had to make the best of it, and of her new circle of relatives living in close proximity. She might have her widowed mother-in-law for years. How welcome these older women felt must have varied enormously. Lapo, a Florentine merchant, had his mother living with him until she was turned 80 (she survived his first wife). When she died in 1416 he recorded that she had remained in 'our' house 67 years, 2 months and 26 days. His twice-widowed sister kept returning home after the deaths of husbands, and Lapo took in sundry family casualties such as orphaned granddaughters. Klapisch-Zuber counts up that he had 10 people, excluding servants, in his house in 1402, and calls a household of 9 to 11 typical of Florentine merchants. In 1410 he had 15. This is a picture of unshirked kin responsibility and women fitting in with the situations they found themselves in rather than moulding them.

Life Cycle

As it is such an outstandingly informative source, the Florentine *catasto* of 1427 may be used to provide a life-cycle framework on which to hang details from there and other places.[13] The sex ratio at birth is naturally around 105, and the ratio of boys to girls in the baptismal registers of San Giovanni 1451–60 is indeed 104.3 to 100. Analysis of the *catasto* and its updates, however, shows a ratio of 128 in babies recorded as up to one year, and one of 119.4 for the under-15 age group. Some of this male excess may be accounted for by careless recording of the male form of a name, rather than a female, and casual treatment of ages. Klapisch-Zuber and Herlihy raise the likelihood, however, that the lower value put on female babies may have led to under-reporting, particularly since more girls were nursed away from home and may have fallen 'out of sight, out of mind'. A further factor which may have removed some girls from the *catasto* was their entry into live-in domestic service at any age from about 8 years old. (Servants were not generally counted in their employer's house, but their parents may not always have included them.) Of the females in service who are recorded in the *catasto*, 34 per cent were aged between 8 and 17, and not uncommonly left service to marry without returning to the parental home. Other indications of girls' inferiority may be cited. Before giving birth, women were encouraged to hope their babies would be boys. Illegitimate male offspring of the family's males were more likely to be acknowledged and reared by the family than girls. The proportion of girls to boys abandoned to the foundling institutions was two to one (61.2 per cent of those admitted at San Gallo hospital in the decade 1404–13). A higher proportion of girl babies was sent away, and further, for wet-nursing, but this was largely confined to upper- and middle-class families and in the lower levels of society children of both sexes would be nursed by their true mothers.

It is not clear what girls did before marriage in their late teens if they were neither sent into domestic service nor convents around 7–9 years of age. (Giovanni Corsini paid 230 florins as a sort of dowry with his 9-year-old daughter in 1412 when she entered the convent of San Piero Maggiore.) Giovanni Villani, writing just before the Black Death, claimed that 8–10,000 children of both sexes were sent to elementary school, and the *Paris Journal* in 1449 describes a procession of children of the mendicant orders and all the schools of Paris, boys and girls totalling 12,500, but however rosy these estimates may seem, by the early fifteenth century Florentine girls' education was at home or convent and pretty much for the elite. According to Nicholas girls in late fourteenth-century Cologne stayed at school for 4 years, half as long as boys; in Ghent he found reference to them being 'sent' to school, but can only say that they learned Flemish.

Florentine girls were first married under 20, indeed under 18, and the most common age was 16. Of the 25 year olds, 97 per cent were already married or widowed, whereas fewer than half the men were married by 25. The average age for first marriage in Florence in 1427 was 17.6 for girls and 30.3 for males, and in Prato 17.6 and 26. The age gap in Verona in 1425 was only around 7 years. Weddings acquired a lot of ritual stages. The dowry was part money (cash/securities) and part trousseau, agreed between the couple's parents at the *giuramento/sponsalia* (a sort of public engagement ceremony) and notarially witnessed, at least in the best Florentine circles.[14] The trousseau was delivered to the husband's home on the wedding day (*matrimonium* or ring day), or next day; this could be some time before the transfer of the bride to her husband's house (*nozze*), and the dowry was sometimes paid by instalments even over years. However, the institution of the *Monte delle doti* influenced marriage practices in Florence because it paid out customarily after the marriage had been consummated, whereas earlier practice had transferred the dowry first. The most detailed accounts of ceremonies and dowries come from upper classes but dowries were not exclusive to them. Lower-class families paid appropriate small dowries and, as noted earlier, some employers agreed to pay them when taking on a servant girl. The charitable objective of giving dowries to poor deserving girls to enable them to marry gained in popularity with benefactors from the thirteenth century – Epstein comments on it then in Genoa – and shows how much a girl was unmarriageable without something appropriate to her status.

Ritually married, and increasingly sooner rather than later taking up residence at the husband's home, the wife entered a period of childbearing. The average age of mothers in Florence was 27.13, the median 25, the modal 20, younger than the countryside equivalents (29.93: 28: 30). The father's average age was 40.20, 38 and 40 in Florence (38.42: 36: 40 in the countryside). Thus the urban father was sometimes twice the age of the mother. Widowers remarried quickly – to younger wives – and kept up procreation. Gregorio Dati married five times and fathered 28 children. But typical households were not necessarily bursting at the seams with many children. Morelli claimed Florentine women before the plague had 4–6 children. Nicholas Corsini's wife had 20 between 1365 and 1389, but only 8 survived childhood. In families which used wet-nurses the wives got physical respite between pregnancies (although they might have conceived again more quickly). Klapisch-Zuber and Herlihy see no sign of artificial family limitation in the wealthy, but suspicion of it in the middle- and lower-class urban families, especially under the 800 florin assessment level.

With childhood mortality rates high it is not surprising that the average lifespan was low. In *ricordi* from 1250 to 1500, 157 males and 63 females have both birth and death recorded. Their average lifespan may be calculated at 37.2 for men and 33.14 for women. (The *catasto* provides 35.6 for men and 36.6 for women as the mean age of those cancelled on account of death in the amendments registered for Florence, compared with 49.1 and 43.5 in the *contado* and 50.8 and 42.7 in the district.) Records show 10 per cent of women were already widows at 40; 25 per cent at 50, 50 per cent after 60, and one in four adult women in Florence was a widow, compared with one in ten in the countryside. The sex ratio settled at a normal 105 from adolescence to the 40s age group, when a decline in male numbers set in, they being fewer than women by age 50. A suspicious reversal of the balance to 105 and 110 in the over 60s may arise from other things than sharply increasing female deaths: such as an anticipatory bunching of men claiming to be over the poll tax age, and the overlooking of impoverished old women. Klapisch-Zuber and Herlihy comment that the Tuscan widow was 'often solitary and usually ignored'. Only the top tax bracket (assessments over 32,000 florins) show old women outnumbering old men, but curiously the wealthy also show the lowest proportion of women in the 30s, with a sex ratio of 174. In this age and class there were still unmarried bachelors around the home, and some of the daughters in marrying were lost from the status group by marrying beneath them. (Their dowries did sometimes lever up an inferior husband's family resources quite noticeably.) Others from this class may have been lost to the *catasto*'s lay statistics by entering convents, for which only a few inmate lists are recorded.

Young widows in Florence had a right to return to the family home and might from there undergo the process of a new marriage with a new dowry. Old widows did hang on with married sons, but some contributed to the many tiny households in Florence, where 20 per cent of the households were single person, bringing the average household size down to 3.8. The percentage of female household heads was 14.3 at Florence, 15.6 at Pisa, 16.7 at Prato, 21 at Pistoia and 24 at Arezzo. (In the Paris *taille* records 15.4 per cent of household heads were women, and in the Venetian *estimo* of 1379, 198 of the 2143 households, 9.2 per cent, were headed by women.) The average age of the married women in urban Florence was 35.2, but the average age of the widows 59.5 and in the listing of cause of death there available for 1424, 1425 and 1430 the undertakers listed 92 men and 226 women as dying of old age. This is about their only statistical 'superiority'.

5

Women and Power: Royal and Landholding Women

Although enormous social gulfs separated queens from the wives of small landowners, the entire landed elite was a class apart from those who were only its tenants, tradespeople and employees. The former lived on revenues from estates, income from investment opportunities, profits from trade carried out by others, and fees from honourable offices, contrasted with the latter's livelihood from the soil tilled by or manufactures made by their own hands, domestic or other service, or trade carried out at the point of sale by themselves. For this reason the womenfolk of the unwieldy group of landowners will be considered together, but in some hierarchical order.

Queens

As in the earlier middle ages, queens were dynastic necessities. Physical fitness for potential child bearing was highly relevant. Marguerite of Austria at the age of 3 was inspected naked by her sister-in-law and her husband, the Beaujeus, when she was first received as future wife for the French heir Charles, and Anne of Brittany was exposed naked to the same couple and two other people at the more embarrassing age of 14 just before her marriage to the same Charles, then king, in 1491. Moral fitness also mattered. The long-term interests of the royal dynasty and the current standing of the king's reputation necessitated the unquestionable chastity of the queen. A huge scandal erupted at the French court in 1314 when the king arrested his three daughters-in-law, accusing the wives of his eldest and youngest sons of intrigue with two knights and the wife of the middle son with being cognizant and not denouncing it. The knights, two brothers, were executed; the dauphin's wife, Margaret, died in prison; Blanche, the wife of Charles, later Charles IV, fought the accusation from prison in Chateau Gaillard, was repudiated by her husband in 1322 and retired to the abbey of Maubisson; her sister Jeanne, wife of Philip V, was cleared. Fawtier commented that the guilt remains doubtful but the fact that royal adultery was to be exposed and publicly punished was significant.[1] It has to be said, however, that this was a moral crusade against adultery when committed by royal *women.* Theirs was a lively generation. Philip IV's own daughter, who may have been the traducer of her sisters-in-law, saw her lover Mortimer arrested in her presence at Nottingham Castle and taken to be tried for treason and executed in 1330, the nearest event England can offer to the fictional discovery of Lancelot with the queen in Camelot. Henry VIII executed Anne Boleyn and Catherine Howard for treasonable adultery and unchastity: unfortunately for these latter day Guineveres no Lancelot snatched them from the scaffold to the safety of *Joyeuse Garde.*

Once married, the obligation to produce healthy, preferably male, children as heirs could prove crushing. Anne of Brittany died at 37 in 1514 having undergone nine more or less full-term pregnancies and at least two miscarriages, but only two daughters survived her, Claude then 14 and Renée then 3. Her last stillbirth, of a son, had been only two years before. It was a terrible drain of repeated physical and emotional effort. Failure to bear children successfully was, as in earlier times and later, a hazard to the durability of a queen's marriage. When royal divorce proceedings were begun, the grounds were usually consanguinity or non-consummation. Louis XII, wishing to rid himself of Jeanne of France, claimed his childless marriage had not been consummated. She fought the nullification of her marriage by claiming that it had. Conversely, Henry VIII's suit against Catherine of Aragon, who had given him only one surviving daughter, hung on whether her earlier marriage to his brother Arthur had been consummated or not; if she was Arthur's full wife then Henry could claim that he should not have married his brother's wife. She swore that the marriage to Arthur had not been consummated. Neither woman, both daughters of kings, could prevail against determined royal husbands. Considering that queens were well nourished and lived in comparatively hygienic conditions (for the time), and that they had the pick of wet-nurses and physicians and more ability than most people to move their children from plague spots, the high death rates among royal children (the four older brothers of Charles VII died under 20), and in the case of Jeanne of France, Anne and Isabeau of Brittany, Claude and Renée, all descendants of Charles V, physical deformities of varying degree, suggest that long inbreeding was taking its toll.[2]

Paradoxically the oldest and most prestigious dynasties politically may have been the most risky to marry into genetically.

To a potential husband, the bride's dynasty was highly relevant politically. Alfonso VIII of Castile and his wife Leonor, daughter of Henry II and Eleanor of Aquitaine, were noticeably successful at exporting daughters into high places. Blanche married Louis VIII and mothered St Louis, for whom she was regent. Berenguela married Alfonso IX of Leon and played a role in uniting the kingdoms of Castile and Leon through their son Fernando, although the marriage was ended by Innocent III because the couple were too closely related. Urraca married Alfonso II of Portugal, and their daughter Alienor became queen of Denmark as wife of Waldemar II. Leonor married Jaime I of Aragon, but was divorced by 1229. Royal dynasties also scooped up brides from the higher international aristocracy. In the mid-thirteenth century four daughters of Count Raymond Berengar IV of Provence were married to kings – Margaret to St Louis of France, Eleanor to Henry III of England, Sanchia to his brother Richard of Cornwall, King of the Romans (but never making it to Emperor), and Beatrice to Charles of Anjou, king of Naples and Sicily.

For the French, for whom the middle ages was a time their kings spent trying to consolidate and extend the kingdom and absorb border territories and potentially disloyal fiefdoms, the ducal heiress to Brittany in 1488 was as attractive a prize as Eleanor of Aquitaine had been to Louis VII and it is quite surprising she was still not irrevocably betrothed when she inherited the duchy in her twelfth year. In December 1490, at 13, she was married by proxy in Rennes cathedral to Maximilian, the 31-year-old King of the Romans, father of Marguerite of Austria, the 10-year-old wife of Charles VIII who was then 20. Franco-Breton politics dictated differently. Maximilian's snatching of Brittany had to be stopped before the proxy marriage with the 13-year-old girl was taken any further. On the first anniversary of her marriage to Maximilian Anne was irregularly married – in the presence of three bishops – to Charles VIII, who had abandoned Marguerite. Married to Charles just short of her fifteenth birthday, Anne proved capable of conceiving almost at once, vindicating the need for haste. By February 1492 she had been crowned; papal dispensations were tardily received in August, and the desired son and heir was born on 10 October. The dauphin, however, died in infancy and subsequent pregnancies ended in grief, one only a month before Charles's unexpected death in 1498. His heir was his cousin Louis XII, who as king needed heirs more desperately than he had needed them as Duke of Orléans. He had previously shown interest in Anne as a potential wife despite the existence of his own earlier marriage to Louis XI's deformed younger daughter Jeanne, to whom he had been contracted by agreement between the couple's fathers when she was 3 weeks and Louis 2 years old, and married, he unwillingly, when she was 12 and he 14. By 1498 they were 34 and 36 and childless. Her spinal deformity made it unlikely that she would bear children successfully, and her husband's more or less forced attentions to her had been more in the nature of public relations visits than cohabitation. He had long desired divorce, and on accession to the throne whose two previous occupants had bullied him into the marriage and pretence of its continuity, Louis immediately opened up negotiations with the pope and sent a messenger to his wife to inform her of the fact. Anne, the dowager queen at 21, was bound by the terms of her marriage contract with Charles VIII (so important was Brittany) to marry only the new king or his heir in the event of being widowed childless. Louis was released from his first marriage on 20 December 1498 and married Anne within the first eight days of January 1499; their first born, Claude, arrived on 13 October.

When kings married foreign brides they were demonstrating their international standing. Always it was politically important for usurpers and new dynasties to show they could marry well. Henry Tudor took the English throne by military force in 1485 and strengthened his position by marrying Edward IV's daughter; to secure Catherine of Aragon as wife for their first born Arthur was a sign of having arrived internationally – no wonder he was unwilling to hand her back when Arthur died. The second son Henry, who eventually took Catherine on (and later still of course repudiated her) succeeded in getting his sister married to Anne of Brittany's widower Louis XII in 1514. There was a recurrent snag with foreign marriages that compatriots of the incoming spouse were often resented, as will be taken up below, but marriage to a subject could also lead to hostilities towards her relatives. Elizabeth Woodville's relations were inordinately resented by the English aristocracy in the reign of Edward IV.

Most queens were queens consort not queens regnant. Fifteen women can be identified from Armin Wolf's study as inheritors of crowns between 1200 and 1550: two queens of Castile, Isabella (1474–1504) and her daughter Joanna (who may be removed from consideration in effect since her husband, father and son successively acted as regents or co-sovereign as she became increasingly insane); two queens of Naples, Joanna I (1343–82) and Joanna II (1414–35); a queen of Sicily, Maria, who died in 1401; two queens of Scotland, Margaret of Norway (1286–90) who drowned aged 7 before reaching her kingdom, and Mary Queen of Scots, who came to the throne aged one week at the end of the period in 1542; two sisters who became respectively queens of Poland (Jadwiga, 1382–99) and Hungary (Maria 1382–95); and a string of queens in Navarre, Joanna I (1274–1305) who was also by marriage queen of France, Joanna II (1329–49), Blanche (1425–41), Leonor (1479) and Caterina (1484–1516). With these, Wolf counts the unique Scandinavian queen Margaret who died in1412 after ruling all three kingdoms with one form of power or another, as will be shown shortly.[3] The two who were most successful at wielding actual power were Margaret of Denmark and Isabella of Castile. Isabella was already married to Ferdinand of Aragon when she succeeded to the throne of Castile in 1474; there his rights were limited, and when he succeeded to Aragon in 1479 she was only queen consort there. Given the title 'the Catholic kings' by Alexander VI, Ferdinand and Isabella are inseparable in history as joint monarchs until her death in 1504. Isabella was of stouter character than her daughter, and campaigned in armour against the Moors, bearing children between sieges. Several of the others were little more than conduits of power to husbands who held on to their thrones when they died, in the Polish and Hungarian cases carefully remarrying cognates of the old dynasty: however, such queens were usually more prominent than mere queens consort, for example being jointly named in documents as was the case with Maria of Sicily and Maria of Hungary.

With the more limited role of queen consort, individuals may be assumed mainly to have played the role their husbands (and local custom) permitted, and indeed they crossed this at their peril. Charles VI of France was subject to bouts of madness and his wife Isabeau of Bavaria, empowered by this abnormal situation, drifted between the royal dukes of Orléans and Burgundy as allies and has been criticized for opportunism and greed for power (qualities which were almost virtues in a king, of course). The unique position of Anne of Brittany as queen consort to two French kings in succession shows contrasting input of personality. Under Charles VIII Anne was removed from her duchy and its independent institutions began to be dismantled. As soon as he died, Anne revived its chancellery, corresponded energetically with it, visited it and presided over its Estates and generally involved herself once more, also erecting a monument to her parents in Nantes. Louis XII seems to have been a more tolerant and indulgent husband and allowed her more leeway in her duchy though (at first secretly) overriding her wish for a Hapsburg match in the matter of the marriage of their daughter Claude. With Louis' 1505 will setting up Claude's marriage to Francis of Angoulême the French heir presumptive Anne was thwarted and it may be significant that she took off on an ostensible pilgrimage through Brittany and was away from her husband for four months. If she felt Louis' action was a slap in the face, she may have realized that she had brought it on herself by interfering in such an important matter. Therein lies exposed the tightrope queens consort walked: if they exceeded themselves there was every likelihood of rebuff. Although there was some tradition for queens' involvement in the arrangement of their children's marriages, even this was being denied to Anne of Brittany.

For queens consort the main opportunity for the exercise of power came if they became regent queen mothers for their sons. One of the earliest in our period was Blanche of Castile, widow of Louis VIII and mother of St Louis, who succeeded to the French throne at the age of 9 in 1226, and one of the latest was Louise of Savoy who, though not previously queen, became regent for her son Francis I when he left the country to pursue war in Italy. Both are treated in the final section below.

Women of the Nobility and Landed Classes

The previous section on queens has already made it clear that there was intermarriage between royal dynasties and the nobility. Royal daughters and younger sons spread out by marriage amid the circle of ducal and comital families which passed its daughters upwards to princely heirs. Thus at the top the nobility was intermeshed with kings and queens. At the bottom the definition of nobility was equally unclear, partly because different areas worked by different principles, depending on whether all a nobleman's legitimate children were noble or only the line of the eldest son, or only noblemen's sons born of noble mothers, or less frequently those born of a noble mother even if the father was not. Where younger children were not noble, the case in England, there was a thriving gentry class equivalent to the lower or petty nobility elsewhere. To make it plain that the widest possible range is considered here the landed classes have been added to the definition to avoid having to test every example for proof of nobility. In towns there was another overlap between what may be called the urban nobility and the non-noble burgher elite, and at the top of the urban nobility a supernobility rose in some situations by economic, ecclesiastical and/or military activities. Within our period Visconti, Sforza and Medici children were all married into European royalty.

The upper class was essentially of independent means, a form of power: the men did not deign to work as farmers or merchants themselves, and wives and daughters lived in comparative luxury and extravagance. But there were also hangers on and impoverished nobles – many nobles did not possess the 250 *lire a grossi* minimum to appear on the Venetian *estimo* assessments of over 2000 households in 1379 (the richest had 60,000). A down-at-heel section of the nobility was ever present. Families which had ever been noble struggled to keep hold of the status, which in many places had tax advantages. Noblewomen benefited from their background but the only ways they could contribute to the furtherance of the family or at least hold it steady was by marriage upwards, or if it had to be downwards at least with some vigorous upthrusting dynasty working its way towards nobility by birth (it usually took three generations to be fully established) from either a ministerial or a military starting point. In the Burgundian Netherlands the newly ennobled firmed their position by marrying a noble wife. The careers leading to upward social mobility – administration and soldiering – were masculine. Marriage was the chief enhancer of status for women, most startlingly illustrated in the promoted mistress. However, Gaunt's mistress who became his last duchess, Catherine Swinford, née Roet, was the daughter of a knight from Hainaut from Queen Philippa's service and Froissart described Catherine as brought up in princely courts.

This is significant for there were perceived standards of behaviour which separated the noble and gentle from the boorish and the money-grubbing. There was some tension in this area, for while literature features noble blood prevailing, a king's son brought up for some reason in a forest or made to serve incognito in a scullery behaving true to birth not true to environment, there was also a view that 'gentle is as gentle does' and that people could learn better manners and be taken for how they behaved. Why else the many etiquette books and 'improving' story collections? The three parts of Christine de Pizan's *The Three Virtues* addressed themselves respectively to princesses, to ladies and maidens of their courts, extending to those who lived on manors and needed to know how to manage their households and estates, and to women of rank in towns and cities, through merchants' wives to artisans' wives, servantwomen and chambermaids, prostitutes, wives of labourers and the poor of both sexes. The Portuguese princess Isabel, third wife of the Burgundian duke Philip the Good sent a copy of this work to her niece Queen Isabel who had it translated into Portuguese, and Queen Leonor had it published in 1518.

In Part One, chapter 20, of the *Three Virtues* Christine wrote that any man of any class is foolish if he sees that he has a good and wise wife and does not give her authority to govern in an emergency. After 1200 aristocrats were less drawn from their home bases by crusading, but wars abroad did still remove them, and their wives or mothers did then cope in some instances – such were the circumstances of Louise of Savoy's two regencies in France in the early sixteenth century. Annexed to her will of 1476 Margaret Lady Hungerford, heiress of William third Lord Botreux and widow of Robert second Lord Hungerford, left accounts detailing expenses arising from her son Lord Moleyns' capture and ransom after Castillon (1453), to explain her comparative poverty: she had taken responsibility for liabilities after her husband's death in 1459 and sold lands particularly from her Botreux inheritance (her father died in 1462) to meet them, impeded by reluctance of her heirs to release their rights.[4] Christine de Pizan would have approved her acceptance of responsibility and wise undertaking of it. Margaret was motivated by a sense of honour and the fear of imperilling her soul by dying in debt. Another of the responsibilities often falling to women of these classes was the fitting commemoration of their deceased husbands. Again Lady Hungerford offers herself as a prominent example, endowing a daily mass for her husband's soul at the St Osmund altar in Salisbury's Lady Chapel and later building the separate Hungerford chantry chapel in the cathedral, the altar consecrated in her presence in 1471.

Not all husbands kept their wives' talents unrecognized until an emergency. Duke Ercole I of Ferrara let his able wife Eleanora of Aragon, daughter of Ferdinand of Naples, deal with affairs in Ferrara while he went riding and played cards. She meantime produced seven infants between 1474 and 1481, two girls followed by five boys, and enjoyed popular approbation. Driven by religious faith she owned devotional books and was much inclined to 'good works' – the sort of princess Christine de Pizan would have applauded.[5]

Lady Hungerford's period of management came in her widowhood and it was in that period of their lives that high-class widows of consequence really came into their own. Margaret Wade Labarge offers a string of illustrations of noble ladies as women who ruled in *Women in Medieval Life*, including Countess Marguerite of Flanders (d 1280) hereditary countess of Flanders and Hainaut; Isabella de Fortibus, Countess of Aumâle and Devon (d 1293), one of the ten richest barons in England in the thirteenth century, her brother's heir to the earldom of Devon and the dowager of William de Fortibus count of Aumâle; Countess Mahaut of Artois (d 1328) who inherited Artois from her father and was dowager Countess of Burgundy after the death of her husband Count Otho in 1302; Elizabeth de Burgh, Lady of Clare (d 1360) one of the three co-heiresses to the Clare estates; Marie of St Pol, Countess of Pembroke (d 1377), daughter of Guy de Chatillon Count of St Pol and wife and widow of Aymer de Valence Earl of Pembroke; and Dame Alice de Bryene (d 1435) widow of a Suffolk knight. All of these were notably active in widowhood and threw their weight about considerably, as will be shown below.

Life Cycle

As the sex of an unborn child was not known a royal or noble birth had to be prepared for regardless of gender. In *Queen's Mate* Matarasso gives a description, from an account roll, of the preparations in 1510 for the birth of the baby who proved to be Renée of France. The birth took place on 25 October, and the purchasing only began on 25 September, late in the pregnancy: the all too often previously disappointed parents may have been superstitious about going ahead sooner in case of prematurity or still-birth. Over a hundred yards of fine cloths were required for making layette and sheets. Carpenters refurbished apartments and made furniture including two rocking cradles and beds for staff including a wet-nurse. The grand royal equivalent of a changing mat, a wooden dais topped with green damask and canopied, was thoughtfully built in the warmest position in front of the fire. Further works took place in the christening chapel. English royal accounts also record lavish expenditure on rooms for royal lyings-in, for example for Philippa of Hainaut in 1335.

The infant Marguerite of Austria's establishment when she was settled in France aged 3 as the bride of the dauphin surely represents the apogee of nursery provision, and is also described by Matarasso. She had a staff of 87 persons, and had ponies, dogs and falcons specially trained for her, and her pet green parrot which had been her mother's. Such an extravagant entourage was special to '*la petite reine*', but there are many other indications of more modest nurseries and specific governesses. John of Gaunt's eldest daughter Philippa, one of his three children by his first wife Blanche of Lancaster, was taken care of at her mother's death by Alyne Gerberge, wife of one of the ducal esquires, who received an annuity from 1370. The three children were described as having a common chamber in 1372 and accounts show purchase of educational books for them. By 1376 the two girls were sharing a chamber and wardrobe in the care of Catherine Swinford, once 'damsel' to their mother and currently the duke's mistress (she bore him four children in the decade). The duke's daughter by his second wife Constance of Castile, Catilina, was brought up separately, at one stage with Lady Mohun. A disjointed childhood with the loss of mother and stepmother and a scandalous governess who became Gaunt's third wife belatedly in 1396 seems to have left Philippa unscathed. At the elderly age of 26 she was married to John I of Portugal; Catilina became wife to Henry III of Castile and co-regent for her son Juan II.

Women of the elite were not uneducated but were excluded from the formal, dedicated, educational institutions available for boys, culminating in the universities. Thus girls of the upper classes, compared with their brothers, generally had less formal tuition in more private circumstances, ending at a younger age. In the courts of fourteenth- and fifteenth-century Italy however, this was becoming a positively academic education. Battista da Montefeltro (b 1384), daughter of Count Antonio, lord of Urbino, her granddaughter Costanza Varano and her daughter Battista Sforza, who married the Count's grandson Frederigo da Montefeltro, were three humanist 'bluestockings'.[6] The senior Battista received a letter from the humanist Leonardo Bruni on the subject of female education in humanist literature, recommending Latin texts of Cicero, Vergil, Livy, Sallust and church fathers, and Latin translations of Greek, and all three women delivered orations – the younger Battista is credited with a short Latin oration given to her uncle Franceso Sforza and his wife in Milan at the age of 4. Later she learnt Greek, and continued studies beyond her marriage at 14 to the 37-year-old later duke in 1460. Within months he entrusted her to rule his vicariates in his absences. In 12 years she bore nine daughters and finally a son, dying 5 months later. In the sixteenth century Henry VIII's daughters Mary and Elizabeth received a humanist education and it was not confined to royalty, as Lady Jane Grey's academic precocity shows.

Royal princesses could have their marriages arranged at any age, at three weeks in the case of the unfortunate Jeanne of France. Marguerite of Austria was held in her governess's arms at her wedding, aged 3. Isabelle, Charles VI's daughter, was married by proxy to Richard II at 8. Anne of Brittany was married to Maximilian of Austria by proxy at 13, and solemnly 'bedded' by the same agent. Girls and boys betrothed young were supposed to be given the chance at 12 or 14 respectively to decline consent before completion of the marriage, and however proper the ceremony, consummation was necessary to render the marriage irrevocable. Marital relations with young girls were, however, realized to be a matter for caution to avoid injury. Mothers seem to have rallied to keep their daughters virgin, even if they were already married, until somewhere in the 14–16 age range, and fathers seem to have been willing to support this. The 'courtesy of England' which allowed a husband life enjoyment of his deceased wife's lands if she had ever borne a living child caused some marriages to be consummated too young. Mary de Bohun who married Henry of Derby (later Henry IV) in July 1381 at 12, bore and lost a son in April 1382, and Margaret Beaufort, who bore the future Henry VII at 13, having been widowed during the pregnancy, never succeeded in bearing another child.

Marriages among the elite involved the giving of dowry from the natal family and the husband's dowering of the bride to secure provision for her widowhood. Evergates's work on Champagne shows that these matters were being written into marriage contracts there from the late twelfth century, and with various qualifying provisions, thus a cash dowry of 6000 livres (of Provins) acquired by the Count of Rethel with his bride Jeanne in 1239 was to be refunded if he died childless, as happened 4 years later. This was a huge dowry by comparison with the 100 livres Evergates thought the typical expectation of a knight's daughter, or the 500 livres 'or more' of a baron's.[7] In Gascony the daughter of the knight Alexander de la Pebree was given a 1000 livres tournois dowry in 1289, and the granddaughter of a doge of Venice had one of 3000 ducats in 1419. The dowry could be in cash or property – the cash value being estimated at ten times the annual revenue in mid-thirteenth-century Champagne. Dowries in property could transfer whole lordships, castles, villages or small amounts of land. The Treaty of Arras brought Artois, Burgundy, Macon and Auxerre into French hands as the dowry of Marguerite of Austria – small wonder she was set up with a splendid nursery. (The dowry had to be unravelled when Charles VIII repudiated her for Anne of Brittany.) Dower was commonly lifetime usufruct of a third or half the husband's property in land, revenue or movable goods. In Champagne and north and east France the customary dower at the start of the period was the principal residence and half the property for life use. The 'half dower' was extended generally over the kingdom in 1214, although the Beauvaisis exceptionally had the third dower when Beaumanoir wrote in the 1280s. However, the various customary provisions could be overridden by the specific making of other arrangements, although they were commonly adhered to and formed the default allocation. By devising specific dower the husband identified particular estates for his widow's support (but these could amount to less than half his assets). Blanche of Navarre, widow of Count Thibaud III, was dowered with seven castellanies which Evergates estimated as about a third of the count of Champagne's revenues. On the other hand, by leaving specific property to his wife by a Roman-style will a husband could make over to his wife whatever he wished her to have.

The desire for a son and heir kept mothers of daughters and lost infants trying again for a son, but although the sorry serials of unsuccessful pregnancies make tragic reading, wives whose children were stronger and included males, did not stop producing more. A strong wife might bear children over 20 years – Blanche of Castile had a dozen children, starting at 17 with a stillbirth in 1205; Margaret of Provence, her daughter-in-law, bore 11; Philippa of Hainaut bore at least 12 from 1330 to 1355; Isabeau of Bavaria 12 between 1386 and 1407. It seems that families which could afford to raise endless children did so: 11 named children of Edward I and Eleanor of Castile are known, 7 of whom survived their father and 6 of whom lived beyond their teens; there were probably about 15 in all. With all these descendants, and the love for his wife which he demonstrated with the Eleanor Crosses, it was nine years before Edward I took a second wife by whom he had 3 more children. But Louis XII of France married again within the year of Anne of Brittany's death, taking Mary Tudor aged 18 when he was 62 and in poor health. He could not have expected to live to see a son old enough to succeed and had already made arrangements for the succession. So in whose interest were the many remarriages of kings? Kings did not need wives to make their meals or hold the shop or stepmother their existing offspring. They were surrounded by company and could pick and choose their entertainment. Plenty in their careers illustrates that they did not have to marry for sex, much though the church, and their mothers, if Berenguela of Castile is typical, may have preferred it to incontinence. Why did they keep on remarrying? Did they remarry to get a wife and personal pleasure, to get a queen and companion functionary, or to use the matrimonial opportunity for political gain? Louis XII was clearly virile in his day – while married to Jeanne he had vaunted his sexuality with other women. With Anne of Brittany and the dignity of the crown he apparently was a faithful husband but a demanding one. Matarasso points out that it was widely reported in Italy within a fortnight that he had consummated the marriage with Anne 20 times in the first night. Widows of independent means who had been through it all often showed less enthusiasm for entering another marital relationship. Marguerite of Austria after three husbands (if the first can be so counted) declined to start again with another.

Royal life was a public peep show then as now, and if the king's virility was a matter of gossip, so were his wife's pregnancies. From Matarasso we learn that when Anne of Brittany was pregnant for the last time, with the son stillborn in January 1512, the Austrian ambassador Andrea da Borgo questioned her straight out, but she would not tell him, leading to his comment that this did not mean anything 'because she never lets on until it shows', so he asked the king, who 'more or less admitted it'.[8] Within the month the queen was keeping to her room and seeing nobody, not surprising if people came out with personal questions like that and were peering at her waistline. While public interest in royal births – including prayers and thanksgivings – might be understandable in the case of needed heirs of national consequence, a similar overboldness on the subject troubled the wives of the aristocracy. In November 1472 John Paston II was having second thoughts that he might have been overfamiliar to his patron's wife, the duchess of Norfolk: 'they say I said that my lady was large and great and that it should have enough room to go out at'.[9]

Anne of Brittany's childbearing misfortunes led to more care being taken in her later pregnancies and so patently did affect her life style, causing her to be left comparatively stationary while the king was more mobile. Childbirth was a dangerous time, and repeated pregnancies sapped women's strength, leading to many young deaths leaving motherless children. But safely out of childbearing some doughty dowagers had a long widowhood – keeping their heirs out of their dower lands. The later lives of Elizabeth de Burgh and Marie de St Pol show them vigorously keeping up grand households and travelling between bases. As they grew older, losing both husbands and children on the way, many upper-class women turned their attention to family monuments and charities. Marguerite of Flanders founded Dominican houses at Ypres and Douai. Jeanne d'Evreux, widow of Charles IV, endowed a chapel at Saint-Denis. Lady Margaret Beaufort founded two Cambridge colleges, Christ's (where she had a room looking into the chapel) and St John's, and latterly lived a quasi-monastic life at Collyweston – beginning this with his agreement while her last husband was still alive. The deaths of queens were marked with suitable processions and obsequies: Edward I had 12 crosses erected to mark the stopping points of the cortege of Eleanor of Castile between Lincoln and Westminster Abbey. With more passion and less gravitas Richard II had the royal lodge of La Neyt and the whole palace of Sheen destroyed after his wife Anne had died there in 1394. Matarasso provides the full details of the rites performed between Anne of Brittany's death and burial in 1514, and her effigy at Saint-Denis reproduces the realistic stitches of the embalmer down her abdomen and that of Louis XII lying alongside.

Transplantation of Women and Ideas

The ancient idea of women as peaceweavers lingered on in the political marriages between royal dynasties. All the kings of England from 1200 until Edward IV married Elizabeth Woodville in 1464 married foreign-born wives and the predominant interchange was with the French royal family which provided wives for Edward I, Edward II, Richard II, Henry V and Henry VI (though in his case only the great-great-granddaughter of a French king). Isabella of France, married to Edward II when she was 12 and he rising 24, was actually dispatched to France as a peacemaker between her husband and her brother the French king Charles IV in 1325 to bring the war over Saint-Sardos to a conclusion. With her son in France to perform homage for Gascony, she went on to plot the revolution which led to the deposition of her husband in 1326. But she is not particularly associated with the import of French ideas, and her French servants were dismissed only when war between the two countries had broken out. Henry VI's wife Margaret, daughter of René I of Anjou, was unfortunate in that the pro-war party in England disliked her because she was associated with the cession of Maine, and seemed rather a 'poor relation' to crown queen consort, but again the men she worked with and who shared her unpopularity were English aristocrats like Suffolk. A bunch of Savoyards who came with Henry III's wife Eleanor of Provence (whose mother was Beatrice of Savoy) were highly unpopular among the English baronage in the mid-thirteenth century, but even the baronial party submitted its case against Henry III to St Louis of France (whose wife was Henry's queen's sister), showing the moral dominance of French influence at the time without any 'party' round the queen being needed to account for it. It was a queen from further afield, Richard II's first wife, Anne of Bohemia, who seems to have had more impact although this may only be because she brought more visibly different ideas. Anne was the daughter of the Holy Roman Emperor Charles IV of Luxemburg and his fourth wife Anne of Pomerania. A cosmopolitan product, with ancestors who had been patrons of the great names in literature, Petrarch, Machault and Dante, Anne spent her childhood years in Prague, where her father had founded the University in 1347. Her father was a patron of the international Gothic style and some of the illuminated manuscripts associated with Richard's court seem rapidly to show Luxemburg and Italianate taste, for example the *Liber Regalis* dated to 1382–3, while the Carmelite Missal of c.1393 has ostriches in the margin, the queen's badge. Anne was quite intellectual and had Czech and German copies of the Gospels, and had an English New Testament ordered. Willard, biographing Christine de Pizan, viewed Valentina Visconti and her entourage as significant importers of Italian influence into the French court. Such innovatory influences were not generally welcome. To counter such tendencies, and make a young wife forget her native customs, aristocratic wives' accompanying attendants were often dispatched back and replaced by persons of the husband's choosing – to the annoyance of Isabella of Aragon when she married Gian Galeazzo Maria Visconti.

It is easier to recognize 'foreign influence' in architecture and painting than in any other sphere and the introduction of French Gothic architecture into the empire has been attributed to St Elizabeth of Thuringia, daughter of Andrew II of Hungary and Gertrud of Andechs-Meranien (sister of Agnes with whom Philip Augustus replaced Ingeborg of Denmark), who married the landgrave of Thuringia in 1221, was widowed in 1227, adopted a Franciscan life style until her death in 1231 and was canonized in 1235. The Gothic style of St Elizabeth's Church in Marburg, built between 1235 and 1283, was innovatory for the empire.[10] Of course sometimes more than the architectural style was influenced – the development of royal family mausolea was passed from Eleanor of Aquitaine (who concentrated Angevin burials at Fontevrault) to her daughter Leonor of Castile who founded Las Huelgas near Burgos with her husband Alfonso VIII; their daughter Urraca was married to Alfonso II of Portugal at the time the Cistercian abbey of Alcobaça was adopted as the royal family burial site. Urraca's sister Berenguela, married to Alfonso IX of Leon, was grandmother of Eleanor of Castile who influenced Westminster Abbey's development in this capacity. Transplanted queens endured phases of unpopularity of a xenophobic kind in the west but were much more consistently subject to hostility in Hungary, where J. M. Bak sees them as characteristically scapegoats, agents of foreign influence and immigration. St Elizabeth's own mother was assassinated for favouring German relatives.[11] At the end of the period Catherine de Medici, a woman who ordered chapters of Machiavelli's *The Prince* to be read to her sons each night, was queen of France but not allowed the input into affairs she would prove capable of (not always advisedly) when regent for her son Charles IX; indeed at this stage in her life she was somewhat eclipsed by her husband's mistress Diane de Poitiers.

The movement of royal brides is the most traceable transplantation of women in this period but sometimes a lesser personage can prove more significant. Christine de Pizan's childhood move to the French court after her father had been appointed physician and astrologer to Charles V gave her the same education her father might have given her had the family stayed in Bologna, but in a splendid court in a vibrant city with a humanist university, and it brought her the contacts which shaped the rest of her life – a young noble husband, secretary and notary to the king, and royal patrons.To her outstanding writings she brought a broader than French perspective, and consciousness of difference – hence the withering comment that some self-made French merchants would only have ranked as retailers in Lombardy. But Christine awaits consideration in Chapter 7 below.

Women and Power

If women are indeed to be associated with power in the middle ages, it is the women of the classes studied in this chapter who must be examined to show it. Recent studies of this topic have redefined the perspective, shifting the focus from 'power' (as conventionally understood, meaning power over others, input into and decisive action in public affairs), to 'agency', or 'empowerment' (meaning ability to pursue one's own strategy, do one's own thing).[12] It was right to challenge the old traditional politically angled history's almost complete disregard for women, and wrong to accept the long-held assumption that women were powerless, with a very few, 'manly', exceptions. But the revisionism may itself have gone astray. Instead of accepting the modern concentration on more restricted spheres of action such as the freedom to pursue a personal strategy even unsuccessfully, or the power to keep silent, it may be worth reconsidering the possibility of women actually wielding power in its more traditional perspective as ability not merely to influence but to force others to follow one's strategy, or ability not only to speak, but to command attention.

Admittedly many conditions constraining women's freedom of action, let alone their power over others, continued through from earlier times. In royal, noble and other landowning classes, generally speaking, daughters were disadvantaged in the laws and customs controlling the inheritance of land. As married women, they had little independence of their husbands even with regard to property they had themselves brought to the marriage. As marriageable women, maiden or widow, they were subject to pressure to marry someone who was deemed the most appropriate by either the family or an overlord. Thus, right into the sixteenth century many women of this class had precious little opportunity to pursue their own strategy, even with regard to their own personal lives. On the other hand, royal aristocratic and lesser landed women in the middle ages wielded a good deal of power in the traditional sense of the word. From his study of Champagne Evergates reckoned women formed a fifth of feudal tenants throughout the thirteenth century – a minority certainly but too many to be dismissed as 'exceptional'. As feudal tenants they had very much the same rights and privileges as men of their class. Blanche of Navarre, pregnant widow of Count Thibaud III, did homage to Philip Augustus within days of her husband's death in 1201. In 1218 she led an army to Nancy and burned the duke of Lorraine's town with the approval of pope and emperor. Women who inherited castellanships responded to military summons. From the early thirteenth century aristocratic women had seals and used them on a wide variety of documents. Women of the landed elite had servants directly on call, and funds of varying quantity to spend on commissions ranging from stone memorials to Books of Hours. Moreover they often had publicly acknowledged influence in areas where direct input was not expected of them – one of the famous vignettes of this is Froissart's portrayal of Philippa of Hainaut begging her husband Edward III for mercy for the burghers of Calais in 1347. Convention expected the queen to intercede in the interests of mercy, to ameliorate the execution of a justice which for political reasons was best presented as that of a justly stern king. Better to have firm rule, subject to dispensation at the behest of a kindlier figure, than a softer regime inviting disrespect. Public role though this gave the queen, it remained essentially subordinate to the king's, begging his attention and mercy, not able to demand it. It was an exercise of influence not authority. But the women of this class sometimes were presented with genuine authority by chance – the chance of their husbands dying leaving only minor heirs or heiresses, or being first absent on military campaign and then prisoners of war requiring ransom.

One of the most successful female regents was Blanche of Castile, regent for St Louis from 1226. Historians seem unable to decide when her first regency ended, which says much for the harmony of relations and policies in mother and son, and Blanche resumed regency again when Louis went on crusade in 1248. She is credited with governing France for most of the period from 1226 until her death in 1252, and Fawtier held that she should be in effect counted among the kings of France, suppressing rebellion, fending off foreign foes, extending Capetian power in the south, raising crusading funds and keeping law and order.[13] Blanche's husband had reigned only 40 months when he died, so she had not had a long apprenticeship as queen consort, but she had had a long schooling in French kingship at her father-in-law's court from her marriage in 1200 when she was 12 and her husband 14.

From the last quarter of the next century Margaret of Denmark is regarded as the ablest Scandinavian ruler of the time, one of the greatest figures in Scandinavian history. Daughter of Waldemar IV Atterdag of Denmark, she was married at 10 to Hakon VI of Norway, who died aged

40 in 1380, leaving a 10-year-old son Olaf IV as his heir to Norway and to his claims to Sweden. Olaf had already succeeded to the Danish throne as Olaf II in 1376. His mother was guardian and regent in both countries, but the boy died in 1387, and she continued to rule both kingdoms, adding Sweden when her elder sister's son Albert of Mecklenburg was rejected there. The constitutional base of her rule was therefore variable and complex: with regard to Denmark she was the younger but sole surviving daughter of Waldemar IV, her son Olaf gained the succession there and left her as his next of kin. With regard to Norway she was the consort of Hakon VI, and again, mother of Olaf. Here she was elected regent for life and empowered to adopt an heir, choosing her great-nephew Eric of Pomerania, born in 1382. Norway claimed power over Sweden, but Albert of Mecklenberg was ruling there until rebellion in 1389. Eric (who was Eric VII in Denmark, Eric III in Norway and eventually Eric XIII in Sweden) was crowned king of the three kingdoms at Kalmar in 1397, approaching his majority, but this did not end Margaret's effective influence over the kingdoms, which continued until her death in 1412. Extracts from advice she sent Eric in 1405 on handling the Norwegians on a forthcoming visit illustrate what Professor Imsen calls 'her masterly way of tackling people and situations, her political genius so to say'.[14] There is no doubt that Margaret wielded real political power despite its varying formal standing.

A century later Louise of Savoy, mother of Francis I, became regent of France.[15] Louise's position was more remarkable for the fact that she was neither daughter nor wife of a king herself. Daughter of a younger son of Louis duke of Savoy, Louise with her brother Philibert had been brought up after the death of their mother in 1483 in the household of Anne of France, elder daughter of Louis XI. Betrothed to Charles of Angoulême when she was 2 years old, Louise was married to him in 1488 at 11, and their son Francis, born in 1494, emerged as likely heir to the throne with the impending failure of male heirs in the senior royal lines which terminated in Charles VIII, who died childless in 1498, and Louis XII who left only two daughters in 1515. Planning for this eventuality as early as 1505, Louis XII had decided Francis of Angoulême should succeed him but on condition of marrying his own daughter Claude, and that the couple's two mothers should be regents if he died before Francis was 14. In the event Claude's mother died first, just a year before Louis, and when Francis succeeded he was already 20, but Louise got her regency, twice, when her son appointed her to take charge during his absence on Italian expeditions in 1515 and again in 1523, when his absence was prolonged until 1526 because of his capture at Pavia. Later Francis appointed her guardian and regent for the dauphin, and she is credited with renegotiating the Treaty of Madrid in 1529. She died in 1531.

It is plain that Blanche, Margaret and Louise exercised real power by any definition. The source material from this later period is sophisticated enough to show that female regents' situation was not an arcane remedy for an accident, but a matter which could be argued about and both attacked and defended on principle. Royals, nobles, councillors and jurists contributed their say to the definition of the powers. In her first regency the Parlement objected successfully to Louise having the right to pardon criminals and appoint to vacant benefices, but in her second Francis ensured her these prerogatives. In her second regency a dialogue was opened up when Louise invited the Parlement of Paris to submit grievances. Conscious and open paralleling of Louise with Blanche of Castile was made, in writings, entry pageants, and manuscript illumination. One way and another the regency of the king's mother in France was ceasing to be something which happened from time to time and had then to work as circumstances dictated, and was becoming institutionalized with a body of citable precedents.

The power queens, or as she preferred 'princesses', might exercise was put into focus in Part I of Christine de Pizan's *Book of the Three Virtues*, for Margaret of Burgundy, the dauphin's wife. Christine's supposition is that in their hierarchical opportunities these women do have some power and also responsibility to exercise it for good. The princess is portrayed as one expected to wish to make peace between her husband and foreign enemies and to keep internal peace to prevent bloodshed (chapter 8). She is expected to practise charity (chapter 9), and there are standards of conduct she is advised to keep in relation to her husband (chapter 12) and his relatives and friends (chapter 13). Christine was a realist, admitting the possibility that the husband might behave badly and the wife have to put up with it, holding out the hope that she would win by endurance. The princess is presented as having large responsibility for her children's upbringing (chapter 14), and her own public relations side is set out in advice on handling those who dislike or envy her (chapter 15) and winning public esteem (chapter 16). She has to control her court women (chapter 17) and watch her finances (chapter 18), while avoiding meanness and avarice (chapter 19). Modern discussions of women in relation to power, authority, empowerment and agency offer less focus on responsibility, and this, the moral aspect of power, comes out strongly in Christine's work, for women and by one. It even extends to the old woman servant's responsibility to try to restrain her headstrong charge hell-bent on indiscretion (chapter 25).

Running through Christine's topics, we may find queens, noblewomen and lesser landed elite illustrative of the situations described. We have already noticed Edward II's wife Isabella acting as a go-between with her brother the French king and Marguerite of Flanders being a notable patron of the Dominicans. Philip IV's wife Joanna of Navarre founded the College of Navarre in Paris in 1304, and Elizabeth de Burgh and Marie de St Pol founded Cambridge colleges, respectively Clare and Pembroke. Mahaut of Artois was a notable alms giver. Louise of Savoy had her two children well educated – her daughter Marguerite wrote *The Heptameron*, and her son Francis I attracted Leonardo da Vinci to the French court. Somewhat disorderly behaviour among Anne of Bohemia's attendants increased her early unpopularity, supporting Christine's view of necessary control of the court women. If Christine seems at times to exaggerate the powers of princesses, reality actually goes further in illustrating them acting in their own right, not merely as husbands' agents. Labarge provides a picture of Countess Mahaut involving herself with Artois in the last ten years of her life through officials and councillors and visiting the county from her main base in Paris. She kept a household of about 40 people, and treated her staff well with medical provision and pensions. Her own yearly expenses were rarely less than 4000 livres a year and often twice as much, which should be set against the 1000 livres she left in her will for dowries for poor young girls. Wealthy wives and widows were visible patrons of the arts, commissioning tombs and chapels, illuminated manuscripts and jewellery and embroidery, becoming dedicatees of written works and eventually patrons of printers (Margaret of York, Duchess of Burgundy, and Lady Margaret Beaufort patronized Caxton). The Englishwoman Alice de Bryene was on a different scale and much less of a 'ruler' but Labarge points out that her day book for 1412–13 and steward's account for 1418–19 echo Christine de Pizan's picture of the lady of the manor's rule of her servants.[16]

6

WOMEN AND RELIGION

By 1200, Latin Christianity was firmly rooted in western Europe and was its most common denominator. This did not prevent Christian kingdoms warring against each other, nor lull Christians into underestimating the threat from Muslims. The infamous Fourth Crusade took place in 1204 and crusading in the Holy Land continued into the 1270s; in southern Spain the Moorish kingdom of Granada only fell in 1492; on Europe's eastern land frontier the Turkish advance across the Balkans led to widespread alarm at critical moments such as the Nicopolis campaign (1396), the fall of Constantinople (1453) and the successfully resisted siege of Vienna (1529). Insidiously, however, the Latin church was decaying from within. Its success had made it enormously wealthy. The discrepancy between the splendour of the church on earth and the simplicity and poverty of the gospel message was obvious. There were always purists urging reform, but until the sixteenth century they were few enough to be stifled as heretics or allowed to establish ascetic followings – which usually became less rigorous with the passage of time. In the early sixteenth century, despite Catholic reformers' efforts, the Protestant Reformation erupted, shattering Catholic Europe and establishing rival churches.

The international careerism within the institutional church, which moved men across boundaries, meant little to women, for they were not office holders except in convents. Crusading did not offer them a military challenge, but some leaders' wives accompanied them on crusade, and like global wives in a foreign posting today, gave birth abroad, St Louis' wife Margaret of Provence for one. (But leaders' wives also travelled and gave birth on non-religious campaigns: John of Gaunt was born in Ghent and Edward IV in Rouen where his father was Henry VI's lieutenant-general in France.) Women remained noteworthy benefactors to the church, founding houses and colleges and making ongoing gifts and bequests to ecclesiastical institutions. They also joined heretical movements which were critical of the visible church and advocated a real church of purer faithful. Eventually the Reformation split both families and communities, not indeed on gender lines, but revealing some women following their own convictions rather than falling meekly behind husband or father.

Professional Nuns

At the start of the period, female monasticism had just passed through a particularly significant century, one of numerous foundations and considerable innovation. Traditional, fundamentally Benedictine and increasingly tightly enclosed convents offered the entrant a secure, structured, spiritually focused life which could satisfy the nun of ordinary attainments and provide an encouraging environment to foster such extraordinary talents as Hildegard of Bingen (d 1179). The reformed orders of Cluny, Prémontré and Cîteaux had spun off imitative women's houses but were increasingly distancing themselves from them. Fontevrault, a unique double house with dependent priories, was flourishing, partly because of its association with the English Plantagenets who concentrated burials there around the turn of the century.

In the early years of the thirteenth century the Dominican and Franciscan mendicant orders burst into very noticeable and vibrant life. Initially they seemed welcoming to women – indeed St Dominic's first foundation was for women, at Prouille in 1206, and St Francis established St Clare and her community at San Damiano in 1212, only 2 years after receiving permission for his own rule – the contrast with Cluny which took 150 years to found its first female house is striking. However, a strong reaction against fostering the female second order soon set in and in any case the Dominican and Franciscan women's houses were significantly differentiated from the men's. The Dominican women were strictly enclosed, in marked contrast with the wandering friars, and despite St Clare's ambitions, the Franciscan 'Poor Ladies' were soon enclosed, and came to be propertied. The Dominican sisters were particularly encouraged to be contemplative in their containment – not necessarily viewed as inferior to the active role of the men (for whom study was also more important from the start than it was for the early Franciscans). Consideration of St Clare is deferred to Chapter 7 below.

The heights to which thirteenth-century women's monasticism could rise may be illustrated by Helfta, particularly during the 40-year abbacy of Gertrude of Hackeborn (d 1291) beginning in 1251. The institution had been founded in 1229, but was twice forced to move to accommodate expansion: Helfta was its third home, from 1258. The house's founders, Count Burchard of Mansfeld and his wife Elizabeth, had intended a Cistercian monastery for women, but the Cistercians were trying to repel female adherents and never acknowledged the house, which must be classed as Benedictine with Cistercian leanings. Under Abbess Gertrude the monastery, about 100 strong in the last decades of the century, became a shining light of mystical spirituality. Three famous mystical works were produced there: *The Herald of Divine Love* assembled from the notes, dictation, writings and teachings of St Gertrude ('the Great') of Helfta (1256–c.1302); *The Book of Special Graces* by the abbess's sister St Mechthild of Hackeborn (1240–c.1298); and *The Flowing Light of the Divinity* completed there by Mechthild of Magdeburg (c.1210–c.1294), an ex-beguine who withdrew to Helfta in 1270. These represent the cream of conventual mysticism (as distinct from the mystical works of lone anchoresses/recluses, to be treated below). Under Abbess Gertrude, Helfta began using Dominican confessors, and the various streams of influence – Benedictine structured orderliness, Cistercian austerity and Dominican and beguine spirituality – came together to be particularly creative there.

Mechthild of Hackeborn and St Gertrude, admitted respectively aged 7 and 5, being schooled at Helfta, testify to its educational attainments as well as its soaring spiritual fervour. Abbess Gertrude was an enthusiast for education, in the liberal arts as well as scripture. St Gertrude's work was much influenced by the liturgical cycle and St Mechthild, attractively referred to as 'the nightingale of the Lord' was the chantress, choir mistress, for 40 years. The Hackeborn sisters came of a baronial family and many other well-born families sent daughters to Helfta; St Gertrude, however, was of unknown parentage, and possibly illegitimate.

Despite its glorious achievement in the late thirteenth century Helfta suffered from problems faced by female houses in particular in disorderly times. Mid-century Saxony was subject to baronial feuds and Mechthild of Magdeburg alluded to physical trials suffered by the community. After St Gertrude's death the house entered a period of trouble and transferred to Eisleben. Its torch was reignited at Engelthal near Nuremberg, where in the early 1240s a group of beguines had transformed their community into a monastery following Augustinian regulations supplemented by Dominican (the house was Dominican from 1246). This monastery had its spiritual apogee in the mid-fourteenth century. The evidence lies in a collection of texts produced there – the *Revelations* of Christina Ebner (d 1356), her biography by an anonymous man described in the text as a brother and probably a chaplain to the nuns, and the *Sister-Book* of the house, most probably Christina's work; the *Revelations* of Adelheid Langmann (d 1375); the *Life of Sister Gertrud of Engelthal* (d 1328) by two of the chaplains; and a biography of Friedrich Sunder (d 1328), chaplain to the nuns for 40 years. In *The Mystics of Engelthal: Writings from a Medieval Monastery*, L. P. Hindsley brings together consideration of the layout of Engelthal's buildings, the 1259 Constitutions for Dominican nuns, the monastic timetable and practices, and the educational standards and scriptural familiarity there to recreate the environment within which specific mystical traditions were taken up and developed. He records that Engelthal fell considerably from grace in the later middle ages, becoming a home for daughters of the nobility who ignored enclosure, neglected Masses and rode for sport – and some gave birth. Slacknesses in convents throughout the period can be picked up from episcopal visitations of religious houses – the records of some nunnery visitations by Archbishop Eudes of Rouen are printed in Amt's *Women's Lives in Medieval Europe.* The faults varied in gravity, including singing the hours too fast, being too comfortably dressed, eating meat in the infirmary, talking too much, keeping animals, being ill famed with men and bearing children. At Villarceaux in 1249 the prioress was reported to be drunk nearly every night.[1]

Sister Bartolomea Riccoboni's chronicle and necrology of Corpus Domini, a Dominican monastery for women in Venice, recently edited by Daniel Borstein, provides a view of life in a medieval convent from within. This is a delightful, loving and intimate recording of a convent's foundation, early expansion, and its sisterhood (including lay sisters) covering 1395–1436, surviving only in eighteenth-century manuscripts. Corpus Domini's first prioress was Sister Lucia Tiepolo. Previously an Augustinian nun for 34 years, after 3 unhappy years as a Benedictine abbess she was inspired by a vision to start up a new convent in Venice. When this was in its infancy, consisting of a wooden church with a stone altar and a wooden dormitory of seven cells, and peopled by herself, another Benedictine and two women in secular dress, it was rescued and transformed by Giovanni Dominici, Lucia agreeing to exchange her position as Benedictine abbess for that of Dominican prioress. Bartolomea Riccoboni, who was enclosed on the first day with 26 others, recorded all their names, plus those of 7 who joined a week later, and of 7 more after nine days, including 6 women from other convents Giovanni was allowed to recruit to Corpus Domini. Bartolomea records with quiet pride that the community reached 40 in nine days, 50 by the end of the year and 72 within two years.

In her initial lists, and in the course of the necrology, Bartolomea reports the age of entry of many of the sisters. Of the founding sisterhood, Orsa da

Noale, one of the seventh-day entrants, was only 7, and 11 of the first-day entrants were virgins between 11 and 16. Bartolomea herself was 25, but Sister Domenica Moro, a widow, was 50. One of the ninth-day transferees, from the Augustinian convent of San Girolamo, was 25 and had been widowed at 13. The prioress must have been over 80, dying in 1413 aged over 100. Sister Maruzza Contari, described as the prioress's companion, had been at Santa Maria degli Angeli for 50 years from the age of 7 and survived another 22 years. Bartolomea wrote up 49 obituaries; the first death, within the first year, was of a founding sister transferred from San Girolamo but still only 13 and not professed when she died. The next recorded death occurred in 1400, when a first-day entrant died at 20, and a month later another San Girolamo transferee died at 21. Many of the sisters seem to have died after long illnesses, and there are many indications that they were lovingly cared for. Sister Piera of Città di Castello, a widow who had entered at 38 and lived in the convent 29 years, specialized in caring for the sick: 30 sisters died in her hands, and Bartolomea noted every one of them thought she was in good company with Sister Piera by her side. Sister Maruzza Bonzi, previously a Franciscan tertiary, was admitted for terminal care close to death at nearly 100. Bartolomea says she was brought in out of respect for her daughter (Sister Francheschira da Noale) but the convent did very well out of it, benefiting handsomely from her will. Giovanni Dominici placed his own mother in the convent at 58; she had been widowed at 17, pregnant with him, her third (and only surviving) child. At Corpus Domini she took on the vilest chores and tended both sick and healthy. Cheerful performance of demeaning chores in the convent is a recurrent feature of the obituaries; other praised attributes were studious reading, singing and writing, assiduous prayer, and dietary self-deprivation.

The necrology is engaging because it reveals the sisters as individuals, revealing appealing characteristics in their personal attempts to lead obedient self-effacing lives of piety, and exercising charity towards each other. It also provides statistics about ages on entry and at death and lengths of illness of members of this small community. But the chronicle part of Bartolomea's text shows their communal spirit, in a regime where 'everything belonged to everyone', and where enthusiasts had to be stopped from excessive scourging and starving. Corpus Domini emerges from this internal record as extremely holy and harmonious. But these chaste enclosed women gazing raptly at the host and inflamed with fervour had their worldly side. Embedded in Bartolomea's effusive obituary of the founder Giovanni comes an unexpected commercial streak – 'after his death he left us all his silver, which we sold for 600 ducats and used the money to buy state bonds'.[2] Convents gave women the opportunity to rise in the sphere of institutional management, an aspect studied by Marilyn Oliva in the Norwich diocese.

In the late fourteenth and fifteenth centuries founders were still experimenting with new or reformed ideals for women's institutional religion. St Bridget (1303–73) founded the Order of the Holy Saviour (Bridgetines) after a struggle with the authorities over 20 years. Vadstena, the mother house, inspired foundations in Norway, Denmark, Poland, Germany and England as well as in Italy where Bridget had lived (at Rome) for over 20 years. Even amid the earthquake of the Reformation, the educational inspiration of Angela Merici (d 1544) was taking shape in the Company of St Ursula in Brescia.

Mystics and Recluses

A characteristic of later medieval religion in western Europe was increased emphasis on personal experience. This can be seen very clearly in the art of the period, where portrayal of the Virgin and Child moves from an authoritative representation to tender maternity, and crucifixions cease to portray a rigid and stylized figure and instead depict physical suffering. The observer is being drawn in to imagining Christ's suffering on the cross, and as a result to appreciate more acutely the magnitude of his endurance for mankind. In tune with this more emotional, affective piety, mysticism had a high profile, and women were particularly prominent as mystics. A series of them is easily enough identifiable: Hadewijch in Brabant in the first half of the thirteenth century, Mechthild of Magdeburg in the second, Christina Ebner and Adelheid Langmann both of Engelthal in the early and mid-fourteenth century, St Catherine of Siena and St Bridget of Sweden in the later fourteenth century, Julian of Norwich and Margery Kempe of Lynn in the early fifteenth and Maria da Santa Domingo (d c.1524) in Spain. Teresa of Avila's achievements belong to after 1550.

The essence of mysticism was achieving union with Christ, and medieval female mystics often represented this in the form of a conventional marriage ceremony (bridal mysticism, *Brautmystik*). This was a comparatively obvious stance to take, since those who were in religious orders had long been cast as brides of Christ, and most secular women married. (The bridal imagery goes back to the Song of Songs.) Some of the women mystics focused their attention on Christ as a baby and saw themselves receiving him from the Virgin to hold sleeping, or even to suckle.

Mystical women were distributed right across the religious spectrum, including cloistered nuns, Franciscan and Dominican lay tertiaries, committed beguines, enclosed anchoresses and the hysterical housewife Margery Kempe (d c.1440). Furthermore, some defy placing in any one of these categories, changing status during their careers. Mechthild of Magdeburg was a beguine before joining the nuns of Helfta, Julian of Norwich (b c.1343) was living at home with her mother when she had her 'showings'; she later had herself enclosed as an anchoress.

Mystical women are treated here in combination with recluses because, although many of the mystics of the period lived in some form of religious community, the mystic's spiritual existence centred round her private relationship with God, which she might make public at his request, often through the mediation of a confessor/scribe. The visionary could be helped to establish circumstances conducive to a receptive frame of mind. The spiritual progression, in various writings termed steps or ladders, involved renouncing the world, avoiding the particular perils of solitary temptation, and submitting to the will of God. The way to lose one's will into God's, or unite one's soul with him, was through intense love of Christ, and the widely recommended way for cultivating this was meditation, particularly on the passion. Angela of Foligno (d 1309) had a vision when she was meditating on Christ's suffering on the cross, concentrating on the nails driving his flesh into the wood; Julian of Norwich had asked God for better understanding of Christ's passion and her first showing was of the ordeal of the crucifixion. Julian is particularly interesting because she wrote an account of her *Revelations of Divine Love* fairly quickly after her visions, experienced in the course of a near-death illness when she was 30, but over the next 20 years continued to meditate over what she had seen and then produced a longer text.

Margery Kempe sought Julian's advice, and other female mystics, in a variety of environments, were resorted to by people in distress or dilemmas. Their clientele included the most powerful individuals. King Charles, later Emperor Charles IV, visited Christina Ebner at Engelthal in 1350 with a retinue of nobles and churchmen. Some mystics were moved to address leaders of church and state without necessarily being approached, in the hope of furthering reform. St Catherine of Siena (d 1380) persuaded Gregory XI to bring the papacy back to Rome from Avignon. After the outbreak of the Schism she supported Urban VI and wrote to three cardinals urging them to acknowledge him, fearlessly upbraiding them as liars and idolaters. St Bridget also chastised the church for its corruption, remaining unscathed because she supported the priestly office and hierarchy and indeed many of the features subsequently attacked at the Reformation such as indulgence trafficking and reliance on good works. Marguerite Porete was less fortunate and was burned in Paris in 1310 after the condemnation as heretical of articles in her *Mirror of Simple Annihilated Souls* which had been referred to the Sorbonne. (Her fatal error was declaring the church's sacramental ministry unnecessary in the final stages of the soul's ascent to perfection.)

Up to around 1200, recluses' cells were mainly attached – physically or supervisorily – to monasteries, but from the thirteenth to fifteenth centuries they became features of towns, sited near town gates, churches or chapels and hospitals. Ivetta of Huy (d 1228) a widow, whose own father and son became Cistercian monks, took up residence in a cell attached to the lepers' church beyond the walls of Huy, where she had already led an informal beguine community. The abbot of her son's monastery, Orval, enclosed her. Over the years as her reputation and age increased, church and cell were rebuilt, and Ivetta acquired a licensed companion and a maid. Recluses were charitably supported by Italian communes – Perugia in 1277 gave assistance to 20 female and 2 male recluses. Sometime after her visions, Julian of Norwich became an anchoress in a cell at the church of St Julian and St Edward at Conisford, Norwich, which belonged to the Benedictine nuns of Carrow. She received bequests in three wills, the latest in 1416. Another Carrow anchoress, Julian Lampett, was there at least 56 years, attracting 67 bequests between 1426 and 1481. In Paris Agnes Durscher spent 80 years as a recluse in a cell at Sainte Opportune, dying in 1483.

Enclosure in an anchorhold or cell was a serious commitment and the church would only permit it after examination of the applicant to ensure personal and financial viability. There was a service of enclosure which was reminiscent of entombment and the entrance was ceremonially blocked up. However, the confinement was not in a claustrophobic cell – anchorholds could run to a suite of rooms and a garden, and while some anchoresses could live in a group of two or three, even the 'solitaries' had servants – Julian had at least two over the years, and a servant was a necessity not a luxury to the enclosed, who had no other means of getting food and water in and garbage out. The cell also had a window through which the inmate could give counsel to those seeking advice.

Beguines and Tertiaries

Monks and nuns, the cloistered professionals who essentially prayed and contemplated, had limited opportunity for extra-claustral activity. The male mendicants were designed for a more active ministry, but the women who were inspired to join them were not allowed to follow the same regimen. It was, however, possible for women to follow a religious life in the community, performing services to fellow beings as well as Christ and supporting themselves by labour. From the late twelfth century women in towns of the Low Countries, later termed beguines, began to attract notice (their male equivalents were beghards and the origin of the term is disputed). In the thirteenth century the Franciscans and Dominicans acquired 'third orders' (tertiaries) of affiliated layfolk.

Beguines and tertiaries, like the friars themselves, were inspired by the biblical apostolic life. These movements had a strong ascetic inclination, combined with practical vocation and in some individuals also visionary fervour. The typical beguine preferred a life of industrious poverty to inherited wealth or being kept by a husband. Many came originally from wealthy or middle-class families. It was practical for them to join up with others of like mind; the commune then lived together in a beguinage (the first was founded in the 1170s at Liège), leading a semi-religious life but free to hold property and free to leave at any time. Jacques de Vitry (d 1240), a protégé of the exemplary Mary of Oignies (d 1213) whose *Life* he wrote, was a supporter, praising the beguines' habitual vigils and fasts, and their poverty and manual work. With even regulated orders of women falling into the laxities revealed in visitations, churchmen were naturally concerned about the more free-floating self-determining beguinages, some of which teetered on the borders of vagabondage, and suspicion of heresy abounded. Gregory IX offered the beguines approval in 1233 but the price was greater control by their diocesans and the Council of Vienne condemned them in 1311 with a saving clause for respectable beguinages. Confusion and clarification followed and the protection of irreproachable beguines in the face of repeated church attacks on extra-regular groups remained a problem throughout the century. From Low Country, Rhineland and north French origins they spread to the south of France, Italy and parts of central Europe, creating communities of religious laywomen active in charitable works. Cologne was a very active centre where it is estimated 15 per cent of the adult female population in 1320 was in beguine communities.

The first so-called third order belonged to the penitent order of Humiliati around 1200, wherein the lay members of both sexes practised monastic virtues while living in their homes. They dressed modestly, fasted and prayed, and performed services to the poor. Next came the Franciscan order of penitents, then the Dominicans' tertiaries; others followed. Before the end of the century tertiary orders had themselves established enclosed communities, allowing a distinction between their inhabitants (regular tertiaries) and the seculars who remained out in the world. Beguines at Strasbourg transformed themselves into tertiaries and many elsewhere did the same: it was a recommended solution for extra-regularity. Female tertiaries included some of the famous visionaries, such as the Franciscan tertiary and hospital founder Margaret of Cortona (1247–97), Franciscan Angela of Foligno, and Dominican St Catherine of Siena. Queen Isabel of Portugal (d 1366) became a Franciscan tertiary late in life after long exercising her influence through many charitable foundations.

The Sisters of the Common Life, developed from a group of poor women in Deventer established by Gerard Groote in 1379, were another unenclosed religious group. The sisters were free to leave the community, and remained members of the parish where the communal house was situated. They dressed plainly, worked hard mainly in dairying or clothworking, and held property jointly. They flourished particularly in the first half of the fifteenth century in the Low Countries.

In the chastisement of current church evils by leading mystical women, and in the 'alternative' religious life style adopted by beguines and tertiaries, it can be seen that women were up in the forefront of the apostolic movement in the late medieval church. Churchmen wrote predominantly in Latin, but the women made their contributions in a variety of tongues: St Gertrude in Latin, Mechthild of Magdeburg in Low German, Sister Bartolomea in Venetian Italian, St Catherine of Siena in Sienese Italian, Marguerite Porete in French, Margery Kempe in English, St Bridget in Swedish and Hindley describes two MSS of Adelheid Langmann's *Revelations* as 'Bavarian with a strong admixture of a Middle German dialect'.

Saints

The written lives of female saints from the period before 1200 are often quarried into by historians in search of passing details for use to illustrate aspects of more ordinary women's lives – family backgrounds, personal motivations for pilgrimages, charitable inclinations and response to church teaching. After 1200 our broader knowledge of the background enables us to see that many of the contemporary saints were actually extraordinary. Their lives present them as marked out for sanctity from early childhood; they often lived awkwardly, even rebelliously, with their families, being excessively emotionally pious and unco-operative with their parents, and once established in their vocation they became zealous in the extreme, exceeding the normal requirements of their chosen life style.

Various calculations indicate that a higher proportion of saints (about a quarter) was female after 1200 than before.

Saints of a period inevitably reflect what was significant in the church of their day. Founders of religious institutions were less likely to be canonized than in earlier times, although this was part of the route to sanctity for some, such as St Clare. Royal dynastic saints were also less common than in the early middle ages, although Elizabeth of Hungary was one. Daughter of Andrew II of Hungary, she was widowed at 20 when her husband, the landgrave of Thuringia, died on crusade, and she took up a regime of excessive fasting and care of sick and poor, under the influence of her confessor Konrad of Marburg. At Marburg she founded a Franciscan hospital in 1228, and there she died and was buried in 1231, at 24, her rapid sanctification in 1235 having more to do with the political pressures exerted by the landgraves of Thuringia and the Teutonic knights than her own activities, meritorious as these were. (Curiously she was promoted as a model wife in the Reformation period.) Less politically significant saints are better guides to what was admired in orthodox circles. Many saints were mystically inclined and regarded as utterers of God's message, either as prophecy or command.

Where saints came of enclosed or tertiary orders their hagiography represents a concentration of the attributes desirably expected in other members. They were not necessarily the careerist high fliers in their communities: indeed if unimpeded by the burdens of authority they could indulge more freely in the ecstasies, weepings, excessive fastings and constant praying which held them in thrall and awed contemporaries. On the more practical side, some earned sanctity by relieving pain and suffering among the poor and sick, prosaically by founding and running hospitals rather than miraculously by divine intervention. Saints in this period were often born in towns, to at least comfortably placed parents, though there is a class identifiable as servant-saints, usually born in the country and serving in the city or local castle, resisting the exploitation of their superiors (whose surplus food they might be diverting to the poor): one such saint was Zita of Lucca (d 1272/8).

St Catherine of Siena was the youngest of more than 20 children of a prosperous wooldyer. She showed her pious inclinations young, at 6 or 7, and defiantly resisted her parents' determination to marry her. She remained in the family home for some years, taking on the lowest chores, and then joined the Dominican tertiaries, still living at home. At 20 she underwent a mystical marriage with Christ, and at 23 a mystical death experience. After this she took up a life of near starvation and penance, dying in 1380 at 33. Although she may have taught herself to read in her late teens, apparently she only learned to write when approaching 30. Some 380 letters from her, dictated or written, are known, and a *Dialogue* between God and a soul. In her letters she harangued political and religious figures. After her death her confessor Raymond of Capua wrote her *Life* to promote her canonization (only achieved in 1461). St Catherine was a virgin, but St Bridget, nobly born in Sweden, had been married and was the mother of eight children.

Saints' influence outlived them, spread widely through their own writings and writings and sermons about them, or localized in places associated, however legendarily, with their lives and deaths, especially burial places. The newly sanctified joined an accumulation of saints from earlier periods who remained interceders and healers and examples to follow. Giunta Bevegnati, confessor and hagiographer of Margaret of Cortona, represented her as a second Magdalen. In this way ancient saints were constantly brought before the eyes of those who would emulate them, while their continued power was demonstrated in the accumulation of miracles registered at pilgrim sites to encourage believers – and to attract offerings.

Laywomen's Devotional Observances

Laywomen in western Europe after 1200 were born into Christian countries with an increasingly organized institutional church visibly present in their communities, with physical buildings and a pastoral workforce allocated to the parishes of the dioceses. To this fixed staff were added from the early thirteenth century the mobile friars. Christianity in western Europe took its lead from the papacy and the basic rites and practices were defined and amended internationally from the top, and imposed downwards. Laywomen's observances were thus swept along by decisions taken far away, and far above their heads, which could not be challenged without risking charge of heresy.

The church's minimal demands on layfolk of either sex consisted of infant baptism, yearly communion (preceded by confession), fasting (principally on Fridays and through Lent), and payment of tithes. Life-cycle events involving clerical participation ran from baptism to confirmation (at 7 plus) to marriage (although a church service was not essential to the validity of the marriage), ending with burial and commemorative masses and anniversaries. But at Montaillou the bishop never got so far from Pamiers to perform confirmation, and this may have been common in remote communities. Unique to their sex was the churching of women after childbirth. In late medieval

English parishes K. L. French claims both sexes were expected to attend three services on Sundays, and could also attend daily mass and other canonical hours said by parish and stipendiary priests. The sexes were separated in church, women on the north side of the nave or at the west end, furthest from the altar.[3] Such a level of observance was not enough for Margery Kempe of Lynn, who after her transforming vision claimed she was shriven two or three times a day, gave herself over to great fasting and vigils, rose at the second or third hour and went to church, was at her prayers until noon and all afternoon, went on pilgrimages and wore a hairshirt.

For most laywomen there would have been little choice of sanctified place or clerical personnel to resort to in these instances. In the countryside problems of accessibility would dictate that the villagers attended the local church and whoever officiated there would be their minister of first resort. Medieval towns supported numerous parish churches, the biggest towns having also perhaps a cathedral, monastery, convent or friary, or several of these, and perhaps a hospital of religious foundation. Here too lay people were more or less constrained to loyalty to one institution, the neighbourhood parish church, or the church where the family head's craft organization had its religious base. Higher up the social hierarchy laywomen had more variety of religious advisers – family chaplains, clergy of churches in the family's presentation, even clerical relatives. There was friction in the English Paston family about the influence exerted over the widowed Margaret by the family chaplain James Gloys, as perceived by her children. Besides the chaplain, the Pastons had presentation to over 20 livings in fifteenth-century Norfolk, and attended St Peter Hungate when in Norwich. Margery junior's secret betrothal to the family bailiff Richard Calle had to be brought before the bishop of Norwich with whom her affronted mother and grandmother spoke.

The reality of choiceless assignment to their parish clergy for most layfolk made attractive the chance to hear visiting friars preach, especially since their sermons were reputed to be more inspiring than many of those by the secular clergy. According to Sister Bartolomea, Giovanni Dominici as lector at San Zampolo had a charismatic effect on the Venetians at large, uprooting many vices. He was a prodigious preacher, and men and women followed him around when he preached three or four times in the day on holidays, marvelling that he could produce four different sermons from one gospel passage. Apparently many men and women left their relatives and children to become friars and nuns at his inspiration. Among the Corpus Domini sisters, Elena Ridolfi had been converted by his sermons while a married woman, and gave herself up to prayer and fasting, wearing a hairshirt and doing penance. After her husband's death she made a practice of feeding seven poor people before she ate her own food. She entered the convent at 40. Another convert of Giovanni's sermons, hearing them in Tuscany, was sister Geronima dei Cancellieri, daughter of the count of Pistoia and widow of a knight, by then 50, whose four adult children objected strenuously to her intentions and tried to have her stopped en route to Venice.

Ardent associations of holy women and their confessors are recorded but it is more difficult to establish the relationship of ordinary laywomen and their parish clergy. Some confessional episodes in early thirteenth-century Bonn and Cologne are culled from Caesarius of Heisterbach by Peter Biller.[4] According to Hindsley as many as three chaplains at a time served Engelthal, also ministering to those laity in the monastery's care. The more ordinary laywoman, not one about to be converted to the cloister, would participate in church services, gazing at the sculpture and wall paintings and representations in stained glass. Latin grammar would have been beyond most of the lay congregation (of either sex) but they would acquire familiarity with the regular repetition of services and some vernacular sermons were preached. The psalms were translated in vernaculars long before whole Bibles; whole Bibles in any tongue were too expensive for widespread purchase, and illiteracy limited readers. Upper-class women might have their primers to hand, to guide their thoughts while the service went on around them. With music, candles, imagery and ritual, services must have been affecting. Processions, occasioned by patronal festivals, Corpus Christi celebrations and other regular feasts of the church as well as occasional public thanksgivings, with banners and figures or the host in some form of container, were something everyone could enjoy, however illiterate, as a participant or spectator. Praying for the liberation of the Holy Land gave women who could not crusade in person an involvement with the cause. Religious plays, widely associated with Corpus Christi – a feast whose recognition owed much to a woman of Liège, Juliana of Mont-Cornillon (1193–1258) – were for popular edification and entertainment. There was always local fund-raising in progress, to raise money for building and maintenance, commemorative services, candles (sometimes expressly wives' or virgins' lights) and new textiles, and women could take part in these charitable activities. Some parishes had wives' and maidens' guilds for channelling their appropriate social activity. At Corpus Domini the woman who became Sister Margarita Paruta (d 1412) had been instrumental with her husband in the renovation of the convent in its early years. After her husband's death she offered herself and her 2000 ducats of possessions to the order and became vicaress. The arrival of such a benefactress and her resources radically affected a convent previously in straitened circumstances. She purchased the convent's vineyard, had windows opened in the cells to let in air, built the new parlour and the old granary and made the cloister, and 'liked the convent have books and everything it needed'. She roped in family and friends to further the making of altar cloths and surplices. In this instance she entered the convent, but the lady bountiful indulging her project was often a wealthy laywoman outside the circle of those who gained from her generosity – think of the female founders of university colleges, and the wealthy patronesses of the Jesuits cultivated by Ignatius Loyola. The practical good works side of charity, as distinct from the more strictly pious good works, also grew more popular in the later middle ages. Countess Mahaut of Artois left money for dowries, and also founded hospitals in her lifetime: the contract for the one at Hesdin (1321) gives details of its size. This hospital was a secular institution, but the motivation for charitable activity was church-inspired.

Margery Kempe must have been a nightmare parishioner, and from her long autobiography it is obvious that some of the clergy she met were more patient and tolerant than others. The anchorite at the Lynn Dominicans believed in her, as did the vicar of St Stephen's Norwich, but the confessor who stood in during the anchorite's absence was 'right sharp' to her. Margery's excesses and wilfulness tried her spiritual advisers to the full. By contrast there were clergy who abused their female parishioners, none more so than Montaillou's womanizing Pierre Clergue. Ogling and seduction by clergy is a recurrent theme in literature, and particularly sensationally presented in the *Heptameron*, whose author, Louise of Savoy's daughter Marguerite of Navarre, furthered reformers of the Meaux group at the French court in the early 1520s. Her clerical fornicators include a bishop, several friars, an incestuous parson, a young clerk and a canon. However, in literature and life, the clergy were more often castigators of women's vices. The Franciscan Berthold of Regensburg (d 1272) acknowledged in a sermon women's reliable religious behaviour – going to church, saying their prayers, and going to sermons more readily than men. In *The Book of the Knight of the Tower*, originally written in French in 1371, a bishop preaching against the wearing of horned headdresses had a good effect.

Women and Heresy

Women were attracted to heretical movements but the suggestion that unorthodox sects tended to give women more freedom (than the Latin church did) has lately fallen from fashion. For women, heresies which appealed to layfolk and welcomed popular participation were more attractive than the arid doctrinal heresies of more abstract thinkers. In the twelfth century two popular movements had particularly troubled the church: the Cathars, alias Albigensians, who had a dualist philosophy, and the Waldensians, originally from Lyons, who had some ideals similar to the Franciscans and were given limited approval as late as the Third Lateran Council (1179), but were subsequently (1184) excommunicated. The Cathars were active in Germany, north Italy and the south of France, especially around Albi; the Waldensians were active in southern France, Spain, Germany, Piedmont and Lombardy. Innocent III took action against both. In the early fifteenth century English Lollardy and the Bohemian Hussite movement were particularly noticeable. There seems little to suggest that women were in any widespread way privileged in most of these movements, although it remains possible that they were more significant than the church authorities realized, and for this reason less a focus of their attention and so less recorded in the documentation of heretical repression.

Concentration on Bishop Fournier's Register has tended, unfortunately, to obscure the earlier twelfth- and thirteenth-century stages of Catharism wherein women seem to have been more important. The Cathars had a thriving alternative church in the French Midi until the Albigensian Crusade (1202–29) and the activities of the Inquisition (from 1233). At this period they had a pastorally active sisterhood of *Perfectae* (Good Women), based in community houses, alongside the *Perfecti* (Good Men).[5] By Fournier's time Catharism was largely a peasant heresy but it had not always been so in the Midi. Detecting Cathars was not that easy, as the Montaillou evidence shows the Cathars going along with Catholic baptism, annual communion and confession. (What is still more confusing is that they were confessing to the Catholic priest Pierre Clergue who was for a time a Cathar and also an informer for the Catholics.) As with Waldensians, heretical sympathizers conforming with the Catholic confessional were economical with the truth with regard to their connections with alternative heretical ministers. As Ladurie phrased it, the frontier between Cathars and the orthodox was 'vague and easily crossed in both directions'. The Cathars saw themselves as the true Christians and condemned the slackness and greed of the church (well exemplified in Pierre Clergue).

Cathar dualism had some life-style consequences. Matter was seen as corrupt, and this included marriage, procreation and meat eating. So their Perfects lived chaste, ascetic and vegetarian lives after receiving the sacrament of baptism called the *consolamentum*. Mere believers only qualified for *consolamentum* at death's door, and so 'final' did it have to be that they were not allowed food after heretication, even if they survived another fortnight. Bishop Fournier's register reveals some women whose maternal instincts were in conflict with these demands on them. Sybille Pierre of Arques, forbidden to feed milk or meat to her hereticated baby Jacotte, under a year old, suckled her after her husband and the Perfect had left her with the child. Of 114 people, mostly Cathar, involved in the 98 cases heard by the Pamiers inquisition court between 1318 and 1325, 48 were women. Ladurie remarks that Catharism showed no great tolerance of women, though 'not entirely antifeminine', but he is commenting on its early fourteenth-century death throes.[6] Although the Perfect did include women who could give the *consolamentum*, in fourteenth-century Montaillou the female adherents were more passive than active, and drawn in by their menfolk rather than influencing them, although Jean Pattisier was converted by his aunt; the Inquisition uncovered more active female participation in the 1240s. By the 1320s in Montaillou Catharism was very much identified with households, although there were vacillating and mixed houses. Cathar believers tended to marry others of the same persuasion and although there were 'mixed' marriages some of these failed, for example that of Fabrisse née Clergue and Pons Rives.

Bishop Fourner's register is more famous for its pursuit of Cathars than for its pursuit of Waldensians, but Inquisition proceedings he began in 1319 against the Waldensians Agnes Francou and Huguette de la Cote, who were both burned at the stake as heretics, are Shulamith Shahar's starting point for her book *Women in a Medieval Heretical Sect*. The Waldensians did not set out with unorthodox beliefs, merely the desire to live in poverty, to wander and preach the Gospel. Because they preached without diocesan permission they fell foul of the church and strictures against them increased as the thirteenth century progressed. This drove them underground, and they deviated increasingly from Catholic conformity. They rejected the doctrine of Purgatory (and with this the use of prayers and masses for the souls of the dead) and papal indulgences, they did not venerate saints, and thought it wrong to sentence criminals to death or mutilation, to make war, including Crusades, and to take oaths. The celibate leaders were called brothers and from them the all-male hierarchy of deacon, presbyter, and bishop or majoral emerged. A class of sisters also taught and preached, but the sisters were cloistered in hospices, paler reflections of the brethren. Most believers still attended the Catholic church at the brothers' recommendation, partly for sacramental purposes, and to be improved by exposure to scripture (even if in Latin), and perhaps partly to allay authority's suspicion. Contrary to widespread assumption the Waldensians did not elevate women to equal rights in the sect.

Agnes Francou was a widow aged around 60 when brought before the Inquisition, the former wet-nurse of the deacon Raymond de la Cote; both were burnt at the stake the same day in 1320. Agnes was illiterate, and though some of her ignorance might have been feigned to protect others in the sect, Shahar believes that she really had not learned much from the brothers. Huguette de la Cote was a more vociferous and provocative respondent in court, a married woman of about 30; she and her husband were burnt the same day in 1321. Huguette was a baker's daughter and her husband a cooper; both were already Waldensian when they married. Huguette mixed orthodox practices with her Waldensianism, but was firm in denying Purgatory, prayers, masses and alms for the dead, excommunication and papal indulgences. Shahar finds gender far less significant within the sect than might have been expected. In some ways Waldensian women were deprived of comforts orthodoxy offered women, such as resort to the Virgin and saints, inclusion in regular companionable parish activities for women such as processions, charitable activities, and watching religious plays. Nevertheless the ordinary female believers were important nurturers of the sect, more free to wander than the cloistered sisters, influential in their own families and circles, and givers of hospitality to travelling brothers.

The puritanical streak in the Waldensians and Cathars was also found among Lollards and Hussites, and the late medieval orthodox church gave ammunition to these movements because there was criticizable luxury in clerical life, immorality among regular and secular ecclesiastics, and a too automative, mechanical, aspect to indulgences, multiple masses and veneration of relics. Most heretical sects aimed at a return to scriptural recommendations and the shedding of superstructures built by the institutional church in recent centuries. Increasingly, contrast was made not between clergy (professionals) and laity (amateurs) but between the institutional or visible worldly church and the invisible true church of God's elect. Scripture was seen as a purer authority than graceless sinful clergy, so John Wyclif (d 1384) advocated translation of the Bible (also a Waldensian project) to make it a more widely available direct guide. The heretical doctrines built up by Wyclif involved very few women while he remained an Oxford academic, but from the 1380s his followers, known as Lollards, increased in the Welsh marches and in Bristol, Leicestershire, Northamptonshire and Buckinghamshire. Lollardy became a lower-class phenomenon in town and country after the Oldcastle rebellion in 1416 scared off gentry support. Records of heresy trials in the diocese of Norwich 1428–31, edited by Norman Tanner, involved 51 men and 9 women, 7 married, 2 single. Hawise Moone, wife of Thomas, confessed comprehensively to keeping company with known named heretics and holding heretical beliefs. She had picked up that many orthodox church rituals were unnecessary – baptism, episcopal confirmation, marriage in church, and extreme unction, along with practices such as pilgrimages, fasting and veneration of images. In denying priests power to remit sins and transform bread at the mass, Lollards were cutting at the spiritual power of the clergy, and in transferring tithes and offerings from them to the poor were sapping their worldly wealth. Extra insults came in declaring the pope Antichrist and every good sinless man and woman as good a priest as any pope, bishop or priest. Lollards shared with Waldensians belief they should not swear or kill. Hawise appears to have known a lot more about her beliefs than Agnes Francou a century before, but unlike Agnes she confessed and abjured. Fewer than a dozen women were burned at the stake as relapsed heretics in England.

Most of Hawise's heresies were those common among the East Anglian heretics of her day, where women appear generally to follow male lead. However, a Lollard burnt in Kent in 1511, Agnes Grebill, had been a heretic for a quarter of a century and used her influence on her husband and sons. In the early sixteenth century wives in the Chilterns and East Anglia are known to have converted husbands to heresy. More extremely, there were accusations of women assuming priestly functions, but as the Lollards tended to demote the priest from his sacramental function to a mere preacher this would not be as radical as might appear. Cross thinks women may have achieved a greater degree of participation in Lollardy than they had previously attained in the orthodox church in England[7] but there is no evidence that the movement attracted women in disproportionate numbers nor proof that their actual participation in Lollard activities was greater than orthodox women's in theirs.

As a religious phenomenon the Hussite movement had much in common with the Waldensians and Lollards. The Bohemian reformer John Hus (burnt at Constance in 1415), one-time confessor to the queen, took up a lot of Wyclif's teachings on predestination and the elect. His followers, particularly active in the two decades after his death, were also interlocked with the Waldensians. Where the Hussites differed was in having a much stronger political, nationalistic, purpose than the other two heresies, which led to military campaigning, not an area where women could be expected to have an important role. But the Hussites did attract women; the Taborite branch recognized women's right to leave husbands and sons to join their urban and hill centres. Full-blown heresies shaded into heterodox ideas and superstitions especially among the illiterate throughout the period.

Witchcraft and Sorcery

Inhabitants of Montaillou clung to superstitions, showing their lack of confidence in the sufficiency of either visible church or Cathar goodmen to ward off all their misfortunes. They regarded things like birdflight as omens, and believed soothsayers who might tell them their animals were dying because of a spell cast on them. Even the parish priest's deceased father had locks of his hair and bits of fingernail and toenail cut off to be kept to prevent the removal of his corpse taking good fortune with it from the house. These relics were given to his widow, and when her time came her ever wily son as usual kept his options open, being rumoured to have taken similar clippings, yet also burying her beneath the Virgin's altar in the church. Beatrice de Planissoles kept the first menstrual blood of her daughter for use as a love potion on some unsuspecting future son-in-law, to bewitch him. She also kept her grandsons' umbilical cords as talismans to help win a lawsuit.

Such practices were not Christian – indeed the soothsayers at Montaillou were more comfortably credited with other-worldly powers if Jewish or Muslim. (In this Pyrenean area access to Jews and Muslims was easier than in northern Europe.) Although the Inquisition had power to deal with witchcraft in the context of heresy, Fournier was busy with Cathars and Waldensians, not witch-hunting. Condemnation of witchcraft and sorcery was consistent in the Christian church and biblically based. Both sexes could be accused of selling their souls to the devil, demon sacrifices, spell casting, attempting divination and generally exercising malevolent preternatural powers. But more female witches seem to have been accused in the fourteenth and fifteenth centuries, and the popular encyclopaedia of the subject, *Malleus Maleficarum* (the Hammer of the [Female] Witches) (1486), which went through 14 editions by 1520, proclaimed that women were more likely to be witches than men. Regarding witches as a dangerous sect of apostates and Satanists rather than as individuals led into mass persecutions which began in continental Europe in the fifteenth century and were pressed even more zealously in the sixteenth, in Catholic and Protestant areas. The sex of 103 of 300 persons accused of witchcraft in Savoy 1415–1500 is known and 88 were women.

Malleus Maleficarum was compiled by Heinrich Kramer and Jacob Sprenger, Dominican inquisitors in Upper Germany. They explained women's greater addiction to evil through their greater credulity and impressionability as well as their feebler minds and bodies and carnal natures and impulsiveness, seen as inherently female flaws. Kramer and Sprenger did not take account of socially conditioning factors for which society in general should share responsibility. Suspicion did not fall on members of busy households. Prime suspects were loners, and the principal loners, professional hermits and anchoresses apart, were older women, many of whom lived on the margins of society, and often, in their loneliness, with an animal (which could be cast as their familiar). Many were probably little more than eccentric. Lone older women were also at greater risk of being persecuted as an annoyance to neighbours. Such old women, if credited with the wisdom of age, and being around all the time, might be resorted to for remedies which could take the form of herbal brews and poultices, but if the patient died suspicion might fall on the unsuccessful healer. Or with lovers wanting their unresponsive object of affection literally charmed, non-therapeutic dosages might be being traded and those wanting to enchant one person might also wish to bewitch that person's current love for the worse. Where society wanted to empower itself against illness, poor crops, unrequited love, or losing a lawsuit, and believed it could be done by potions or incantations and suchlike, motive and opportunity crossed the divide between harmless and harmful practice. The seriousness of the matter was much increased when the surface activity was seen as a manifestation of inner complicity with the devil, a development of the fifteenth century. The confession of a tortured Savoyard, Antoinette, wife of Jean Rose of Villars-Chabod, in September 1477 is offered by Rowland as typical. She admitted to renouncing God and the Catholic faith and taking a devil called Robinet as her master. She was marked by the devil on her left little finger, and gave him her soul. Using a wand and ointment she flew through the air to the synagogue or witches' sabbath where the assembled company feasted, honoured the devil and indulged in an orgy of intercourse. She identified people present at different covens. She produced illness with the devil's ointment and killed a cow with his powders (made from children's body parts).[8]

Accusations of witchcraft or sorcery could be used for what would seem to be primarily political and even economic purposes as well as in defence of the faith. Countess Mahaut of Artois was accused of sorcery after her daughters' indiscretions, although her innocence was proclaimed in 1317. In 1419 Henry V of England arrested his stepmother Joan of Navarre for sorcery, her own confessor accusing her of compassing the death and destruction of the king. Henry needed money at the time and appropriated her dower of 10,000 marks a year. After three years of reasonably luxurious captivity Joan was released without the charge being pressed and the dower or its equivalent restored. Joan of Arc, treated below in Chapter 7, was called by the English the witch of France, though she was not convicted of witchcraft. Eleanor Cobham, Duchess of Gloucester, faced ecclesiastical and secular authorities in 1441 on charges which included sorcery, necromancy and treason. Condemned, she was divorced from the duke, forced to perform public penance and incarcerated for life. Her associate Margery Jurdane, the witch of Eye, burnt at Smithfield, claimed she had concocted medicines and potions for Eleanor to win Duke Humphrey of Gloucester's affections.

Non-Christian Religions

Two sets of women continued to exist in western Europe in this period practising non-Christian religions under varying degrees of difficulty: Jews and Muslims. At the start of the period the Jews were widely spread in western Europe but gathered in towns where they lived as a minority amid Christians (although tending to be gathered together in a distinct Jewry district); by contrast the Muslims were primarily concentrated in areas where they had been dominant as parts of the Arab Mediterranean empire – the Iberian peninsula, the Balearics and Sicily. For both groups, times were getting harder. The Crusades had heightened Christian hostility to Jews everywhere, and the Christians were on the offensive against Arabs on the north side of the Mediterranean as well as in the Holy Land.

Hostility had already taken the form of intermittent rioting against Jewish homes and synagogues in individual towns, and more military offensives to recover territory held by Muslims particularly in the Iberian peninsula, where the battle of Las Novas de Tolosa in 1212, capture of Cordoba in 1236, fall of Seville in 1248, and loss of the Balearics in the early 1230s and Valencia by 1245 restricted Arab independence to Granada, but left many Muslims as minorities in Hispanic Christian kingdoms. Philip the Fair had expelled Jews from the royal domain in 1182, and Edward I expelled them from England in 1290, and there were further expulsions from France in 1306 and 1394, Spain in 1492 and Portugal in 1497, while individual towns expelled Jews from time to time; many moved east and ended up in Poland. The Black Death triggered attacks on Jews in towns all over Europe. Widely blamed for poisoning wells, Jews were set upon and thousands killed – at Narbonne and Carcassonne in 1348, Strasbourg and Frankfurt in 1349 for example. As at the time of the Crusade massacres, many burned themselves to death in their homes (as at Speyer) or synagogues (as at Esslingen) in preference to awaiting death at the hands of mobs, and it was seen as heroic for Jewish mothers to throw their children into the flames to escape forced Christian baptism. The Jews were thinner on the ground in northern Europe but still suffered, for example in the Hanse towns. Mobs seized Jews' possessions, burnt their homes and synagogues and forced Christianity on them wherever they could, or killed them, or simply drove them away. Usury, religion and race were points of conflict. That women and children might be spared (even if forcibly converted) suggests their religion (which Christians desired to eradicate) was more a *casus belli* than their race (which could not be altered but could after conversion be seen as irrelevant).

In their own communities Jewish women continued to live by the Talmud, interpreted by male rabbis. The code of behaviour offered them considerable protection: Rabbi Meir of Rothenburg's pronouncement on a thirteenth-century case even entertained amputation of the arm for persistent wife-beating. Victims were entitled to divorce and their *ketubbah* (the marriage contract's defined widow's portion of her husband's estate also due to divorcees unless forfeited for certain reasons). Jewish men were expected to honour their wives and sustain them (even if they were propertied themselves). It emerges from rabbinical rulings that many problems arose from the Jewish men's mobile commercial life style. Husbands could force their wives to move with them to a similar sized town or home, but not from a town to a city or from a poor to rich home, or vice versa. If a wife had to borrow to provide for herself during the husband's absence in a foreign country he should pay the debts. Rabbi Meir (d 1293) favoured declaring one doubtful betrothal void rather than requiring a divorce lest the husband refuse divorce and travel to a distant country, making it impossible for 'the unfortunate woman' (note the sympathetic tone) ever to marry again. However the same rabbi was one of the main figures in contemporary attempts to restrict women's participation in circumcision and other rituals. Meir ruled that creditors had priority over the widow's *ketubbah,* which underlines the importance of secure credit transactions in the Jewish community but undermined a widow's security.

Eleazar of Mainz (d 1357) set down moral instructions for his sons and daughters, incorporating traditional Jewish women's practices in his ethical will, printed in Amt, *Women's Lives.* Jewish wives and daughters were expected to be modest and industrious, staying at home not gadding about, and spinning, cooking, sewing and keeping a clean house. They had to attend prayers and keep the Sabbath, and observe ritual bathing and diet. Eleazar urged his sons and daughters to live among other Jews in the interests of bringing up their children in the faith. Obviously it was less easy for isolated families to stick to proper religious and dietary requirements. Jews were fastidious – for religious reasons – about cleaning meat, food plates, and wearing clean clothes. Amt cites a couple of examples of their sumptuary restraint from Forli in 1418 and Valladolid in 1432. To the outside world Jews would show charity, discretion and moderation. Nevertheless Judah Asheri's reference to a cousin having 500 relatives at his wedding in Germany invites suspicion that Christians might have seen such gatherings as provocative. Asheri (d 1349) praised his female relatives as devoted to the Torah, thrifty, and helpful to their husbands' scholarship.

Had Jewish women lived peaceably entirely within their own communities they would present merely a picture of women living by 'other' standards, but because they were also living surrounded by Christians interface complicates the picture. Christian legislation against Christians socializing with Jews – eating or bathing with them, letting houses to them, working for them and women having sexual intercourse with their men – indicates that admixing did go on and Baumgarten stresses some commonality of practice and belief.[9]

The argument elevating women's importance in the internal, household practice of heretical religion, now rather played down, has been successfully transferred to their role in the maintenance of politically proscribed religious practices in the case of both Jews and Muslims, particularly in sixteenth-century Spain, where these populations, under increased Christian pressure, were large enough to be significant. The predicament of a particular group of women of Jewish descent in the later middle ages has recently been revealed in Melammed's *Heretics or Daughters of Israel: the Crypto-Jewish Women of Castile.* Anti-Semitic riots in Spain in 1391 resulted in perhaps a third of Spain's Jews being killed and another third forced into Christian conversion. Some of the converts (New Christians) stayed with Catholicism but others conformed minimally and preserved their old religion with the co-operation of the remnant of openly Jewish inhabitants. It was to counter this clandestine judaizing that the Inquisition at Seville was set up in 1481. It persisted tenaciously with its work long after the 1492 expulsion of Jews by Ferdinand and Isabella. Melammed illustrates the continuous challenge to women trying to keep the dietary regulations and Jewish calendar furtively amid snooping neighbours, and facing the acute challenge of defending themselves to the Inquisition. She details the procedures against Maria Lopez and her daughter Isabel, begun in 1516, and their husband/father in 1518. All three were burned as heretics; both women had been tortured but gave nothing away.

The Muslims in Spain were differently distributed, in dispersed families in the north, clustered in rural communities in Aragon and Valencia and highly concentrated in towns such as Cordoba, Seville and Granada. Within Muslim communities free to live by their inherited traditions the women continued to be generally disadvantaged, and there is little sign of their position improving. Their submission can be summed up in the Qur'an's 'Good women are obedient'. Women came last in the social classifications in the mid-fifteenth-century *Sunnī Breviary* of 'Isā b. Jābir. The Qur'an's recommendations were at the base of Islamic law and allowed a man up to four wives. A husband took responsibility for a wife, dowering and maintaining her. He was allowed to beat her for persistent opposition, and repudiation seems to have been comparatively easy for him. Women had inheritance rights, but only half the share of a man. The better off Muslim families kept their womenfolk in seclusion but poorer ones had to be allowed out to work. Muslim women were also transported and sold as slaves in Europe – in thirteenth-century Genoa the slaves were mainly 'Saracen'.

As with the Jews, interface was a problem. Christians allowed their men to touch Jewish and Muslim women, but did not want their own women to be available to the others' men. The Muslims took the same stance: their men could breed from Christian women, but their women were not to fall into Christian hands. In 1258 the Cortes of Valladolid banned Christian women from becoming nurses to Jewish or Muslim children, and Jewish or Muslim women from nursing Christians. The Christians were treating Jews and Muslims alike as 'other', and Jews and Muslims made some common ground against Christians. Thus Muslims would not touch meat slaughtered by Christians but would take meat slaughtered by Jews, and the Jews in Spain when their own meat was unavailable sometimes took halal.

The Catholic church in Spain found the co-existence of Jews and Muslims and Christianized converts from both religions challenging and the Inquisition handled them similarly. Within a decade of the fall of the kingdom of Granada in 1492 the Muslims were faced with the choice of conversion or expulsion, a policy pursued through the rest of the period and beyond. When Muslims were converted, voluntarily or by force, women were able to preserve rites and customs in the home, discreetly avoiding forbidden foods and keeping Ramadan, privately maintaining birth and death customs.[10] This all became very much more difficult with tightened Christian 'policing' in the last decades of the period.

The Reformation and Women

Despite widespread attestations to the vitality of Christian life in pre-Reformation Europe, there was much that was criticizable in the late medieval church and both orthodox and heretical thinkers had drawn attention to similar points throughout the period. An institution which constantly attracted endowment generation after generation, and in principle did not let go of what it ever received, was inevitably going to grow inordinately wealthy. The monastic life style by 1200 seemed incompatible with Christ's insistence that his followers should give up their wealth: hence St Francis' stress on poverty. The wealthiest monasteries were usually male, therefore the nuns did not attract much criticism on this score, but neither did would-be Franciscan women succeed in establishing equally non-proprietorial institutions for themselves. The church, so well endowed with lands and the income therefrom, was busy in this period expanding its income from dues and services: annual tithes, fees such as mortuary fees, charges for anniversary services and suchlike, and fines for misbehaviour. Growth areas were dispensations and indulgences. These payments roused more resentment against the visibly male collectors than against women in the church. The gap between church teaching (the apostolic life, chastity and moderation) and all too visible practice (standard of living among the higher clergy, clerical concubinage and indiscriminate whoring, gluttony, simony and absenteeism) did extend to the nunneries, where individual property, pet keeping, socializing through inward visitors and outward excursions, excessive comforts and sexual indulgence sometimes resulting in pregnancy were reported in visitations, which were of course looking for trouble.

Individual heretical groups recurrently raised dissatisfaction with such practices, and while the church had been able to suppress these outbreaks with its own mechanisms (Inquisition) and at times with sought military aid (Albigensian and Hussite crusades), in the 1520s and 1530s the pent-up dam burst in too many places at once and formed an ecclesiastical revolution, the Protestant Reformation. Catholic evangelicals pressed for reform within the established church, playing down external activities such as pilgrimages and relic veneration, indulgence trafficking and good works relied on mechanically, but they were overtaken by radicals whose inspiration led to the complete overthrow of Catholicism in some areas. This is not the place to discuss the distinctive teachings of Luther, Zwingli and Calvin, but their variations meant that the Reformation was not as united as the structure it attacked, and remained distinctly flavoured in different areas. Whether the old church or one of the new persuasions triumphed in an area depended greatly on the attitude of the local authorities. By the end of the period the Counter-Reformation was reshaping the old church in response, but the Roman church was not going to recover the position it had held in the middle ages.

As Wiesner-Hanks has recently underlined, scholars are now less inclined to generalize about the impact of the Protestant (or the later Catholic) Reformation on 'women' than they were a few decades ago.[11] Women in different social classes and geographical settings experienced things differently. But some basic issues must be raised: how the Reformation affected women by changing the demands made of them and attitudes towards them, and how they responded to it, encouraging or resisting or carried along bemused. For women the upheaval brought by the Reformation was most striking for those who were enclosed nuns when it began. As the furore grew, some nuns who had entered convents unwillingly or had become disillusioned were inspired to escape, among them Luther's future wife Katherine von Bora (d 1550). Ursula von Münsterberg (d c.1534), granddaughter of George Podiebrad of Bohemia, escaped from her convent at Freiburg in 1528 and published her reasons. Other nuns were allowed to leave at a stage when the convents were remaining for those who wished to stay. Then, in areas committed to Protestantism, when some convents came to be closed, nuns had to be disestablished and relocated, or allowed to stay as an establishment ran down. Engelthal was banned by the Nuremberg authorities from admitting new novices and dwindled away until the prioress and last nun surrendered in 1565. Nuns' families were affected by the dissolution of convents for they lost at a stroke a traditional placement for daughters, and in some cases received daughters and sisters back. Pious laywomen were faced with changed rituals and doctrines imposed with varying degrees of radicalism. Literally the habits of a lifetime in terms of devotion to the Virgin and Saints and funerary proprieties were swept away. Women's reception of these changes must have varied hugely, but some would be helped by their parish priests embracing the new religion and still visibly leading their devotions in the same, if transformed buildings.

As most women were married at some point in their lives the Reformation teachings on marriage and the family had perhaps the most significant sociological impact. The Protestant Reformation increased emphasis on the family, reinforcing patriarchy. Lyndal Roper considers it a misreading to view the Reformation as beneficial to women, in terms of progressiveness, individualism and modernization. In *The Holy Household: Women and Morals in Reformation Augsburg* she noted Protestantism's heritage for women as ambiguous. Wives were kept firmly submissive to husbands. The economy was dominated by the guild ideal of the household workshop and the reformers entrenched this with wives being subordinate to husbands, children to parents and servants to masters. Instead of a Utopian harmony of the couple's interests, Roper sees a relentless gendering of labour, and a personal stifling of the wife in deference to a supposedly wiser husband, who had the disciplining of the household and could chastise its members. Steven Ozment, on the other hand, views the period *When Fathers Ruled* rather more optimistically, with the wife as mother of the house and thus of high standing, and the Reformation leading into a period of unusually level shared parenting. The medieval church's monopoly of matrimonial business was broken and towns set up tribunals usually dominated (in numbers) by laymen, even if still advised by clergy. Where the old church's disciplinary machinery for moral lapses was overthrown it did not mean unreined moral anarchy. The policing of Zurich, Basel and Geneva was intrusive into civil rights and the Discipline Lords of Augsburg survived the 1548 restoration of Catholicism. The Protestant reformers tended to take a proactive morally righteous stance and the old double standard of sexual morality was condemned by preachers, but less obviously a principle for action. Zurich allowed wives to divorce adulterous husbands in the late 1520s. Remarriage after divorce came to be cautiously allowed under certain conditions. In extreme circumstances, the Anabaptists in besieged Münster in July 1534 introduced polygyny, and forced women over 12 to marry, although many resisted. (With regard to women's position in the various movements categorized as Anabaptist historians' opinions differ and it seems women's opportunities for participation varied with the different complexions of the groups.)

With clerical marriage allowed in the reformed churches, a new figure emerges: the pastor's wife. Katherine Luther in Wittenberg and Katherine Zell (née Schütz, d 1562) in Strasbourg backed their husbands to the full (showing just how wrong the idea of a wife and children impeding a priest or philosopher was). Luther repeatedly showed loving appreciation of his wife as did many others of the first-generation married clergy. The role of reformer's wife had its attractions: Wilbrandis (née Rosenblatt, d.1564) married three successively, John Oeclampadis, Wolfgang Capito and Martin

Bucer. Women were no more going to become priests in the reformed churches than in the old, but the reformers' wives were better placed to be a professional partner with their husbands than priests' concubines could ever be, and sometimes the wife was the steadier and more reliable of the couple, entertaining visiting reformers (and wives), and Katherine Zell published herself: Wiesner-Hanks calls her a Strasbourg reformer in her own right.

At the same time wives of involved German, Italian, and French princes, dukes and other nobles can be seen being influenced by Reformers and sometimes as patrons of them. Religious allegiance was tied up with politics and diplomacy: the East Friesland regent Countess Anna von Oldenburg, widowed in 1540, tried to pursue a middle way between Lutheran and papalist extremes in religion and politics. Where wives and husbands took different stances there could be difficulties. Elisabeth of Brandenburg (1485–1545), after 25 years of orthodox Catholic wedlock to the Elector Joachim I, took up with Lutheranism in 1527 and fled his recriminations. Her brother was Christian II of Denmark, whose wife Isabella was Lutheran, although her brother was the staunch Catholic Emperor Charles V. The activities of Renée Duchess of Ferrara (daughter of Louis XII and Anne of Brittany, d 1575) caused her husband to ask Henry II of France in 1554 for a theologian to win her back from the influence of what he called Lutheran rascals. Polarization within couples was of course suffered more during the first generation of the Reformation: later generations tended to marry within their known persuasions, or at least with awareness of the differences between them.

7

Women Who Exceeded Society's Expectations

For most medieval women there was a huge educational gap between what was available for, and expected of, their brothers and themselves. In the later fifteenth century some of the daughters of the Italian Renaissance nobility received an advanced humanist education and, as shown in Chapter 5 above, attained precocious levels in childhood and went on to participate in diplomacy and literary and artistic patronage. Christine de Pizan, as will be shown later in this chapter, was brought up in an unusually intellectual atmosphere for a girl, and it shows in her extraordinary literary career.

While many women rose above society's expectations to some extent, the three women selected for focus in this chapter were exceptional individuals transcending by far the norms for their class. Christine was the most rarefied, because her father's professional career catapulted her into a royal court background and launched her into association with important and culturally influential people. She embraced her opportunities and joined in at the highest literary level despite her sex. Clare of Assisi was born into the urban nobility – a particularly Italian phenomenon – and brought up with her family's intention of marrying her well. Her mother was a woman of apparently more than average piety, combined comfortably enough with marriage, but Clare was inspired by St Francis not to be satisfied with merely following her example. Joan of Arc, a peasant girl from Lorraine, had a much more 'ordinary' childhood. With no advantages of birth or environment, what brought her out came from within, a driving force that God was telling her to rally the Dauphinists and save France. Joan was brought up with exposure to the normal religious provision of a French village. What was unusual about her as a child was her reaction to her religious opportunities, and the testimony of her childhood friends at her rehabilitation trial tells of an excessively pious child, even teased about it by her contemporaries.

Christine was pioneering as a professional woman writer and it is by her writings that she is known. Clare left the Poor Clares their rule (but it incorporates much of St Francis' design for the women) and a very few letters; her life style and inspiration, attested by others, would have influenced more people than her words did. Even more is this the case with Joan the Maid, to whose few strictly business-in-hand letters she is known to have penned her Christian name in just three surviving examples. The records of Joan's trials, before and after her death, and the comments her extraordinary career elicited from Christine, chroniclers and letter writers, provide most of our knowledge of her. Joan's career is the most outstanding of the three (although she only lived a third of the lifespan of each of the other two) because it crashed through the strongest glass ceiling – military command of men – and took the obscure peasant girl in a matter of months to the king's side at his coronation in Reims cathedral.

St Clare of Assisi (1193/4–1253)

The western church had from earlier history examples of sainted women who founded convents in which they lived as the first abbesses. St Clare exceeded these, being popularly regarded as the founder of an Order (the Poor Ladies, later Poor Clares) and creator of the first religious Rule written by a woman, given papal approval in 1253. Both claims for Clare, however, are simplifications of a rather complex process, and bolder than she would have made for herself. Clare, as she always acknowledged, was a disciple ('little plant') of St Francis of Assisi. The Franciscan Second Order (its women) essentially followed the first (the men). Francis in 1212 placed his first group of women followers in Assisi's San Damiano church which he had restored, giving them a form of life similar to his own. The papal confirmation of 1253 was for the text described as 'this form of life and the manner of holy unity and highest poverty which your blessed Father St Francis gave you for your observance in word and writing', emphasizing the Franciscan derivation. Thus 'co-founder' might be a better description of Clare's role regarding the Poor Ladies. Similarly, their form of life, commonly referred to as the 'Rule of St Clare', was only one of several rules and adaptations applied to the order before 1263, one stage in the evolution of the order's regulations, which had been initiated by St Francis and subjected to overriding alterations by the appointed cardinal protector of the Franciscans, Hugolino di Segni, who also secured for the sisters the title 'Second Order of St Francis'. Clare resisted some of the watering down of the Franciscan ideals for its women vigorously but with limited success. Incidentally, Heloise's involvement in the evolution of the rule for the order of the Paraclete makes a woman's wrestling with the regulation of an order not unprecedented.

However, these qualifying remarks hardly detract from St Clare's extraordinary enough achievements. She was born into the noble family of Offreduccio of Assisi around 1194, the eldest of three daughters. Her mother Ortolana had a pious disposition, had been on pilgrimages, was inclined to charitable good works, and eventually, widowed, joined Clare at San Damiano. Clare was expected to lead a secular life and to marry well, but in her teens came under the influence of the charismatic Francis. On Palm Sunday 1212 she left home with concealed intent, and was placed by Francis successively in two local Benedictine nunneries before he established her and her sister Catherine (Agnes) at San Damiano, despite their family's attempts to recover them. Other young women of the town were soon attracted. They had all chosen to emulate the Franciscan ideals and life styles, heavily centred on absolute poverty. However, Clare evidently suspected that the church authorities were going to step in and alter the group's definition and she secured from Innocent III a papal bull guaranteeing the Poor Ladies the privilege of poverty, that is, that they could not be forced to receive possessions. Thus at around 21, Clare was astute enough to realize the single point which was going to be most at issue for the Poor Clares over the next half century, and enterprising enough to approach the pope, no less, for a buttress against the decision going contrary to the principle which was so dear to her.

Unfortunately for Clare, Innocent III died almost immediately. In a series of moves between 1217 and 1219, acting on the Fourth Lateran's thirteenth canon which tied new developments to already approved religious rules, di Segni imposed on San Damiano a basically Benedictine rule, breaking the privilege of poverty. Clare resisted, with some support from Francis, who died in 1226, and eventually in 1228 the privilege was permitted, just for San Damiano, by Gregory IX (as Hugolino had become). However, the matter was still critical. Innocent IV tried to impose uniform regulations on the whole order, and Clare's response was to produce the 'rule' of 1253, approved by the pope two days before her death, an event which drew pope, cardinals and bishops from Perugia in her honour. About two months later the pope commissioned the archbishop of Spoleto to collect evidence of her virtues and miracles preparatory to canonization. His successor Alexander IV canonized her in 1255.

Clare lived all her professional life at San Damiano, renouncing her wealthy background and selflessly directing her community for over

40 years. When she died there aged around 60 she had been a physical invalid for about half her life, her body weakened by her excessive fastings and ascetic living. Much of her career is merely a good illustration of what might be expected of a holy woman attaining the perfection of religious life as contemporaries idealized it. Where Clare exceeded contemporary expectation was in standing up to the highest church authorities in a resolute defence of her followers' right to live in the corporate poverty originally envisaged for the group. Her *Legend*, written c.1255–6, preserves the story of Gregory IX trying to win her over to community property by offering to absolve her from her vow if this was what was hindering her, and receiving the unanswerable response 'Holy Father, never will I consent to be absolved from following Christ'.[1] Physically frail, Clare was iron willed and able to discomfit her opponents by such disarming sweet reason. If Clare had been less strong willed, or less intensely convinced of the necessity to persist with her cause, the early definition of the Poor Clares could have been rather different. In this respect her particular contribution was unique.

There are writings attributed to Clare, and writings about her. Attributions include four letters to Agnes, the pious daughter of Ottokar of Bohemia, beginning c.1234/5, and a cluster of texts from the end of her life, the Rule or Form of Life credited to 1252–3, returned with papal approval just hours before her death, and the Testament and (final) Blessing both credited to 1253. The letters to Agnes are seen as the most authentic; the Form of Life is accepted by most scholars (acknowledging that passages from earlier rules are incorporated into it), the Testament and Blessing are widely accepted but have less secure textual history. After Clare's death came the Process of Canonization, and shortly after that the anonymous *Legend*, attributed by some to the Franciscan Thomas of Celano who had written the first *Life of St Francis*. The first letter to Agnes contains an often quoted hymn to poverty.

Drawing from the letters to Agnes, Form of Life, Process, and *Legend*, a picture can be pieced together of Clare at San Damiano, practising what she laid down. The Form of Life placed the Poor Clares' abbess in an unusually democratic constitution. The abbess was not only elected but, if she appeared incompetent to the entire body of the sisters, had to be replaced. She should preside by strength of virtues and holy behaviour rather than the authority of office. Sisters had to be consulted on matters of conventual welfare and on the incurring of debt, and at least eight discreet sisters were elected whose counsel she was bound to use; sisters could and should remove and re-elect other officials and discreets if this became expedient. There could not be a stronger contrast with the imperious behaviour of the Benedictine abbess

Hildegard of Bingen in the previous century. Clare's abbess was to be so familiar with the sisters that they could speak and act with her 'as ladies do with their servant' – a telling indication of the social class of early recruits. Clare's abbess was a kindly matron to sisters who were ill. In the canonization process Sister Pacifica testified she had many times seen Clare, when well, serving her sisters, washing their feet and giving them water for their hands, and washing the seats used by the sick.

The regimen in the house was austere – the sisters were to fast strictly (but were allowed to eat twice at Christmas whatever day of the week it fell), go to confession at least 12 times a year, and receive communion 7 times on specified feasts. The Rule mercifully dispensed fasting, at the abbess's discretion, for younger sisters, weak ones and those serving outside the monastery, and in time of manifest necessity. The third letter to Agnes contains the information that on 'ordinary' Thursdays the nuns could please themselves whether they fasted or not; it also cautions against excessive austerities, 'our flesh is not of brass nor our strength stone', advising that sacrifice should be 'seasoned with the salt of wisdom'.[2] The reference to sisters serving outside the monastery is interesting. The friars were of course essentially mobile among laypeople. The church authorities from di Segni onwards shrank from giving women religious free rein to wander outside convent walls, and the second orders became cloistered, but Clare left open some external activity, hedged with restrictions not to linger outside, to behave there in an edifying manner, and to maintain discretion – not repeating the world's gossip inside the monastery or repeating outside anything from within that could cause scandal. Entrants had their hair cut, set aside secular dress and thereafter could not go outside the monastery except for 'some useful, reasonable, evident and approved purpose'. The literate sisters celebrated divine office like the friars, the illiterate were prescribed set repetitions of the Lord's Prayer at the different hours. Those who did not know how to read were not to be eager to learn, but rather devote themselves to the spirit of the Lord – not an attitude to education the abbess Gertrude of Helfta would share. That Clare's rule is based on two earlier Franciscan rules of 1221 and 1223 does not detract from Clare's inventiveness; obviously she would be anxious to preserve as much conformity with Franciscan regulations as possible.

Both Francis and Clare were in tune with their times as their recruitment success proves. San Damiano had reached apparently 40–50 sisters by Clare's death, and there were over 20 Poor Ladies' monasteries, with another 100 or so within another 10 years. Some Benedictine houses converted to the more austere regime, including one at Florence to which Clare's sister Agnes was dispatched, to direct it. Francis and Clare had charisma which affected their contemporaries. A rather more devious reaction Clare inspired in the church has recently been suggested. The bull of canonization referred to her as the 'new woman of the valley of Spoleto' and the 'new leader of women'. Seemingly the church did not wish to let such a new woman give rise to a whole breed of them. Both the Franciscans and the Dominicans went through a phase of resisting responsibility for their second orders in the thirteenth century, and in 1298 the bull *Periculoso* tightened the enclosure of monastic women, which was reinforced at Trent. The brief vision of religious women as religious men's equal was being obliterated. More subtly, ecclesiastical writings about Clare have been interpreted as deliberately manipulative. Catherine Mooney, in *Gendered Voices: Medieval Saints and their Interpreters*, shows how Clare was increasingly characterized as a follower of Mary, whereas her own works refer to the footprints of *Christ* as the ones to follow. Mooney suggests that Clare was connected with Mary because Mary was the great mediatrix, and female saints (more than male ones) were seen as mediators, conduits, channels, vessels between the human and divine. It suited churchmen to portray men imitating Christ while women had their own (lesser) model to imitate in Mary, and the friars, desiring to distance themselves from responsibility for and relationship with their female branch, did not want its 'parity' implied. To make such effort to present a saint in a way she did not apparently see herself (and ignoring the way she did, that is as a direct follower of Christ) looks suspicious, and is certainly open to the interpretation that the church wanted Clare tucked back harmlessly into the old mould of holy but conformist women. Mooney points out that, of course, where so often we only have later, male-authored writings about women saints and not their own words to compare with the presentation, there may be similar gender bending.[3]

Clare's charisma still dazzles some of those who write about her, inducing an uncritical frame of mind, promoting what they want to believe about Clare, rather than what is substantiable. Reading about Clare, it seems more difficult to obtain a balanced view of her than about Hildegard, another holy woman (from the twelfth century) who has attracted a lot of attention recently. Writers enthusing over Hildegard seem more willing to acknowledge her faults and failures than Clare's enthusiasts are to imagine she could have any. The Brookes tell us her life ended in a quiet but dramatic triumph with the pope confirming her version of her own rule, but Ranft calls this approval 'a token gesture at best', limited to the two houses of Clare and Agnes, and pointing out that within 10 years the papacy had imposed a rule forbidding absolute poverty on the other 120 houses. Sister Thom believes

Clare did not oppose ecclesiastical dignitaries and counted popes and cardinals among her dearest friends, while Innocent IV considered her surpassing 'all the women of our time'; the Brookes say it is commonly assumed there was considerable friction and conflict between Clare and the curia.[4] Clare's modern treatment illustrates the dangers to readers when neither problems with the evidence, nor the existence of alternative interpretations are admitted (or are obscured in bald footnote references). This state of affairs is not Clare's fault, and in a paradoxical way it strengthens her case to be considered extraordinary – still.

Joan of Arc (c.1412–1431)

Joan of Arc did not simply exceed the expectations of her day. She was a phenomenon. Few individuals have changed the course of history so noticeably in so short a time, and probably no other woman in Christian times. She performed her feats in the masculine military world, and created such uproar on the political scene of the Hundred Years' War that two of the three participating factions had to co-operate to have her burned alive as a heretic, after a travesty of a trial, as the only way to get rid of her. She was only about 19 when she died; 25 years later the trial was nullified for procedural flaws. A little short of 500 years after her death she was canonized. Her life was astonishing, the effecting of her death was extraordinary and her reputation has been remarkable. Furthermore, her career is comparatively well evidenced since so noticeable a person inspired contemporary record (not without bias) and the reconsideration of her trial a generation later, with many of her associates still alive, delved into recollections (not all accurate). However at least there is plenty for historians to consider: letters sent in her name, the treasurer's accounts recording expenditure on her armour, contemporary written comment (on both the French and Anglo-Burgundian sides), letter reports circulating in more distant places as her fame blazed across Europe, transcripts and other records of her trial at Rouen, and its subsequent investigation, and a secondary literature about her beginning soon after the rehabilitation.

Joan's story is well known. She emerged from obscurity in May 1428 when she descended upon Robert de Baudricourt, captain of Vaucouleurs, the local fortress near her home village of Domrémy on the Meuse, asking to be taken across France to the dauphin Charles, then at Chinon, her mission being the recovery of the kingdom of France. Not taking no for an answer, Joan persisted and in February 1429 had her way, being escorted to Chinon and meeting the dauphin on 6 March. Here too she was sufficiently convincing – surely against all odds – to persuade the dauphin (disinherited in favour of the English king by the 1420 Treaty of Troyes) to dispatch her to raise the siege of Orléans. She reached the city, besieged by the English with every prospect of success, on 29 April, and on 8 May the siege was raised. A keynote change of fortune for the Dauphinists, this event was followed by a series of successes for Joan in June, the taking of Jargeau, and the bridge at Meung-sur-Loire and victory at the set battle of Patay. Joan then overpowered doubts and resistance to her vision and pushed the dauphin into travelling to Reims for anointing and crowning as King of France, which was achieved on 17 July 1429, with Joan standing in the cathedral at the king's side bearing her standard. Some position for a teenage girl, who 6 months earlier was in rural Lorraine. After the coronation Joan remained in arms but lost her predominance, and was set to some military tasks which were not to her conviction. It was on 31 July 1429 that Christine de Pizan wrote her *Ditié de Jehanne d'Arc*, waxing lyrical over 'a maiden sent from God', 'a little girl of 16', 'a simple shepherdess – braver than any man ever was in Rome'.[5] Then 10 months later Joan was captured by the Burgundians at Compiègne, trying to raise its siege. Sold to the English for 10,000 livres tournois by John of Luxembourg whose vassal had taken her, she was brought to ecclesiastical trial at Rouen and burned alive there on 30 May 1431, her ashes being dropped into the Seine to ensure there would be no relics. Thus Joan's public career was only days longer than 3 years.

Joan influenced experienced military men to change their tactics; she rode armed into battle brandishing her highly targetable standard, and participated in the thick of artillery and scaling ladders. Her inspiration changed the course of the war and her insistence on getting the dauphin crowned in the traditional setting at Reims (and anointed with the traditional holy oil kept there) strengthened his position in the balance of politics. Although the church handed her over for burning as a relapsed heretic, it saw the error of its ways and eventually canonized her for her holiness not her heroism. Later canonization is always to some extent irrelevant to a particular saint's story, indicating later interpretation rather than confirming lifetime facts. But in Joan's case the canonization probably takes us back nearer to the girl as she saw herself.

Joan's common identification of herself was as Jehanne la Pucelle, Joan the Maid. Her father was Jacques Darc; Christine and history use his surname for Joan, but she did not use it for herself. Her own choice of identification was highly significant. She was presenting herself relevantly to her situation as she saw it; she came as a young inspired virgin, not as her father's daughter or a village girl from Domrémy. Her virginity was a major part of her integrity, for she believed herself to be the recipient of instructions from God, sent through voices (sometimes identified as St Catherine, St Margaret or St Michael). Holy women uttering God's messages were highly regarded in the middle ages but they were handled cautiously by the church which could not afford to accept any ranting trollop's self-proclamation as God's messenger. So Joan was subjected to examination as she advanced towards her goal. Robert de Baudricourt needed reassurance before forwarding her under escort. He sent her for preliminary interview with Duke Charles II of Lorraine at Nancy, and she was exorcised by the priest at Vaucouleurs before setting out to Chinon. After meeting the dauphin, but before being let loose on her plan, she was examined for 11 days at Poitiers by theologians of the University to test her religious soundness, and at Tours by the dauphin's mother-in-law (or her ladies) to test her virginity. After capture, her virginity was tested again at Rouen. The virginity was crucial because Joan's claim to be listened to was otherworldly. What was unusual about her divine message was that it was political (that the English had no right to France and should be ejected, and the rightful king's position should be strengthened by having him properly crowned and anointed at the proper place) and military (that the immediate task was to raise the siege of Orléans). Joan was possessed by these aims and she could only get them widely accepted and brought to fruition if those in power accepted that she was sent by God to direct them. Only after they had grudgingly or generously accepted her moral right to an astonishing level of leadership for a young girl, were the existing military leaders faced with having their immediate strategies and technical decisions overruled by her. Belief in her solidified when she began to reverse the French failures. She was not simply an army's lucky mascot; she proved in her own talent a shrewd positioner of artillery and an inspiring leader of men in the thick of battle, all without previous military training, though not apparently without lance and riding practice. To her own side Joan as God-sent Maid, radiating innocence and purity, fearless in battle and even imperious in diplomacy, gave them confidence as no battle-gnarled veteran could, and to the opposition this supernatural aura (though they preferred to consider her a fiendish witch) made her and the troops with her seem much more dangerous.

Everybody knew that living amid soldiers endangered a woman's chastity, and that armies attracted prostitute followers. It suited the English and Burgundians to assume the worst and insult Joan as a whore; the French, sensitive to what normal people would think, later recollected her disarming power – men said they had never felt carnal impulses towards her, or had never dared own up to such, or give them vent. In fact two of Joan's brothers, Jean and Pierre, were with her a good deal of the time – both were with her from Tours, and Pierre was captured with her at Compiègne, so she may not have been as defencelessly exposed to men as is often suggested. Joan helped men and herself obliterate awareness of her sex by dressing in male armour. (At first nobody seemed to bother about this, but at her first trial it became enormously important as defiance of church teaching.) Estimated (from fabric orders) at about 5 feet 2 inches tall, she could well have appeared, in male dress, like a slight page, but of course it was not her intention to merge unnoticed in the throng – her banner drew attention to her wherever she was. She needed to transcend gender, so that her male colleagues ignored her physical body, but to be known to be a woman, so that respect for her untouchable difference added to her reputation.

The problems facing a respectable woman living among soldiers Joan seems to have surmounted by ignoring them, and the men who were being asked to submit themselves to a woman giving orders, and of all places on the battlefield, did so without loss of face by accepting her as inspirational. Joan's fears of sexual assault seem only to have arisen once she was imprisoned by the hostile English, and in the hands of male guards, with no longer a brother to hand. Here her position was difficult because she was being held as a military prisoner while being tried by an ecclesiastical tribunal. Her English gaolers did not have the respect for her as God's Maid, and bore her hatred, as an enemy who had done their side harm. The aura of God's protection was somewhat dimmed by the fact of her capture anyway, and the thankless Charles VII's failure to ransom her further emphasized her powerlessness. Nobody influential seemed to want to do anything to help her. Cut down to size, Joan was pitiably incarcerated in leg irons, in a cell virtually 'bugged' (with eavesdropping space outside), and was even an object of display for the earl of Warwick's dinner guests.

Like other conduits of God's word before her, Joan's confidence lay in her driving self-belief that she had to carry out divine instructions. Earlier visionaries had also been emboldened by their conviction that God was using them. But the gap Joan had to bridge was far wider than theirs. Most of the church's leading female visionaries up to Joan's day were nobly born, and had relatives in authoritative positions in church or state. Communicating with this level of people was inbred in them. Furthermore, though they conventionally claimed illiteracy or lack of learning, they were often convent educated. But Joan was an illiterate peasant girl, telling peers of France how to conduct war. Many of the top French generals were aristocrats, of royal or noble blood (even if bastard), and had been reared for a career in arms. The Hundred

Years' War opened opportunities for lesser born fighting men to rise up the ranks by talent. But for these established military men, whichever way they had reached command, to accept a peasant girl's instructions was asking much. Some never overcame resentment. In the circumstances Joan's illiterate peasant origins could be advantageously stressed to make her extraordinary emergence at the top all part of her miraculous image. DeVries asserts in *Joan of Arc: A Military Leader* that her family was a bit wealthier than most contemporary peasants (with about 20 hectares of land to farm). They were only village farmers, but probably reasonably comfortably placed in their community, since her father had been village headman, collecting rents and taxes, commanding the watch, guarding prisoners and enforcing local decrees and it may be surmised such responsibilities normally went to the better off peasantry. 'Honest husbandmen' was one description of the family from the rehabilitation trial. Joan's mother Isabelle came from the nearby village of Vouthon; one of her brothers was a roofer and another a parish priest. Isabelle was known as Romée which may indicate she had been on pilgrimage to Rome, which in turn would imply she could afford to. However, by 1440 when she had lost her husband and eldest son Isabelle had fallen on hard times and was rescued by the grateful citizenry of Orléans who took her in, gave her an allowance of 48 sous a month and paid her doctor's fees when she was ill. Joan's surviving brothers Jean and Pierre benefited from the ennoblement of the family bestowed by Charles VII in 1429 in gratitude for Joan's services. Her parents were also rewarded with admission to the coronation, where they witnessed their daughter's triumph at the king's side. As her family prospered with her success, so too did her community and in successive generations: Joan gained tax relief for Domrémy and neighbouring Greux.

Although some 17 letters and references to others from Joan have been distinctly identified, some imperious in tone ('I am commander of the armies … I am sent from God … to chase you out of all of France'[6]) they do not throw light on Joan's own literacy. Only three originals appear to bear her signature, in the single word Jehanne. These were written on 9 November 1429, and 16 and 28 March 1430. The signature on the first is much more hesitant than on the others, suggesting her writing ability improved in the next 6 months, which in turn implies she was raw to writing when she wrote the first signature. The long, threatening, letter to the Hussites written on 23 March 1430 was signed by her confessor Pasquerel, who may have written it all. What is never known about a letter not demonstrably all autograph is how much it was dictated to a mere scribe and how much composed by an executive secretary. Even allowing for the fact that

Joan's background and comparative lack of education would have made her seem easily classable as peasant and illiterate at the dauphin's court, and acknowledging that stressing this would also add lustre to her miraculous emergence as the power behind the throne, it seems to be a reasonably accurate description.

Thus Joan's career was extraordinary enough; from obscure farm daughter to the topmost councils of war. The way she died was also quite exceptional. Captured at Compiègne, Joan was passed upwards by her captor, the Bastard of Wandomme, to his lord John of Luxembourg, as was customary with prisoners of war in the Hundred Years' War. Joan was a valuable prisoner – the price for her was up at royal levels. John could expect to sell her on to the English, or deliver her to Charles VII for a ransom. He kept her 4 months before selling her to the English. The money was raised by the estates of Normandy, then under English occupation, and it was paid to secure Joan's handing over for religious trial under the Bishop of Beauvais, in whose diocese she had been captured, the bishop (Cauchon) being backed by the University of Paris, supporting the English king on this issue. 'Owing to her evil reputation she is by no means to be dealt with as a prisoner of war' was the prevalent policy.[7] Her trial lasted 5 months.

Joan could easily have been killed at the siege of Orléans or at the battle of Patay or at other moments in her military career (she was wounded at Orléans and again at Paris). Taken prisoner, she could have been ransomed by her own side (though the Anglo-Burgundians would have been unwilling to let her free to fight another day). Kept in gaol in irons she could have died of natural causes or by murderous treachery. There was a scare in April 1431 when she was suddenly very sick after eating a carp sent by Bishop Cauchon – doctors were sent for to ensure she recovered because the English king did not wish her to die a natural death. (He was nearly cheated of his prize when Joan abjured on 24 May in circumstances obscured by seeming alteration of the trial record.) Any of these deaths would have released Joan from longer suffering and left us with less information. But the 1431 trial left both French transcripts of the court session notes and Latin translations of them, and much of Joan's career was raked over. Immediately after her burning, the English king wrote a justificatory letter attacking her and optimistically commenting that the case was closed. It was not. Twenty-five years later the business was reopened. Surviving witnesses from all stages of Joan's life were sought out over four years from 1452 to 1456, leaving another set of transcripts of oral recollections. From these come many of the affectionate reminiscences of Joan as a child, a good, simple, pious, God-fearing, humble sweet girl, generous with alms, working round the house, spinning, watching over animals. Her old mother testified that she had been baptized and confirmed, and went to church frequently, receiving the Eucharist every month after confession, and gave herself to fasting and prayer. Her godfather testified to her piety. A man who called himself her companion as a boy admitted he and his fellows had teased her about her piety. Another said he had accompanied her on pilgrimages to a local hermitage. A girlfriend remembered spinning with her. Though subject to the vagaries of oral testimony, and laid down with knowledge of what Joan had gone on to do and how she had died (as her mother said 'most cruelly by fire'), these are plausible stories of a country childhood in days before compulsory education, when children of both sexes occupied themselves with chores suitable to their age, and socialized across the sexes, and when this girl's only abnormality was excessive piety.

Joan's reputation remains high to this day. 'Almost alone' writes DeVries, Joan transformed a losing French side into the victorious one which drove the English out of all their French territory except Calais by 1453. She turned the tide, and it was the unexpected change of the balance when the siege of Orléans was raised that did it. French MS 23018 in the Bibliothéque Nationale, printed in *The First Biography of Joan of Arc* as the first chronicle to record Joan's exploits, has almost all the long familiar elements of the story: Joan the Maid, farmer's daughter and shepherdess, innocent, divinely inspired, taken up by the dauphin, working wonders at Orléans, inspiring the dauphin, striving to render the army god-fearing, riding before the king after the coronation, working wonders at Paris and Compiègne, burnt and her ashes thrown into the Seine. The chronicler saw the 'Joan-effect' clearly: 'with the Maid in arms ... the Dauphin ... acquired new courage'. Christine de Pizan's ambitions for her swelled: 'she will restore harmony in Christendom and the church ... destroy unbelievers ... and heretics ... [and] the Saracens by conquering the Holy Land'.[8] Throughout Europe, in France, the Empire, Low Countries and Italy, Joan was recognized as the saviour of Orléans. The Anglo-Burgundians also sensed the change, though with inverse reaction: Bedford wrote to Henry VI that all was prospering for him until the siege of Orléans, when fortune was reversed 'by a disciple and follower of the fiend called the Pucelle'.[9] Orléans did not forget its deliverance, celebrating it annually on 8 May with a procession. In 1435 the pageant drama *Mystère du Siège d'Orléans* was produced there for the first time. Somewhere around the 1460s the *Chronique de la Pucelle* and *Journal du Siège d'Orléans* were produced, probably at Orléans, and around 1500 the first *Life of Joan of Arc*, written anonymously, in French, by order of Louis XII and the Admiral of France. The literary accretions just went on growing. Her impact is still remembered, which has been a truly remarkable destiny for a girl born into a very ordinary country family, dead before 20, and only three years in the limelight, one of these in gaol. It is ironic that a girl with such medieval piety should also show us, through the records about her, recognizable manifestations of modern inhumanities to political prisoners.

Christine de Pizan (c.1365–c.1430)

Christine de Pizan was born in Venice, but spent most of her life in France. Her father, Thomas de Pizan, astrologer and physician, had accepted Charles V's invitation to his court where his family joined him in 1368. At 15, Christine married Etienne de Castel, a noble courtier and royal secretary/notary, and she was widowed at 25, by which time she had three children and her widowed mother and an unmarried niece to support. She made a remarkably successful career as a professional writer of both French verse and prose, peaking 1399–1405. She was commissioned by Philip the Bold to write the biography of his brother, *The Book of the Deeds and Good Customs of King Charles V* (1404). She wrote on politics (*The Book of the Body Politic*, 1406–7), and arms (*The Book of the Deeds of Arms and Chivalry*, date disputed, 1405 or possibly 1410) in prose, and in verse *The Tale of Joan of Arc* (1429), but for the study of women her most interesting writings are her contributions to the *Roman de la Rose* debate from 1401 to 1403, and, in particular, *The Book of the City of Ladies* and its follow up *The Book of the Three Virtues* (both 1405). Biographical material is contained in the verse *Book on the Mutability of Fortune* (variously dated between 1400 and 1404) and prose *L'Avision Christine*, a dream vision from 1405.

In the early fifteenth-century French literary world Christine held her own amid male writers. Her education, as a woman, lacked the institutional opportunities available to her male peers. In the *Book of the City of Ladies* reference is made to her parents. Her father did not believe that women should not know science, and took pleasure in her inclination to learning, but her mother stood as an obstacle to her greater involvement in the sciences, preferring her daughter to be reared traditionally to spend her time spinning and in what Earl Richards translates as 'silly girlishness'. The French court was showing humanist leanings and as the astrologer's daughter Christine was brought up in stimulating surroundings and read French and Italian; her Latin skills seem less certain, she preferred French translations of Latin authors, but if she had read Boccaccio's *Genealogia Deorum Gentilium* which seems to have affected her view of the nature of poetry, she must have read it in the Latin. It is believed she had access to the royal library at the Louvre. Apparently her husband encouraged her learning, and after her widowhood she embarked on a crash course in self-education, reading histories, science and poetry, beginning her writing career with poetry in the 1390s.

The two books on the City of Ladies formed a universal history of women, ending with practical behavioural advice for women of every social class in contemporary society. *The Book of the City of Ladies* is not history written chronologically: it is set out as an indignant defence of women, faulting the hostile arguments of male writers, and taking up the literary challenge of constructing an edifice (the City of the title) to form a refuge for virtuous and valiant women against sundry assailants. Christine claimed to be put to this task by three crowned ladies identified as Reason, Rectitude and Justice, who help her. As they create 'a New Kingdom of Femininity' more attention is paid to talk than the tasks as the figures answer Christine's inquiries about the malignment of women, and cite good examples of excellence in women from mythical, pagan and early Christian times and more recent history. In the three successive parts Christine converses respectively with Reason, Rectitude and Justice, raising such questions as why different authors had written against women, why women were not in the legal profession, whether God had ever wished to ennoble women with scientific knowledge and so on. Christine was a literary writer not a sociological researcher, and allowance has to be made for her use of various literary devices which may seem odd to us but in fact show her technical mastery of her art and her ability to recentre material constructively. Periodically a discussion ends with reality cutting off further progress: that some men do not want women educated is met simply with the comment 'these men are wrong'.[10] The generally positive perspective on matrimony, with its reference to Christine's own happy marriage, is tempered with acknowledgement that there are bad husbands, and the final chapter of the book underlines wives' powerlessness. The married woman is told sometimes it is not best for a creature to be independent. Wives with good loving husbands can thank God for them; wives with husbands neither wholly good nor bad should praise God that they are not the worst, and wives with 'cruel, mean and savage' husbands should strive to endure them, and try to overcome their vices and bring them back to a reasonable behaviour – some chance! This imaginary refuge for women offers no real help to the battered wife, although the book's treatment of rape, from the women's standpoint, at least refutes the old masculine 'excuse' that women want it.

Although the *Book of the City of Ladies* is seen as revolutionary, and the first book by a woman in praise of women, it has to be seen in its medieval literary context. About three-quarters of the material was derived from Boccaccio's *De Mulieribus Claris* (itself well worth reading, especially for the moral lessons Boccaccio draws from history and sets out for girls and widows of his own day).

The third part, in which Justice brings the Virgin Mary and her noble company to rule the City, is stuffed with saints' lives, largely of virgins or chaste wives most horribly butchered in martyrdom for the Christian faith, and Christine reproduces the grisly details of breasts torn off, a body slashed, a tongue cut out, a girl hanged by the hair, and the frenzied attempts of torturers and executioners to crush, burn or drown their victims. The *Book of the Three Virtues* was more practical. Material from its three sections was used for illustration in Chapters 4 and 5 above. For historians it seems safer to quarry in, being less rhetorically misleading than the more artful *Book of the City of Ladies*, and more closely rooted in shrewdly observed real life.

Christine sallied into her works on women convinced that women's voice should be heard, so naturally her writings on women are of central interest in a study of women in medieval Europe. Of course she has been seized upon and praised for her 'feminism', and criticized for not carrying this far enough (both interpretations being anachronistic in relation to Christine's own times). She was equally outstanding in the areas where she tackled male writers' subjects, giving and expecting no quarter on account of her own sex. Her commission to write Charles V's biography was extraordinary for a woman, and that she should tackle military theory, and update Vegetius by comparing Roman with contemporary siege tactics, and be accepted as worth reading on this most masculine of subjects, is testimony to her authoritative style and reputation. Caxton, a publisher with a talent for salesmanship, did not try to conceal her sex when he printed translations of her works in England. The moral proverbs she collected for her son were published in Earl Rivers' translation by Caxton as *The Moral Proverbs of Crystine* in 1478, and Caxton's *Feats of Arms and Chivalry* (1489) contains in the epilogue 'thus ends this book which Christine of Pyse made and drew out of the book named *Vegecius De Re Militari* and out of the *Tree of Battles* ...' *The Book of the Body Politic* rather daringly contains some critical asides about the current French situation in relation to clerical promotion and behaviour, rampant soldiery, unfair taxation, and the use of influence in the making of official appointments. *The Book of the Body Politic* was written for the dauphin Louis and belongs to the moral mirror genre, associated over the centuries mainly with ecclesiastics writing for princes. As a laywoman advising a dauphin, Christine was demonstrating her characteristic disregard for any designation of serious matters as inappropriate for women to engage in. In the ninth century the noblewoman Dhuoda of Uzès had also ventured into the genre, less ambitiously aiming her moral guidance at her son with her *Handbook for William*. The two texts enable us to see how vastly more sophisticated Christine's writing was.

8

Conclusions

Expectations and Achievements

Women were expected to marry in the middle ages. Sexual continence was a highly esteemed virtue and to become a virgin of Christ the highest of callings, but the life of perpetual virginity was not expected of most medieval women. Desiring it, some pious girls had to resist family intentions to marry them off; however, others were forced by family pressure to take the veil against their inclination. However they had come to be professed, society was more concerned about nuns' chastity than monks', and fallen nuns were a cause of scandal and attracted opprobrium. Nuns whose behaviour did not attract disgrace normally drew little other attention either, being somewhat anonymously corporate within convent walls, but outstanding individuals acquired extra-mural fame. Not to enter religion and yet to remain never-married was unexpected and such individuals were an awkward fit in society. Girls were not generally trained to earn their own living as a permanent prospect, although the less well off commonly worked in domestic service in their youth, saving up to marry. In southern Europe young brides tended to marry older men, and began married life as the junior partner. In northern Europe the ages tended to be closer and the brides older, resulting in a more companionable pairing. But the church preached at women to be obedient, docile and of course chaste wives, and ribald literature showed men's fears of being henpecked or cuckolded.

Class made a great difference to the behaviour expected of both sexes. The fourteenth and fifteenth centuries saw the production of several behavioural guides for laywomen, either openly instructive or masquerading as story collections but with morals to the tales. These of course were written for an audience with access to the written word. Boccaccio's *Famous Women* included notorious as well as good women, almost all from classical times, so not immediate role models. But intermittently he underlined express lessons for his own times, warning against girls being let roam freely, or throwing themselves at men, and widows' frequent remarriage. In his story of the poetess Cornificia he berated slothful women and pitiful creatures who lacked self-confidence for convincing themselves that they were only useful for men's embraces and giving birth and raising children 'as if born for idleness and the marriage bed'. The youthfulness of Italian brides from wealthy families in a city like Florence could account for this perspective, for a girl who had never had to earn her living passing at around the age of 15 from father's to husband's house amid expensive ritual might seem spoilt daughter transforming into pampered wife. The royal wives cited in the present work bearing a dozen children over a score of years illustrate the reality of the procreational cycle. Boccaccio was not questioning reproductive usefulness, he was rather denying it as the sole or sufficient role for women, which he accused them of convincing themselves it was. Was this fair? The church was constantly railing against the enjoyment of sex and urging it as a procreational duty. Were not women conditioned to see themselves as childbearing wives? Similarly, was it surprising women lacked self-confidence when a church preaching meekness and obedience and a patriarchal society's laws conspired to give them no confidence? In the same passage Boccaccio expressed approval ('how glorious') of a woman scorning womanish concerns and turning her mind to the study of great poets. For how many women could this have been a fair chiding? How few would have had books of great poets to hand, that they were merely unwilling to read? Most houses had no books, and indeed no literacy. One would conclude that Boccaccio was thinking of the more bookish social elite but readers will recollect he criticized the freedwoman Epicharis for lacking taste for good literature, so how far down society did he direct this criticism? Furthermore, if a woman was not studying literature was she being slothful? A wife with a household staff might have only a supervisory role and thus have the leisure, but a wife coping with all sorts of demands including child rearing (presumably scorned 'womanish concerns') would have no piece of work, or mental improvement, to show for it, but would not have been idle.

Christine de Pizan, in *The Book of the City of Ladies*, rightly shifted the focus from unwillingness to learn to educational deprivation. But in her sequel, *The Book of Three Virtues*, she ignored women's lack of education and set out to provide a splendid contemporary window on women's defined position, their room for inventive manoeuvre and their potential scope for ameliorating their situation, and this for women class by class from princesses down to paupers. This was positive teaching, because its emphasis was on what a woman could do to make the best of a situation. It accepted many of the restrictions on women (disappointing some later feminists), and recommended ways of smoothing situations, even ways of improving husbands, by tolerance, charm and earned respect. (The charm offensive also features in Book III of Castiglione's *The Courtier* (1528) in discussion of the court lady.) Christine's book comes recognizably from the same world as the Ménagier and Knight of La Tour Landry but instead of giving a wife and daughters instructions to obey, it treated women as rational beings, showing them how to rise to responsibilities and offering advice to be gracious about what they have to endure. (Education for responsibility had also been a concern of the 1380s *Livre de la Vertu du Sacrament de Mariage* of Philippe de Mézières.) Christine was a woman of spirit. In the *Mutation of Fortune* (1403) she developed the idea of Fortune changing her into a man to cope with sailing her pilotless craft after the loss of her husband. She recognized and rejoiced in the spirit shown by Joan of Arc, crediting the achievements to the *intelligence* of the maid, and commenting 'what honour for the female sex'. For Christine Joan was women's potential made flesh. It is not known whether she lived long enough to know of Joan's death at the stake, a fate which shows only too well the dangers a woman courted when putting herself into prominence in a men's world.

Continuity and Change

Throughout the later middle ages there was discrimination between the sexes following from the teachings of the church and legal customs and generally working to women's disadvantage. The authorities took their discriminatory attitudes from earlier times and to some extent from biology where the woman's body is usually smaller and less strong and where the female of the species (at least in mammals) gestates and then suckles the next generation. Physical 'manpower' is at a premium in more primitive societies which are fighting other tribes for territory and hacking at new ground to colonize. By 1200 western European societies were well beyond the primitive, but manpower was what agriculture, armies, the church and the growing bureaucratic administration of nascent states and towns required. Men were physically stronger than women by nature and intellectually superior by nurture. Formal education was an offspring of the church and its purpose was to teach choirboys Latin, and then draw the more apt into further grammatical study, without which they were not equipped to study the liberal arts or theology, canon and civil law, music and medicine. Women were not accepted into the church ministry on principle, it was not thought fit for them to practise law in public courts, nor proper for them to practise medicine, so there was no purpose in teaching Latin to secular women. But without this universal language of European scholarship, women were condemned to the world of vernacular communication, written or heard. The women who entered convents had the most professional status and some reached proficiency in Latin, but they were restricted to advancement within the conventual world. Abbess was the top of the profession for the nun, whereas abbot was not for the monk.

Inequality of educational opportunity long outlasted the period, but within it at least it came to be openly recognized and put in perspective. In 1362 Boccaccio had said women would share with men the ability to do everything which made men famous if they were willing to apply themselves to study. Forty years on Christine de Pizan moved the argument from unwillingness to lack of access. In chapter 27 of Book I of the *City of Ladies* she had Reason point out that if it were customary to send daughters to school like sons, and if they were then taught the natural sciences, they would learn and understand as thoroughly as men. But they were not so sent, and thus did not learn.

Although this educational discrimination prevented women from reaching their full intellectual potential except in very rare cases, it must not be imagined to be a disadvantage most women at the time would have been aware of. In the vast majority of rural households neither men nor women received any formal education in reading and writing. Most received only minimal religious education from parents and parish priests, and informal apprenticeship doing agricultural tasks. Here husbands and wives, and brothers and sisters, shared an equality of ignorance unless a boy was caught up from the church choir and groomed for the priesthood.

It is generally agreed that the literacy level was higher in towns, and there an alternative practical curriculum for managing a business, keeping its records and casting accounts was evolved. Did this create a wider educational gap between the sexes in towns? Probably it did. The merchant of Prato's wife was illiterate in the early years of her marriage and dictated her letters to her husband and had his read to her. But Nicholas suggests women kept accounts in family businesses and we have seen evidence of some schooling for girls in Cologne, Florence, Ghent and Paris. Another aspect of education in the towns was formal apprenticeship and this was definitely much more commonly arranged for boys than girls. Women's opportunities for work in towns were either unskilled services or spin-offs from connection with the business of a husband or father. Only in the demographic shortfall after the Black Death was women's labour more welcome in towns, and when the population began to recover they were eased out.

The Renaissance brought less change to the prevailing idea of woman than might have been expected. Theologians kept woman subordinate to husband and church, although they did see marriage as more companionable. Experimental anatomy was advancing medical knowledge and the unclean connotations of womanhood were being outmoded but woman's inferiority remained. Law continued her containment (for her own protection). Vives' *Institution of the Christian Woman* (1523) held up the chaste, modest, silent, submissive, hardworking, soberly dressed, pious and long-suffering wife as the model. No change here then: women did not have a renaissance while men were liberating their minds. The surge of humanist scholarship in Italy did create a cadre of learned women – high-born, well married, able to be dedicatees of works of literature and art and to correspond in Latin and give speeches in it. Perhaps these comparatively few 'bluestockings' turned Boccaccio's vision of women otherwise idle taking to literary study and becoming as famous as men into reality. (They were not, however, content to be otherwise idle.)

The Protestant Reformation, in urging translation of the Bible and its study in the vernacular by both sexes might, along with the new medium of printing, have promoted vernacular literacy to the benefit of some women, but for others it brought a sharp termination to their cloistered life, casting adrift those who were content with it, though bringing freedom to the unwillingly veiled or those who had grown critical of the life. In the countries which remained Catholic the Council of Trent was in process of overhauling conditions as our period closes.

If Renaissance and Reformation seem to have had surprisingly little effect on the place of women by 1550, it should perhaps be more accurately reported as surprisingly little visible effect. There was about to be much wider voicing of women's equal right to education, based on equality of virtue and intellect. Mary and Elizabeth Tudor, Mary of Guise and Catherine de Medici, all educated in our period, were about to force rule by women to controversial prominence. Times were changing, and for want of better nomenclature they become labelled 'early modern'. The world described in this book was receding into the past.

Notes

Introduction

1. First published in *Becoming Visible: Women in European History*, ed. R. Bridenthal and C. Koonz (Boston, MA, 1977), pp. 137–64.
2. Figures are from K. Fowler, *The Age of Plantagenet and Valois* (London, 1980), pp. 155–6.
3. J. Evans (ed.), *The Flowering of the Middle Ages* (London, 1966), pp. 164–5.
4. S. Rees Jones, 'Women's Influence on the Design of Urban Homes', in *Gendering the Master Narrative: Women and Power in the Middle Ages*, ed. M. C. Erler and M. Kowaleski (Ithaca, NY, 2003), pp. 190–211.

Contemporary Gender Theory and Society's Expectations of Women

1. R. D. Hale, 'Joseph as Mother', in *Medieval Mothering*, ed. J. C. Parsons and B. Wheeler (New York, 1996, 1999), pp. 101–16; D. and H. Kraus, *The Hidden World of Misericords* (London, 1976), p. 135.
2. L. Guzzetti, 'Separations and Separated Couples in Fourteenth-Century Venice' in *Marriage in Italy 1300–1650*, ed. T. Dean and K. J. P. Lowe (Cambridge, 1998, 2002), pp. 265–7.
3. T. Evergates (ed.), *Aristocratic Women in Medieval France* (Philadelphia, PA, 1999), p. 96 (Evergates on 'Aristocratic Women in the County of Champagne') and pp. 133, 135–6 (K. S. Nicholas on 'Countesses as Rulers in Flanders').
4. A. Blamires, *The Case for Women in Medieval Culture* (Oxford, 1997), p. 199.
5. R. L. Krueger, 'Transforming Maidens: Singlewomen's Stories in Marie de France's *Lais* and Later French Courtly Narratives', in *Singlewomen in the European Past 1250–1800*, ed. J. M. Bennett and A. M. Froide (Philadelphia, PA, 1999), pp. 171–80.
6. *The Book of the Knight of the Tower*, trans. M. Y. Offord (London, 1971), 'How a woman sprange vpon the table', pp. 35–7.
7. E Power, 'The Position of Women', in *The Legacy of the Middle Ages*, ed. C. G. Crump and E. F. Jacob (Oxford, 1929/1962), p. 408.
8. L. Roper, *The Holy Household: Women and Morals in Reformation Augsburg* (Oxford, 1989), p. 40.

The Practical Situation: Women's Function in Rural Communities

1. G. Duby, *L'Économie Rurale et la Vie des Compagnes dans l'Occident Médiéval* (Paris, 1962), trans. C. S. Postan as *Rural Economy and Country Life in the Medieval West* (London, 1968), pp. 119, 121. All references to Duby in this chapter are to the English translation of this work.
2. P. Franklin, 'Peasant Widows' 'Liberation' and Remarriage before Black Death', *Economic History Review*, 2, xxxix, ii (1986), 196.
3. Duby, *Rural Economy*, pp. 485–6.
4. S. Shahar, *The Fourth Estate: A History of Women in the Middle Ages*, trans. C. Galai (London, 1983), p. 242; E. Le Roy Ladurie, *Montaillou: Cathars and Catholics in a French Village*, trans. B. Bray (Harmondsworth, 1980), p. 5; Duby, *Rural Economy*, p. 153.
5. Duby, *Rural Economy*, pp. 146–7, 350–1; Ladurie, *Montaillou*, p. 106.
6. J. M. Bennett, 'Medieval Peasant Marriage: an Examination of Marriage Licence Fines in *Liber Gersumarum*', in J. A. Raftis (ed.), *Pathways to Medieval Peasants* (Toronto, 1981), pp. 197, 205.
7. B. A. Hanawalt, *The Ties that Bound: Peasant Families in Medieval England* (Oxford, 1986), pp. 145–6.
8. S. Shahar, *Childhood in the Middle Ages* (London, 1990), p. 127.
9. Duby, *Rural Economy*, pp. 283–4, 505–6.
10. D. Herlihy, *Medieval Households* (Cambridge, MA, 1985), p. 140.
11. S. Shahar, *Growing Old in the Middle Ages*, trans. Y. Lotan (London and New York, 1997), p. 156.
12. Duby, *Rural Economy*, p. 510.
13. Ibid., p. 519.

The Practical Situation: Women's Function in Urban Communities

1. *A Parisian Journal 1405–1449 translated from the Anonymous Journal d'un Bourgeois de Paris*, by Janet Shirley (Oxford, 1968), p. 155.
2. D. E. Queller, 'The Venetian Family and the *Estimo* of 1379', in *Law, Custom and the Social Fabric in Medieval Europe: Essays in Honor of Bryce Lyon*, ed. B. S. Bachrach and D. Nicholas (Kalamazoo, MI, 1990), p. 190.
3. D. Nicholas, *The Later Medieval City 1300–1500* (London, 1997), pp. 203–4.
4. K. L. Reyerson, 'Women in Business in Medieval Montpellier', in *Women and Work in Preindustrial Europe*, ed. B. A. Hanawalt (Bloomington, IN, 1986), p. 121.
5. These facts come from Nicholas, *Later Medieval City*, p. 264. References to Ghent in this chapter normally come from his *The Domestic Life of a Medieval City: Women, Children and the Family in Fourteenth-Century Ghent* (Lincoln, NE, 1985).
6. C. M. Barron, 'Johanna Hill (d 1441) and Johanna Sturdy (d c. 1460) Bell-founders', in *Medieval London Widows 1300–1500*, ed. C. M. Barron and A. E. Sutton (London, 1994), pp. 99–111.
7. S. A. Epstein, *Genoa and the Genoese 958–1528* (Chapel Hill, NC, 1996), p. 267.

8. C. Klapisch-Zuber, 'Female Celibacy and Service in Florence in the Fifteenth Century' in *Women, Family and Ritual in Renaissance Italy*, trans. L. G. Cochrane (Chicago, IL, 1985), pp. 165–77.
9. Easiest access to the relevant text is through the extracts printed in *Women's Lives in Medieval Europe*, ed. E. Amt (New York and London, 1993), pp. 317–30.
10. Klapisch-Zuber, 'Blood Parents and Milk Parents: Wet Nursing in Florence 1300–1530', *Women, Family and Ritual*, pp. 132–64.
11. M. E. Wiesner, 'Midwifery: a Case Study', in *Women and Work in Preindustrial Europe*, pp. 94–110.
12. Klapisch-Zuber, 'Kin, Friends and Neighbors: the Urban Territory of a Merchant Family in 1400', *Women, Family and Ritual*, pp. 68–93.
13. In the remainder of this chapter the Florentine *catasto* data is taken from D. Herlihy and C Klapisch-Zuber (eds), *Tuscans and their Families* (New Haven and London, 1985).
14. Klapisch-Zuber discusses the nuptial rites and aspects of the dowry in 'Zacharias, or the Ousted Father: Nuptial Rites in Tuscany between Giotto and the Council of Trent' and 'The Griselda Complex: Dowry and Marriage Gifts in the Quattrocento', in *Women, Family and Ritual*, pp. 178–212 and 213–46.

Women and Power: Royal and Landholding Women

1. R. Fawtier, *The Capetian Kings of France: Monarchy and Nation 987–1328*, trans. L. Butler and R. J. Adam (London, 1966), pp. 53–4.
2. A point made in P. Matarasso, *Queen's Mate: Three Women of Power in France on the Eve of the Renaissance* (Aldershot, 2001), p. 109. The lives of Anne of Beaujeu, Anne of Brittany and Louise of Savoy are interwoven in great detail in this work, to which all citations of Matarasso in this chapter refer.
3. A. Wolf, 'Reigning Queens in Medieval Europe: When, Where and Why', in *Medieval Queenship*, ed. J. C. Parsons (Stroud, 1998), pp. 169–88. The years in brackets are years of rule.
4. Margaret's activities are the subject of several articles by M. A. Hicks, particularly 'Counting the Cost of War: the Moleyns Ransom and the Hungerford Land-Sales, 1453–87' and 'The Piety of Margaret, Lady Hungerford (d. 1478)', reprinted in Hicks, *Richard III and His Rivals: Magnates and their Motives in the Wars of the Roses* (London, 1991), pp. 185–208, 99–118.
5. W. L. Gundersheimer, 'Women, Learning and Power, Eleanora of Aragon and the Court of Ferrara', in P. H. Labalme (ed.), *Beyond their Sex: Learned Women of the European Past* (New York, 1980), pp. 53, 48.
6. C. H. Clough, 'Daughters and Wives of the Montefeltro: Outstanding Bluestockings of the Quattrocento', *Renaissance Studies*, 10, 1 (1996), 31–55.
7. T. Evergates, 'Aristocratic Women in the County of Champagne', in *Aristocratic Women in Medieval France*, ed. T. Evergates (Philadelphia, PA, 1999), pp. 74–110.
8. Matarasso, *Queen's Mate*, p. 262.
9. N. Davis (ed.), *Paston Letters and Papers of the Fifteenth Century* (Oxford, 2 vols, 1971–6), I, no. 269.

10. P. Crossley, 'The Architecture of Queenship: Royal Saints, Female Dynasties and the Spread of Gothic Architecture in Central Europe', in *Queens and Queenship in Medieval Europe*, ed. A. J. Duggan (Woodbridge, 1997, repr. 2002), pp. 263–300.
11. J. M. Bak, 'Queens as Scapegoats in Medieval Hungary', in Parsons, *Medieval Queenship*, pp. 223–33.
12. The introduction, 'A New Economy of Power Relations: Female Agency in the Middle Ages', in *Gendering the Master Narrative: Women and Power in the Middle Ages*, ed. M. C. Erler and M. Kowaleski (Ithaca, NY, and London, 2003), pp. 1–16 is a good discussion of perspectives.
13. Fawtier, *Capetian Kings*, p. 28.
14. Her career is discussed in S. Imsen, 'Late Medieval Scandinavian Queenship', in Duggan, *Queens and Queenship*, pp. 58–61.
15. E. McCartney, 'The King's Mother and Royal Prerogative in Early Sixteenth-Century France', in Parsons, *Medieval Queenship*, pp. 117–41 discusses Louise's role as the heir's mother and regent. Matarasso, *Queen's Mate*, also considers her earlier life and experiences.
16. M. W. Labarge, *Women in Medieval Life* (London, 2001), pp. 87–8, 95.

Women and Religion

1. E. Amt (ed.), *Women's Lives in Medieval Europe: A Sourcebook* (New York and London, 1993), pp. 245–52.
2. Sister Bartolomea Riccoboni, *Life and Death in a Venetian Convent: the Chronicle and Necrology of Corpus Domini, 1395–1436*, ed. and trans. D. Bornstein (Chicago and London, 2000), p. 84. All references to this convent and its sisters are from this work.
3. K. L. French, 'Women in the late medieval English Parish', in M. C. Erler and M. Kowaleski (eds), *Gendering the Master Narrative* (Ithaca, NY and London, 2003), pp. 162–3.
4. P. Biller, 'The Common Woman', in *Women in the Church*, ed. W. J. Sheils and D. Wood (*Studies in Church History*, 27: 1990), 133–4.
5. See A. Brenon, 'The Voice of the Good Women: an Essay on the Pastoral and Sacerdotal Role of Women in the Cathar Church', in *Women Preachers and Prophets through Two Millennia of Christianity*, ed. B. M. Kienzle and P. J. Walker (Berkeley, Los Angeles and London 1998), pp. 114–33.
6. E. le Roy Ladurie, *Montaillou, Cathars and Catholics in a French Village 1294–1324*, trans. B. Bray (Harmondsworth, 1980), pp. 212, 324, ix.
7. C. Cross, '"Great Reasoners in Scripture": the Activities of Women Lollards 1380–1530', in *Medieval Women*, ed. D. Baker (*Studies in Church History*, Subsidia 1,1978), pp. 359–80.
8. R. Rowland, '"Fantasticall and Devilishe Persons": European Witch-Beliefs in Comparative Perspective', in *Early Modern European Witchcraft: Centres and Peripheries*, ed. B. Ankarloo and G. Henningsen (Oxford, 1990), pp.162–3.
9. Amt, *Women's Lives*, pp. 292–3. The extracts from Eleazar and Asheri are also in Amt, but more of the latter is in J. Murray (ed.), *Love, Marriage and Family in*

the Middle Ages: A Reader (Peterborough, Ont, 2001) which also provides the extracts from Rabbi Meir; E. Baumgarten, *Mothers and Children: Jewish Family Life in Medieval Europe* (Princeton, NJ, and Oxford, 2004), pp. 8–13.

10. M. E. Perry, 'Behind the Veil: Moriscas and the Politics of Resistance and Survival', in *Spanish Women in the Golden Age: Images and Realities,* ed. M. S. Sánchez and A. Saint-Saens (Westport, CT, 1996), pp. 37–53.
11. M. Wiesner-Hanks, 'Women, Gender and Sexuality', in A. Ryrie (ed.), *Palgrave Advances in the European Reformations* (Basingstoke, 2006), pp. 253–72.

Women Who Exceeded Society's Expectations

1. F. Hart, 'Following in the Footprints of the Poor Christ: Clare's Spirituality', in *Peace Weavers, Medieval Religious Women,* vol. II, ed. J. A. Nichols and L. T. Shank (Kalamazoo, MI, 1987), p. 181.
2. Ibid., p. 192. The rule is printed in E. Amt (ed.), *Women's Lives in Medieval Europe: A Sourcebook* (New York and London, 1993), pp. 235–45.
3. C. Mooney, '*Imitatio Christi* or *Imitatio Mariae*? Clare of Assisi and her Interpreters' in *Gendered Voices: Medieval Saints and their Interpreters,* ed. C. M. Mooney (Philadelphia, PA, 1999), pp. 52–77.
4. R. B. and C. N. L. Brooke, 'St Clare', in *Medieval Women,* ed. D. Baker (*Studies in Church History,* Subsidia I, 1978), pp. 285, 276; P. Ranft, *Women and the Religious Life in Premodern Europe* (Basingstoke, 1998), p. 68; F. A. Thom, 'Clare of Assisi: New Leader of Women', in *Peace Weavers,* p. 207, quoting *The Legend and Writings of St Clare of Assisi,* ed. I. Brady (St Bonaventure, NY, 1953), pp. 129–30.
5. C. de Pisan, *Ditié de Jehanne d'Arc,* ed. A. J. Kennedy and K. Varty (Oxford, 1977) (includes translation), pp. 44, 46.
6. R. Pernoud and M-V. Clin, *Joan of Arc: Her Story,* trans. J. duQ. Adams (London, 2000), pp. 33–4.
7. Quoted in *The First Biography of Joan of Arc,* ed. and trans. D. Rankin and C. Quintal (Pittsburgh, PA, 1964), p. 43.
8. Ibid., pp. 113–25. The quotation is from p. 115; de Pisan *Ditié,* p. 47.
9. K. DeVries, *Joan of Arc: A Military Leader* (Stroud, 1999/2003), p. 90.
10. C. de Pizan, *The Book of the City of Ladies,* trans. E. J. Richards (New York, 1982), p. 153.

Further Reading

Introduction

Amt, E. (ed.), *Women's Lives in Medieval Europe: A Sourcebook* (New York and London, 1993).
Davis, N. Z. and Farge, A. (eds), *A History of Women in the West. III Renaissance and Enlightenment Paradoxes* (London and Cambridge, MA, 1993).
Dinshaw, C. and Wallace, D. (eds), *The Cambridge Companion to Medieval Women's Writing* (Cambridge, 2003).
Ennen, E., trans. E. Jephcott, *The Medieval Woman* (Oxford, 1989).
Kelly-Gadol, J., 'Did Women have a Renaissance?' in *Becoming Visible: Women in European History*, ed. R. Bridenthal and C. Koonz (Boston, MA, 1977), pp. 137–64.
Klapisch-Zuber, C. (ed.), *A History of Women in the West. II Silences of the Middle Ages* (Cambridge, MA and London, 1993).
Labarge, M. W., *Women in Medieval Life* (London, 1986 and 2001).
Larrington, C. (ed.), *Women and Writing in Medieval Europe* (London and New York, 1995).
Mitchell, L. E. (ed.), *Women in Medieval Western European Culture* (New York and London, 1999).
Rosenthal, J. T. (ed.), *Medieval Women and the Sources of Medieval History* (Athens, GA and London, 1990).
Shahar, S., trans. C. Galai, *The Fourth Estate: A History of Women in the Middle Ages* (London, 1983 and 1990).
Ward, J., *Women in Medieval Europe 1200–1500* (Harlow, 2002).
Wilson, K. M. (ed.), *Medieval Women Writers* (Manchester, 1984).
Wilson, K. M. and Margolis, N. (eds), *Women in the Middle Ages: An Encyclopedia* (Westport, CT and London, 2 vols, 2004).

Contemporary Gender Theory and Society's Expectations of Women

Blamires, A., *The Case for Women in Medieval Culture* (Oxford, 1997).
Blamires, A. with Pratt, K. and Marx, C. W. (eds), *Women Defamed and Women Defended* (Oxford, 1992).

Brown, J. C. and Davies, R. C. (eds), *Gender and Society in Renaissance Italy* (Harlow, 1998).
Brundage, J. A., 'The Merry Widow's Serious Sister: Remarriage in Classical Canon Law', in *Matrons and Marginal Women in Medieval Society*, ed. R. R. Edwards and V. Ziegler (Woodbridge, 1995), pp. 33–48.
Bullough, V. L. and Brundage, J. A. (eds), *Handbook of Medieval Sexuality* (New York and London, 1996).
Dean, T. and Lowe, K. J. P. (eds), *Marriage in Italy 1300–1650* (Cambridge, 1998).
Erler, M. C. and Kowaleski, M. (eds), *Gendering the Master Narrative: Women and Power in the Middle Ages* (Ithaca, NY and London, 2003).
Farmer, S. and Pasternack, C. B. (eds), *Gender and Difference in the Middle Ages* (Minneapolis, 2003).
Fenster, T. S. and Lees, C. A. (eds), *Gender and Debate from the Early Middle Ages to the Renaissance* (New York and Basingstoke, 2002).
Ferrante, J., *Women as Image in Medieval Literature* (New York, 1975).
Goody, J., 'Inheritance, Property and Women: Some Comparative Considerations', in *Family and Inheritance: Rural Society in Western Europe 1200–1800*, ed. J. Goody, J. Thirsk and E. P. Thompson (Cambridge, 1976), pp. 10–36.
Hale, R. D., 'Joseph as Mother: Adaptation and Appropriation in the Construction of Male Virtue', in *Medieval Mothering*, ed. J. C. Parsons and B. Wheeler (New York and London, 1996), pp. 101–16.
Howell, M. C., *The Marriage Exchange: Property, Social Place and Gender in Cities of the Low Countries 1300–1550* (Chicago, IL and London, 1998).
Krueger, R. L., 'Transforming Maidens: Singlewomen's Stories in Marie de France's *Lais* and later French Courtly Narrative', in *Singlewomen in the European Past 1250–1800*, ed. J. M. Bennett and A. M. Froide (Philadelphia, PA, 1999), pp. 146–91.
McLean, I., *The Renaissance Notion of Woman: a Study in the Fortunes of Scholasticism and Medical Science in European Intellectual Life* (Cambridge, 1980).
Nolte, C., 'Gendering Princely Dynasties: Some Notes on Family Structure, Social Networks and Communication at the Courts of the Margraves of Brandenburg Ansbach around 1500', in *Gendering the Middle Ages*, ed. P. Stafford and A. B. Mulder-Bakker (Oxford, 2001), pp. 174–91.
Tomalin, M., *Features of the Warrior Heroine in Italian Literature: an Index of Emancipation* (Ravenna, 1982).

The Practical Situation: Women's Function in Rural Communities

Duby, G., trans. C. Postan, *Rural Economy and Country Life in the Medieval West* (London, 1968).
Franklin, P., 'Peasant Widows' "Liberation" and Remarriage before the Black Death', *Economic History Review*, 2nd series, 39 (1986), 186–204.
Hanawalt, B. A., *The Ties that Bound: Peasant Families in Medieval England* (Oxford, 1986).
Ladurie, E. le Roy, trans. B. Bray, *Montaillou: Cathars and Catholics in a French Village 1294–1324* (Harmondsworth, 1980).

Razi, Z., *Life, Marriage and Death in a Medieval Parish: Economy, Society and Demography in Halesowen 1270–1400* (Cambridge, 1980).
Shahar, S., trans. Y. Lotan, *Growing Old in the Middle Ages* (London and New York, 1997).

The Practical Situation: Women's Function in Urban Communities

Bachrach, B. S. and Nicholas, D. (eds), *Law, Custom and the Social Fabric in Medieval Europe: Essays in Honor of Bryce Lyon* (Kalamazoo, MI, *Studies in Medieval Culture*, XXVIII, 1990).
Dillard, H., *Daughters of the Reconquest: Women in Castilian Town Society 1100–1300* (Cambridge, 1984).
Epstein, S. A., *Genoa and the Genoese 958–1528* (Chapel Hill, NC and London, 1996).
Hanawalt, B. A. (ed.), *Women and Work in Preindustrial Europe* (Bloomington, IN, 1986).
Herlihy, D. and Klapisch-Zuber, C. (eds), *Tuscans and their Families: a Study of the Florentine Catasto of 1427* (New Haven, CT and London, 1985).
Howell, M. C., *Women, Production and Patriarchy in Late Medieval Cities* (Chicago, IL and London, 1986).
Howell, M. C., *The Marriage Exchange: Property, Social Place and Gender in Cities of the Low Countries 1300–1550* (Chicago, IL and London, 1998).
Killerby, C. K., *Sumptuary Law in Italy 1200–1500* (Oxford, 2002).
Klapisch-Zuber, C., trans. L. G. Cochrane, *Women, Family and Ritual in Renaissance Italy* (Chicago, IL and London, 1985).
Kuehn, T., *Law, Family and Women: Toward a legal Anthropology of Renaissance Italy* (Chicago, IL and London, 1991).
Meek, C., 'Women, Dowries and the Family in Late Medieval Italian Cities', in *The Fragility of her Sex: Medieval Irishwomen in their European Context*, ed. C. E. Meek and M. K. Simms (Dublin, 1996), pp. 136–52.
Nicholas, D., *Urban Europe 1100–1700* (Basingstoke and New York, 2003).
Nicholas, D., *The Later Medieval City 1300–1500* (London and New York, 1997).
Nicholas, D., *The Domestic Life of a Medieval City: Women, Children and the Family in Fourteenth-Century Ghent* (Lincoln, NE and London, 1985).
Origo, I., *The Merchant of Prato* (Harmondsworth, 1963).
Pisan, C. de, trans. S. Lawson, *The Treasure of the City of Ladies or the Book of the Three Virtues* (London, 1985).
Rossiaud, J., trans. L. G. Cochrane, *Medieval Prostitution* (Oxford, 1988).

Women and Power: Royal and Landholding Women

Boruchoff, D. A., *Isabel La Catolica, Queen of Castile* (New York and Basingstoke, 2003).
Cohn, S. K. jr, *Women in the Streets: Essays on Sex and Power in Renaissance Italy* (Baltimore, MD and London, 1996).

Duggan, A. (ed.), *Queens and Queenship in Medieval Europe* (Woodbridge, 1997).
Erler, M. C. and Kowaleski, M. (eds), *Gendering the Master Narrative: Women and Power in the Middle Ages* (Ithaca, NY and London, 2003).
Labalme, P. H. (ed.), *Beyond their Sex: Learned Women of the European Past* (New York and London, 1980).
McCash, J. H., *The Cultural Patronage of Medieval Women* (Athens GA and London, 1996).
Matarasso, P., *Queen's Mate: Three Women of Power in France on the Eve of the Renaissance* (Aldershot, 2001).
Nicholas, K., 'Countesses as Rulers in Flanders', *in Aristocratic Women in Medieval France,* ed. T. Evergates (Philadelphia, PA, 1999) pp. 111–37.
Parsons, J. C. (ed.), *Medieval Queenship* (Stroud, 1994).
Rezak, B. B., 'Women, Seals and Power in Medieval France 1150–1350' in *Women and Power in the Middle Ages,* ed. M. C. Erler and M. Kowaleski (Athens, GA and London, 1988), pp. 61–82.
Taylor, A. S., *Isabel of Burgundy* (Stroud, 2002).
Tomas, N. R., *The Medici Women: Gender and Power in Renaissance Florence* (Aldershot, 2003).

Women and Religion

Bainton, R. H., *Women of the Reformation in Germany and Italy* (Minneapolis, MN, 1971), *in France and England* (1973*), from Spain to Scandinavia* (1977).
Baumgarten, E., *Mothers and Children: Jewish Family Life in Medieval Europe* (Princeton, NJ and Oxford, 2004).
Biller, P., 'The Common Woman in the Western Church in the Thirteenth and Early Fourteenth Centuries', in *Women in the Church,* ed. W. J. Sheils and D. Wood (*Studies in Church History,* 27, 1990), 127–57.
Bornstein, D. (ed. and trans.), *Sister Bartolomea Riccoboni: Life and Death in a Venetian Convent: the Chronicle and Necrology of Corpus Domini 1395–1436* (Chicago, IL, 2000).
Hindsley, L. P., *The Mystics of Engelthal: Writings from a Medieval Monastery* (Basingstoke, 1998).
Jansen, K. L., *The Making of the Magdalen: Preaching and Popular Devotion in the Later Middle Ages (*Princeton, NJ, 2000).
Karant-Nunn, S. C., 'Reformation Society, Women and the Family', in A. Pettegree (ed.), *The Reformation World* (London and New York, 2000/2002), pp. 433–60.
Kienzle, B. M. and Walker, P. J. (eds), *Women Preachers and Prophets through Two Millennia of Christianity* (Berkeley and Los Angeles and London, 1998).
Kors, A. C. and Peters, E. (eds), *Witchcraft in Europe 1100–1700: A Documentary History,* revised edn by E. Peters (Philadelphia, PA, 2001).
Ladurie, E. le Roy, trans. B. Bray, *Montaillou: Cathars and Catholics in a French Village 1294–1324* (Harmondsworth, 1980).
McDonell, E. W., *Beguines and Beghards in Medieval Culture with Special Emphasis on the Belgian Scene* (New Brunswick, NJ, 1954).
Meek, C. E., 'Men, Women and Magic: Some Cases from late Medieval Lucca', in *Women in Renaissance and Early Modern Europe,* ed. C. Meek (Dublin, 2000), pp. 43–66.

Melamed, R. L., *Heretics or Daughters of Israel? The Crypto-Jewish Women of Castile* (Oxford, 1999).
Mooney, C. M. (ed.), *Gendered Voices: Medieval Saints and their Interpreters* (Philadelphia, PA, 1999).
Nichols, J. A. and Shank, L. T. (eds), *Medieval Religious Women. Vol. 1 Distant Echoes: vol. 2 Peaceweavers; vol. 3 Hidden Springs* (Kalamazoo, MI, 1984, 1987, 1995).
Oliva, M., 'Aristocracy or Meritocracy? Office-holding Patterns in late Medieval English Nunneries', in Sheils and Wood (eds), *Women in the Church,* pp. 197–208.
Ozment, S., *When Fathers Ruled: Family Life in Reformation Europe* (Cambridge, MA and London, 1983).
Ranft, P., *Women and the Religious Life in Premodern Europe* (Basingstoke, 1996).
Roper, L., *The Holy Household: Women and Morals in Reformation Augsburg* (Oxford, 1989).
Rowland, R., '"Fantasticall and Devilishe Persons": European Witch-Beliefs in Comparative Perspective', in *Early Modern European Witchcraft: Centres and Peripheries,* ed. B. Ankarloo and G. Henningsen (Oxford, 1990), pp. 161–90.
Shahar, S., trans. Y. Lotan, *Women in a Medieval Heretical Sect: Agnes and Huguette the Waldensians* (Woodbridge, 2001).
Simons, W., *Cities of Ladies: Beguine Communities in the Medieval Low Countries 1200–1565* (Philadelphia, PA, 2001).
Voaden, R., '"All Girls Together": Community, Gender and Vision at Helfta' in *Medieval Women in their Communities,* ed. D.Watt (Cardiff, 1997), pp. 72–91.
Warner, M., *Alone of All her Sex: the Myth and Cult of the Virgin Mary* (London and New York, 1976).
Wiesner-Hanks, M., 'Women, Gender and Sexuality', in *Palgrave Advances in the European Reformations,* ed. A. Ryrie (Basingstoke, 2006), pp. 253–72.

Women Who Exceeded Society's Expectations

Boccaccio, G., ed. and trans. V. Brown, *Famous Women* (Cambridge, MA, 2001).
Brooke, R. and C. N. L., 'St Clare' in *Medieval Women,* ed. D. Baker (*Studies in Church History,* Subsidia I, 1978), pp. 275–87.
DeVries, K., *Joan of Arc: A Military Leader* (Stroud, 1999).
Mooney, C. M., '*Imitatio Christi* or *Imitatio Mariae*? Clare of Assisi and her Interpreters', in Mooney, *Gendered Voices: Medieval Saints and their Interpreters* (Philadelphia, PA, 1999), pp. 52–77.
Pernoud, R. and Clin, M-V., *Joan of Arc: Her Story,* rev. and trans. J. du Q. Adams, ed. B. Wheeler (London, 2000).
Pisan, C. de, trans. S. Lawson, *The Treasure of the City of Ladies or the Book of the Three Virtues* (London, 1985).
Pisan, C. de, *Le Ditié de Jehanne d'Arc,* ed. and trans. A. J. Kennedy and K. Varty (Oxford, 1977).
Pizan, C. de, *The Book of the City of Ladies,* ed. and trans. E. J. Richards (New York, 1982).
Pizan, C. de, *The Book of the Body Politic,* ed. and trans. K. L. Forhan (Cambridge, 1994).

Rankin, D. and Quintal, C. (eds), *The First Biography of Joan of Arc* (Pittsburg, PA, 1964).
Richards, E. J. with J. Williamson, N. Margolis and C. Reno (eds), *Reinterpreting Christine de Pizan* (Athens, GA, 1992).
Willard, C. C., *Christine de Pizan: Her Life and Works* (New York, 1984).
Willard, C. C., 'A Fifteenth-Century View of Women's Role in Society: Christine de Pizan's *Livre des Trois Vertus*' in *The Role of Women in the Middle Ages*, ed. R. T. Morewedge (Albany, NY and London, 1975) pp. 90–120.
Willard, C. C., 'The Franco-Italian Professional Writer Christine de Pizan', in *Medieval Women Writers*, ed. K. M. Wilson (Manchester, 1984), pp. 333–40.

Index

NB Persons, places, sources and concepts handled in the text would swell this index unmanageably if all were individually entered into it and on each occurrence. Therefore the index is pruned to guide the reader to pages where the reference has particular importance as information, illustration, comment or for cross-reference purposes.